TARGET: THE PRESIDENT

Saffran and Sewell decided to bring their JetRanger to a hover next to the Huey. Perhaps they thought they could somehow communicate with the pilot. But as they came up alongside the rogue ship, it dashed away and made for the large building dead ahead. The White House. And by the reckless way the Huey was being flown, it looked as if the pilot meant to smash the aircraft into the building.

Saffran and Sewell followed close behind.

It took only a minute for the Huey's short flight, but now the two lawmen were faced with the rogue military ship on the White House lawn. The two troopers felt they had no option but to place their JetRanger between the Huey and the President's home.

If the two ships came into contact, the Huey's four hundred pounds of whirling rotor blades would shred their aircraft—and them along with it. But they had a duty to protect the White House.

They took a deep breath and prepared to make what appeared to be an unavoidable sacrifice. . . .

SKY COPS

Stories from America's Airborne Police

RICHARD ROSENTHAL

POCKET BOOKS

New York   London   Toronto   Sydney   Tokyo   Singapore

An *Original* Publication of POCKET BOOKS

 POCKET BOOKS, a division of Simon & Schuster Inc.
1230 Avenue of the Americas, New York, NY 10020

ISBN: 0-671-79516-3

First Pocket Books printing October 1994

10 9 8 7 6 5 4 3 2 1

POCKET and colophon are registered trademarks of Simon & Schuster Inc.

Cover photos: top, Joe Azzara/The Image Bank; bottom, Walter Bibikow/The Image Bank

Printed in the U.S.A.

Acknowledgments

This book was possible only because of the generous amounts of time given me by the many members of the airborne law-enforcement agencies whom I interviewed. I have tried to recount the incidents they shared with me as accurately as I could. Any errors or omissions in their stories are unintentional and my responsibility, for which I apologize.

A number of fine stories did not make the final cut. I regret this. Only so much space could be allotted to the book, and some tough choices had to be made. Perhaps in *Sky Cops II* ...

The Airborne Law Enforcement Association's president, Los Angeles Police Department Air Support Division Pilot Charles "Chuck" Perriguey Jr., and the association's magazine publisher, Roger Crescentini, were both most helpful to me in seeing to it that this project succeeded. Chuck also took the time to show me around the impressive LAPD Air Support Division offices as well as the unit's heliport, the largest such facility in the world.

I would like to thank Sergeant Steve Hinton, of the San Diego Police Department Air Support Unit, for the time he gave me at the unit. Also pilots Teresa Clark and Kevin Means of that agency were most hospitable as well, taking the time to share their thoughts on police aviation with me.

And finally I would like to thank Associate Editor Eric Tobias for his patience and advice.

Contents

CONTENTS

BOOK TWO

Maryland State Police Aviation Division

BOOK THREE

Georgia State Patrol Aviation Section

CONTENTS

BOOK FOUR

Arizona Department of Public Safety Aviation Division

CONTENTS

BOOK FIVE

Los Angeles Police Department
Air Support Division

CONTENTS

Preface

Maryland State Trooper Lou Saffran watched as the pilot of the stolen Army Huey began to perform pirouettes atop the Washington Monument. This was not your approved Army maneuver, Saffran mused. The green, red, and white running lights of the helicopter were not lit. Nonetheless, Saffran could clearly see the machine silhouetted against the starry blackness of the one A.M. Sunday sky. Saffran and his partner, Trooper Don Sewell, had been vectored to the stolen Army Huey by ground controllers. They had just come onto the scene, and for the moment could only stand by in their much smaller JetRanger and keep the big military aircraft under surveillance.

The other guy must have read the two troopers' thoughts. Tiring of toying with one national monument, he flew down to ground level, pointed his aircraft in the direction of the White House, and started for the President's home. Saffran and Sewell followed close behind.

It was a flight of only a couple of minutes from the monument to the White House lawn. The troopers managed to set their JetRanger between the Army machine and the big white building. Neither man had any way of knowing what the pilot of the larger helicopter had in mind or what his motives were. But the way Saffran figured it, the Huey pilot's antics were becoming progressively more bizarre. Even suicidal. And now those two tons of aluminum and jet fuel were pointed *at the door of the country's first residence. He was sure that hadn't happened by accident. The two troopers made their decision in an instant. They weren't going to let that bastard destroy the White House.*

Sewell put power to the engine and started for the Huey. . . .

Never before has a book been written specifically about airborne law enforcement. *Sky Cops* is the story of America's airborne police, the men and women who have taken the fight for this country's cities to the air. Police aviation unit members have been depicted as cartoonlike heroes in the movies. And their machines perform maneuvers and stunts that have little basis in fact in the actual world of aviation.

But the stories you are about to read do not come out of someone's imagination. They are real.

This book was written from the perspective gained by my personal experiences and knowledge as to how the missions and jobs are flown by these officers. I served as both a sergeant and lieutenant with the New York City Police Aviation Unit, flying Bell JetRangers and Army surplus Hueys. The reader will share an insight into a facet of the airborne law-enforcement function impossible to come by except from someone who was there, sweated out the missions, and took part in the day-to-day life of a police aviation unit.

Whether the flying unit is situated in a city the size of Los Angeles, with its seventeen Air Support Division police helicopters, or is among the nation's many dozens of other smaller police and airborne law-enforcement units, these men and woman harbor incredible stories. Be it snatching people from the roof of a bomb-damaged building a quarter of a mile above city streets, taking and exchanging ground fire as if flying over the jungles of Vietnam, or piloting helicopters in suicidally dangerous fog to rescue plane crash survivors, this is the first time these exciting tales are being told in a single place.

Police officers tend to be nervous around reporters and journalists. I don't think I ever met anyone in the law-enforcement profession who didn't have a horror story about someone in the print or news media twisting the facts of a particular story to suit their editorial needs. Putting it simply, cops soon find it is best to keep their mouths shut. After a few years on the job, they discover that there is just no advantage gained when talking to "outsiders" about what they do.

When first beginning to work on this book, I met resistance from potential interviewees who thought I was just some guy wanting to write a bunch of cop stories. I had to make it clear to them that I was a full-time chief of police, an appointment I took after having served in the same kind of unit they were now in. I am sure my position and background proved to be of more than a little value in putting the various law officers I spoke with at ease.

The stories gathered here are more than a series of anecdotes about flying exotic aircraft. They are really about the officers who operate and crew these machines. And they are very much about lives saved and lives lost.

This book profiles cops from five aviation units around the country: New York, Georgia, Maryland, Arizona, and Los Angeles. The stories run from the humorous to the melodramatic. The law officers have involved themselves in missions ranging from the rescue of stranded white-water rafters to the investigation of kidnappings and homicides.

Who are the men and women who make up these elite units? Where do they come from and how are they trained?

Most start out as police officers who just happen to have an interest in flying. Most aviation units, however, require their applicants to possess, at minimum, a Commercial Pilot license (often privately earned). These licenses, earned in conventional aircraft, cost between eight and ten thousand dollars, due to the great expense of flight time. To secure such a license in a helicopter would thus cost someone nearly $25,000, and that would be without any turbine-powered helicopter training.

To successfully fly these aircraft, the person at the controls must continually make hundreds of minute, almost imperceptible corrections. *Continual* is the key word here. It is a never-ending process, and one of the reasons helicopters are somewhat tedious to fly for long distances. A fixed-wing pilot, when their aircraft is properly trimmed up in cruise, can let go of all the controls and be confident the machine will tend to remain in stable and level flight. After a few moments, sometimes for as long as several minutes, a fixed-wing aircraft might tend to veer a bit, perhaps even enter a gentle spiral. But its airspeed will remain fairly constant— indeed, if properly trimmed initially, the airplane will try to remain at the speed the pilot last chose—and the ship's attitude will not likely degrade to a dangerous level. There have even been documented cases where aircraft have either taken off by themselves (the pilot had started the machine, but for whatever reason, left the cockpit unattended) or the on-board pilot had become incapacitated and the airplane(s) had managed—once they ran out of fuel—to land themselves, with varying degrees of success.

Not so for the person flying a helicopter. Once that machine's controls are released, the helicopter will immediately diverge from its course and, within a very few seconds, go out of control. The problem is exacerbated when such machines are in a hover situation. With the ship so close to the ground, there is little room for error.

To gain the skills necessary to become a member of one of these flying units—and to face the dangers inherent in the job—is a daunting task. Ten thousand dollars is a hefty sum for a person living on a police officer's salary to spend in the hopes of qualifying for a flying position. It's clear that airborne cops often must show great commitment to their work before spending an hour on the job.

However the men and women of law-enforcement aviation come to find their way into the cockpit, they ultimately discover themselves working at all hours, sometimes around the clock. Their missions frequently have them out in appalling weather conditions. They are often the only ones up flying, the civilian pilots having prudently found a safe place to land. Thus it is that the Sky Cops who make up these very special police units constantly live up to the motto coined by the New York City Police Aviation Unit, "Above All Else."

BOOK ONE

*New York City Police
Department Aviation
Unit*

CHAPTER 1

**Captain Joseph Mottle
Sergeant/Pilot Tom McManus
Detective/Pilot Gregory Semendinger
Detective/Pilot John Fagan
Emergency Service Unit Sergeant
Timothy Farrell**

World Trade Center Bombing
February 26, 1993

WITH THE ACQUISITION OF A PAIR OF UNDERPOWERED WOOD-and-fabric-covered amphibious biplanes, the New York City Police Department heralded the start of airborne law-enforcement sixty-five years ago. That police department, as well as the dozens of other local, state, and federal flying units that came after them, have come a long way since the official beginning of police aviation on October 24, 1929. Today, aircraft flown by police and law-enforcement agencies may be found in virtually every state in the union.

For the sixty-five years the NYPD unit has flown the skies over New York City, its pilots and crew members have responded to literally thousands of life-and-death jobs. Whether it be threading a big-bodied helicopter between

3

lamp posts to make a landing on a city street to pick up an injured child, rescuing kids from an ice floe on the East River, or dangling from inside the belly of a Huey to hand over needed emergency equipment to other officers atop a 300-foot smokestack, the members of the Aviation Unit have done it all.

The most recent compelling incident that the unit was involved in was the tremendous rescue work done during the World Trade Center terrorist bombing. Facing unknown perils, unit members responded to the site of what could have been a disaster of the first order. Once there, they lived up to their unit's motto, "Above All Else," which also makes this a good place to begin the story of America's Sky Cops.

The man driving the truck took his time as he threaded his way through the crowded streets of lower Manhattan. He patiently waited at each of the red lights he came upon before he moved on, and at every stop sign made certain his van came to a complete halt. The last thing he wished was to be pulled over by a police officer. Not with what he was carrying in the back of his vehicle.

As he neared his destination he once more glanced nervously into his rearview mirror, relieved to see his friend following behind in their getaway car. Once the truck was parked and the device set, he didn't want to be anywhere near the thing.

As he passed City Hall he mused to himself that it had all been so easy. Everything needed to make the hundreds of pounds of explosive that rested in the back had been purchased locally. It consisted of a petroleum-oil-based mixture of organic compounds and a timer-activated detonator. Every part had been homemade or bought through legitimate sources. Even securing the vehicle had been no problem. He had rented the van with a four hundred dollar deposit a day earlier in New Jersey. To explain why it was missing, he would only have to report the vehicle stolen as soon as it was no longer needed.

Whatever money they had required for the mission had come from friends overseas. He smiled and reflected that for what would be accomplished, their friends' investment would turn out to have been a great bargain.

The driver was aware that were the mixture in the truck composed of some sophisticated plastic explosive, it would be many times more powerful then what was there now. But getting that kind of material into the United States would have been both time-consuming and dangerous. What they had made would do nicely.

The driver stopped at the next red light and flicked on his right-turn signal. Drumming his fingers nervously on the steering wheel, he considered how easy it had been for all the people involved in this mission to do what they believed they had to do. Even getting into the United States proved to be child's play. No papers were needed, all a person had to do was get on a jet, and once in America, ask for political asylum by claiming they were fleeing political persecution in their own country. Not that that was a false statement. After all, since other members of his group had machine-gunned and bombed civilians in his home country, their government had been trying to stamp them out.

And now that they were in the United States, they would get busy and do to this country's citizens what they had been doing to their own. After all, wasn't it God's will they were fulfilling?

The light turned green. The man moved his foot from the brake and gently pressed down on the accelerator. This last turn had brought him to within a block of the World Trade Center complex. The large towers loomed ahead, their tops invisible in the overcast sky.

He drove on only a few more blocks. Slowing at the entrance to the towers' large, belowground parking garage, he turned in, picked up his parking ticket, and made his way into the facility. Nobody even so much as glanced at him. Behind him followed the other car, driven by his colleague.

The man passed by a number of open spaces. He had been told where to seek a place to park the van, a place where the most damage would be accomplished by the explosion.

Several levels down he found a good location. Pulling into the parking space, he shut the van's engine off, reached back and set the timer. It wouldn't be long now.

He jumped from his vehicle and into the waiting car. His friend, more nervous then he, sped toward the exit. The man wished his friend wouldn't drive so quickly, it would only call attention to them.

A minute later they were back out on the street. Now they would go to a local police station, to report the van stolen. It had been so simple.

As they drove along the city streets, the man silently considered the four hundred dollars he had put down as a security deposit on the van the day before. He could use that money. Maybe tomorrow he would try and get it refunded.

Detective/Pilot Gregory Semendinger has enjoyed fiddling with electronic and mechanical gear for as long as he can remember. At the Aviation Unit, where he has been assigned for eight of his twenty-six years in the department, he worked on the delicate but necessary equipment found on and around the department's helicopters, which inevitably got out of whack with use. It annoyed him that an otherwise perfectly good aircraft could be put out of service for some relatively trivial and, at least for him, easily repairable problem. So it was that other members of the unit would often find him out in the hangar area, fixing some radio or avionics glitch, mending a defective door latch or repairing broken wires in one of the unit's several dozen headsets.

Semendinger vividly recalls one particular day at work. It was just after noontime, on Friday, February 26, 1993, and he was designated as the air/sea rescue pilot. The multimillion candlepower Nightsun spotlight on one of the helicopters had been reported as malfunctioning by a pilot. So, as flying weather wasn't particularly good that day, with light-blowing snow and a low ceiling, Semendinger busied himself working on the problem inside the hangar.

It was Semendinger's habit to carry around a portable radio with him when he was the air/sea rescue pilot. The job meant that, were a water-related emergency called in— a sinking vessel or some other trouble on the ocean—it would be his responsibility to fly the scuba team out to the mission. He figured having the radio nearby gave him those extra few seconds of time, as well as that little bit of additional information, that sometimes can mean so much in a life and death emergency. He had just traced the electrical fault down to a connector and was engrossed in the process of finishing up the repair job when he heard the first of a series of unusual radio calls come in.

Initially the Communications Unit transmitted reports of a transformer explosion and ceiling collapse in lower Manhattan. Within a few moments of the first radio broadcast, multiple calls started to come over for the same job. And to Semendinger's ears, whatever the problem was, it began to sound serious. But at first he didn't think it likely that Aviation would be required to help deal with the emergency.

As he listened, the pace of the changing information quickened. Finally it was reported that whatever had happened was the result of a bomb. Emergency Service Units (ESU) were requesting that Scott packs (rescue breathing apparatus), portable lighting, and generators be rushed to the scene.

Semendinger, still unsure as to the role his unit might play in the situation, decided to head for the Operations room, a small walled-off area next to the commanding officer's office, which held several telephones as well as an assortment of police and aviation radio equipment. It would be the place where all calls would be coming for whatever was going on in the street. He figured that if they were in a hurry for specialized gear, the fastest way to get around New York City was by helicopter. Semendinger never made it to Operations. Lieutenant Steven DiAntonio—ranking officer of the shift—met him on the way and ordered, "Get the 412 out. Get it out now!"

Semendinger didn't debate the order. He grabbed his equipment, and seeing one of the unit's two Bell 412s being wheeled out to the flight line, jumped on its dolly. While the ship was still in motion, mechanics and pilots set it up in a multiple Medevac configuration. Someone among the mechanics decided it would be prudent to put the high-rise fire kit in place. Whoever thought of the idea turned out to be right on the money.

The kit included a long rappeling rope, crowbars, and axes. The rope was to be used to put ESU personnel on a rooftop otherwise occupied by antennas and assorted other obstacles. The tools would be employed by the officers to flatten those same antennas and obstacles to enable the helicopter to land.

As the unit members worked, Semendinger's radio spoke of a fire and a large number of injured persons. There was also some concern being voiced about people trapped in the building. Semendinger got in and began to run through the Bell 412's complicated start-up procedure. With him for the flight was Police Officer/Pilot Tom Defresco as well as mechanic and Crew Chief Richard Troche.

Semendinger quickly brought the 412 to life. When he was just about to pull power and head for the scene, he received a radio transmission telling him to hold in place. Established protocol said Semendinger had to wait until the arrival of a crew from an Emergency Service Unit. It was the ESU team that would rappel onto the roof of the burning building if that were deemed necessary. ESU Seven Truck was reported to be only a few minutes away.

A few minutes later—though it seemed much longer to Semendinger—the ESU truck came into view.

ESU Sergeant Timothy Farrell had just pulled into Seven Truck—referred to by members of ESU just as it's written, "Seven Truck"—quarters, adjacent to the 75th Precinct, situated in Brooklyn. Assigned to one of the unit's squads, he'd been in Emergency for seven years. He liked the work. He liked it so much that on his off-duty hours out in Long Island he was a deputy fire chief for his local fire department, and fully expected to be promoted shortly to chief.

The reason for the existence of Seven Truck was, quite logically, its large rescue truck. This vehicle held virtually every possible tool that might be needed for whatever emergency the citizens of New York City would need to be rescued from. It held hydraulic Hurst tools for tearing things apart—a wrecked car, for example—chain saws, circular saws with carbide tipped blades, come-alongs, a generator and lights, as well as the usual axes and Haligan tools. It also held a veritable arsenal of rifles, shotguns, and submachine guns.

Whatever was needed, cops could find it in Seven Truck. The day had been a normal one for Farrell as a member of ESU. That morning he'd already been to several "jobs." Farrell and his officers had just returned from the scene of a double homicide, where they helped detectives search for evidence. Someone had tried to dispose of two dead bodies by burning them. One of the victims was female. Farrell hadn't been able to tell the sex of the second individual—the body had been burned beyond any possibility of recognition.

But now it was time for lunch. He got out of the truck and helped the driver back the vehicle into quarters.

Over the radio it was reported that information had been received from a Port Authority police officer regarding a building collapse at the PATH train tunnel in lower Manhattan. The train runs under the World Trade Center buildings. Farrell figured it might entail an interior ceiling collapse. Maybe even a train wreck. From what he was hearing from the radio, he figured it might turn out to be a big job. And there he was, stuck in Brooklyn.

Still, he continued to listen carefully. And he told the truck's driver to stop backing into the garage.

It sounded like additional manpower was going to be needed in Manhattan. He called to the ESU officers already in the station to get in their smaller rescue vehicles and head out to Manhattan. Nobody had called for them yet, but it looked to him like there was a strong possibility added personnel would be needed at that site. The Williamsburg Bridge connecting Brooklyn to Manhattan was far enough away so that if in fact the extra officers weren't required, there would be ample time to recall them.

Then over the radio came the report of smoke coming into the Twin Towers. Farrell, part of the high-rise fire rescue team, now figured that the team might be activated. Which meant he would have to get his equipment and people over to the Aviation Unit at Floyd Bennett Field.

He got back into the truck and directed his driver to head for Aviation.

By the time they got to the Belt Parkway, Farrell heard over the radio the call for Aviation to get a helicopter ready for either a Medevac or a high-rise rescue. He picked up his microphone and told Central—the term used by cops to refer to their Communications Unit—to have the ship wait. The high-rise rescue team was only "five minutes" away.

A somewhat long "five minutes" later, Farrell and his truck pulled into Floyd Bennett Field. As they approached the 412 on the dolly, Farrell saw that Crew Chief Richard Troché was waving them onto the tarmac. That was unusual. In Farrell's experience, pilots and crew generally liked ground vehicles to keep their distance from the helicopters, especially when the ships had their rotor blades turning over.

The big truck had barely come to a stop next to the helicopter when Farrell and four other officers jumped out. They opened up side panels on the vehicle and Semendinger watched as they removed Scott packs plus about ten spare air bottles. There was an additional rappel rope, handheld lights, and other pieces of assorted equipment used by ESU officers.

The material was tossed on board the 412 and five officers climbed into the ship, each taking a seat atop their gear. One ESU officer remained with the truck and drove it on to lower Manhattan.

Semendinger finally was able to pull power. The heavily laden 412 lumbered into the air. He flew no higher than five hundred feet over the city, as it made little sense to go any higher when he knew he would be descending as soon as he came onto the emergency site.

En route to the scene little communication went on inside the helicopter. Farrell and his team silently rigged up the ship for a possible rappel mission. Two 200-foot-long lines, each capable of holding 9000 pounds, were tied in place. Safety lines were made secure and carabineers fastened. Everyone knew exactly what they were doing, because they had drilled and practiced doing it so many times in the past.

The closer they came to the LZ, the more serious were the reports coming in over the police radio about the magnitude of the destruction they were going to have to deal with at the Twin Towers.

It took only a few minutes to arrive over Battery City Park, located to the north and at the base of one of the

World Trade Center buildings. Semendinger could see where a temporary landing zone and command post had been set up by ground units in an empty parking lot. He pointed the nose of his helicopter in its direction.

As Semendinger began his approach to the snow-covered LZ, he had no thought of rooftop landings or anything else. At that moment his first thought was to get the badly needed equipment and personnel down to the ground. When he came close to his touchdown point, the downwash of his rotors forced the parking lot's layer of fresh snow to swirl around the ship, causing an almost complete loss of vision. Semendinger found he had just enough eye contact with the ground from his side window and chin bubble to safely continue the landing. He gently eased the more than five tons of aluminum, jet fuel, and people to a touchdown.

Careful to roll the power off slowly—the machine rested on what appeared to be a solid sheet of ice, and an abrupt change in rotor torque could easily whip the heavy helicopter around like a top—the ESU officers jumped out and unloaded all their equipment. While those personnel worked at removing their things, Semendinger took a moment to look around. He could see one of the World Trade Center buildings to his front. Curtains were blowing from open windows a hundred stories overhead. It took a few seconds before he remembered that the windows in the Twin Towers weren't designed to be opened. The billowing curtains suggested that the windows had been smashed open, either by people or events. Semendinger guessed that the building's occupants had forced them open in order to get air to breathe. Which meant that somewhere in the lower levels there was a fire.

Examining the scene more closely, he saw that the Vista Hotel, situated between the two towers and directly over the shared underground garage, had substantial amounts of smoke coming from its windows as well. Semendinger figured that as soon as all the ESU stuff was unloaded, he had better do an aerial survey of the roofs of those buildings.

Now that Farrell was on the ground, he had his ESU officers unload their equipment from the helicopter. Crew Chief Troche informed him that once the ship was cleared of ESU officers and equipment, they were going to conduct a survey of the damage. Farrell suggested that two ESU members stay with the helicopter and that they keep some of their rappel equipment, as well as a number of their tools, aboard the 412. That way he and ESU Officer Robert Schierenback could take a look at the situation and, when they reported directly back to the ESU commanders, enable the bosses to make the decision as to whether to deal with the problem with an immediate rappel to the roof.

Little more than half an hour had passed since the explosion, and Semendinger's radio continued to spill out a jumble of information. There was a good deal of talk of a fire, with reports of people trapped in the upper floors of the big buildings. Semendinger decided Farrell's idea about keeping two of the ESU officers with the helicopter when the 412 went to see what was going on was a good one. After all, if somebody was going to have to rappel onto the tower roofs, it would be them. Sergeant Farrell and Officer Schierenback prepared for the possible job as Semendinger lifted off from the LZ.

Semendinger wanted to take a look a the roof of the Vista Hotel. As he climbed higher he noted that although the hotel was lower than the two large towers on either side, there seemed to be more dense black smoke spewing out from the hotel's insides. Passing above the top of the Vista, the 412 continued to climb. Looking down on the hotel's roof—the small building was dwarfed by the two 110-story towers—he and his crew could see that no one waited on the smaller building's roof for rescue. Relieved that at least that location didn't need his attention, Semendinger continued to gain altitude to the roofline of the northern tower.

As he cleared the top of the building, he didn't see anyone standing around. Good, Semendinger thought. Everybody followed the directions of the fire department and didn't go to the roof. Barely a minute later, as the 412 moved over to the southern tower, Semendinger could see nearly two hundred people on that building's observation deck.

He took a deep breath, figuring this would be a big operation.

He could see that he was going to have a couple of problems. First and foremost, though there was a helipad on top of the building, it had never been put into operation. Instead, nearly fifty assorted antennas and mushroom-shaped microwave towers had been fastened around the pad. Semendinger wasn't at all sure he would be able to fit the 412's big blades between all the protruding equipment.

He told his copilot, "I think I'm going to put it in position over the helipad to see if it'll fit."

The two hundred people on the observation deck and catwalk around the helipad stared up at the helicopter as it came nearer. Semendinger's copilot attempted to wave them off and away from the area. They cheerfully waved back! It was obvious to Semendinger that those people hadn't a clue as to what was going on around them. It had been clear from what he'd seen coming up from ground level that the tower they were hovering over hadn't been hit nearly as hard as the northern one had. It was apparent that the people under them were simply tourists enjoying the day.

Semendinger came to a twenty-foot hover over the helipad and began to permit the 412 to settle down. It looked real close from where he sat—his crew later measured the antennas' clearance from the blades' tips. He had all of twelve feet to play with—but he figured he could make it. Then an unusual thing happened. While still fully engrossed in the landing attempt, something—to this day he doesn't know what—told him that he should be over at the other tower. He aborted the approach.

Making a right-hand turn into the wind, he made his way over to the northern tower. There was still nobody in view. But in this tower, Semendinger saw a hell of a lot of smoke coming from the building—too much not to have at least a few people seeking shelter on the roof. It just didn't seem right.

On one of the corners of the building, Semendinger caught sight of a helipad sign painted on the roof. And on this building he saw a hundred-odd antennas crowding the helicopter pad. He'd never make the landing without suffering a blade strike.

Farrell looked out his side of the 412. He noted that nobody was on the roof. To him that was a bad sign. Farrell told Troche as much, adding that if the helicopter couldn't land because of all the equipment sticking up around the pad, it would be no problem for him and Schierenback to rappel down and find out for sure what the story was. The helicopter could then return to the LZ and pick up more ESU officers if need be.

Troche and Semendinger discussed the option and decided to go for it. Semendinger set the 412 up in a forty-foot hover over the cluttered landing pad area. "Let's rappel," his crew chief, Richard Troche, called over the intercom.

"Let's do it," Semendinger replied.

Farrell and Schierenback "hooked up"—attached themselves to the rappel rope—and, taking up the heavy duty cutting and prying tools they thought they'd need, prepared to drop down the fifty feet of the rappel line which now stretched from the helicopter to the roof.

From the open door Farrell tossed out the bag of tools so that they were lowered down the rappel line. With a final okay from Semendinger, Farrell stepped outside onto the ship's skid, turned in to face the open doorway, and kicked off into space.

He had performed rappeling dozens of times in the past, but that had been in training. Without conscious thought, he used his left hand to loosely hold onto the line a foot or so above his head. Using that hand as a guide on the rappel line, with his right hand he pressed the rope against his side to control the rate of descent. A few seconds after exiting the helicopter, his feet touched down on the roof. At the time, Farrell didn't think anything special of the event, but in fact with that rappel he became the first New York City police officer to actually perform a high-rise rappel that wasn't a drill.

The moment he hit the deck, he loosened the rope around him, lest he be pulled back up in the air by the now lightened helicopter. Or maybe worse, have a gust of wind shift the big aircraft, with him being dragged along as a hapless passenger.

Farrell noticed that the wind was pushing him around a bit. Concerned, he looked up at the 412 hovering overhead. It appeared to be rock solid. With that, his confidence increased significantly in Semendinger's ability to handle a helicopter.

Grabbing onto the rope and holding it steady—called "belaying"—Farrell prepared for Schierenback to come down. As Farrell had been the first man out of the helicopter, there had been nobody below to steady the rope. That made his descent the more precarious of the two. Had Farrell had some problem, such as hitting his head as he exited on some part of the helicopter and rendering himself unconscious, he would have fallen the nearly fifty feet to the roof below. But now that he was safely on the roof, he would hold onto the end of the rappel line. Should some problem arise that caused Schierenback to slide down at too rapid a rate, Farrell would pull the rope tight. Even were the other man unconscious, he could literally stop Schierenback midway between the helicopter and the roof, and then, by varying the amount of pressure he put on the line, lower him down at whatever rate of descent Farrell thought best.

Farrell, line in hand, watched as Schierenback backed out of the door of the 412 and let himself fall back into empty space. With the deft skill of someone who had practiced his art, Schierenback gently slid down the rappel line, coming down as surely as had Farrell before him. With Schierenback on the roof, Farrell tied off the remainder of the rope into a neat package around the now empty equipment bag, which had been lowered earlier and held the heavy cutting tools, and signaled for Troche to pull it back aboard the helicopter.

Farrell walked over to the edge of the roof and called over to the people on the tower to his south to find out if they were okay. A man yelled back everything was all right. A comedian shouted over the question, "Do you have any Grey Poupon?"

With that crack Farrell figured they'd hold for a while. In the meantime he wanted to find some way to get into the building. The two men walked down a stairwell and found a door, but it was locked. With one of his tools, Farrell pried the security plate off the front of the lock and forced the door open.

As the door came open, Farrell was struck by the amount of thick, heavy smoke he encountered. As the first assistant chief in his Williston, Long Island, fire department, he knew all about fires and smoke. The good news, Farrell thought, was the smoke was cold, meaning it probably came from a lower floor and had cooled off as it rose to the top of the building. Farrell knew it was unlikely he would face a fire on the upper floors. Before he moved forward, he wedged open the door. He wanted to ventilate the building, and besides, he didn't like the idea of having the door locked behind him in case he needed to get out in a hurry.

As he entered the building, Farrell had to come to terms with the bad news. Smoke, Farrell knew, was the reason most people die in fires, and he was unprepared for all the smoke at the top of the building. Neither he nor Schierenback were equipped with the Scott-pack breathing apparatus. Undaunted, the men crouched low to avoid the smoke, and this allowed them to breathe and see—well, sort of see. There was no electricity in the building, so Farrell and Schierenback pulled out their flashlights and began to conduct a survey of the floor.

With the two officers out of the helicopter, there was no more Semendinger could do over the tower. He started back down to the LZ. As he did so, he found himself bumping up against and even going a bit into, the bottom of the cloud base. After all, they were over 1500 feet above sea level when he did the rappel, and he now worried that should the ceiling get any lower, he might be shut out from picking the two cops up if they needed to get off the roof in a hurry. Nonetheless, he figured he'd better get a few more ESU people up there with more equipment in case Farrell and Schierenback required assistance.

Four ESU cops were already waiting at the LZ for the pickup. Semendinger noticed one of them in particular. He was the son and namesake of a former member of the Aviation Unit, Joe Zogbi, the man who had been in charge of maintenance. But there was no time for a chat.

Unknown to the rescuers, eight people had been trapped in an office on the floor just below Farrell and Schierenback. It was the CBS communications room, and, as it was a high security area, whoever designed the facility used a high-tech solution to make sure only authorized people could get in or out. Each of the people in the room had magnetically coded credit-card-size plastic passes which unlocked the room's doors to the roof. They could go down but not up.

The cards worked great, so long as there was electricity to operate the locks. With the power to the building cut off, there was no way they could now escape to the roof. They knew that they could make their way to the ground floor via the down stairwell, which was situated behind the room's emergency door. At the first sign of trouble, they had tried to get out by that exit, only to come face-to-face with a wall of thick black smoke. The people inside the room slammed that door shut and quickly stuffed rags underneath to keep the smoke out. Which then left them with no place to go.

Farrell and Schierenback made their way down the stairs and through a service hallway, which led them to an office hallway. To their left Farrell saw an office door. First feeling the door to make sure it wasn't hot—which would mean there was a fire on the other side—he pulled it open. Rags had been shoved underneath in an attempt to keep out the smoke. But as it opened he found there was the same amount of the dark gray stuff inside the room as in the hallway.

Walking among the office cubicles, in the distance he could see a couple of flashlight beams dancing ahead of him. Farrell had found eight people. Most were from that office, part of the CBS corporation. A woman, Debbie Menut, emerged from the group and exclaimed, "Thank God the fire department is here."

Farrell corrected her. "Not the fire department, the police department."

To which she replied, "I don't care. Somebody's here for me!"

As Schierenback spoke to the others, Farrell's attention was drawn to the woman. She told him she was pregnant, and was visibly upset over having already breathed in so much smoke. Farrell, with two sons and a pregnant wife who was due in less than a month, understood her feelings.

He told her to grab her coat, he was going to take her outside. Leading everyone in the office back up the stairs and onto the roof and fresh air, he had her stay in the stairwell, to keep her out of the wind until other help could arrive.

And Farrell knew that at that moment the only thing that was going to be able to get Debbie Menut down from the roof of a World Trade Center tower was a helicopter.

Farrell returned to the building and went back to the CBS office. He had been told by one of the individuals that the telephones there were still functioning in a marginal way. Those in the office could call out, but the disruption to the building had stopped all incoming calls.

Farrell knew the cellular telephone number used at any scene requiring a temporary headquarters. This post should have been set up by now and the telephone placed into operation. It was standard operating procedure (SOP) at the scene of disasters. He dialed it, expecting that if he were lucky enough for the cell phone to have somebody on the other end, he'd still be calling right in the middle of a very chaotic situation.

To his relief, not only was the number being manned, but the person who picked the call up turned out to be someone he knew well, Sergeant Steven Berger, head trainer for the department's K-9 unit. Both men had grown up together and had been members of the same volunteer fire department. It permitted Farrell to give a brief situation report to Berger without need of detailed explanation. He told Berger there were eight civilians on the roof, and explained that as he spoke Schierenback was finishing cutting down the assorted antennas surrounding the roof landing pad. In a few minutes it would be safe for a helicopter to set down.

Farrell also told Berger that he wanted to get those civilians back down on the ground soon, as he had a survey to conduct to see who else was in trouble in the building.

The ESU sergeant began his task of searching out survivors of the explosion by working his way down Stairwell A. His intent was to conduct a primary survey. This basically entailed having him move quickly from office to office, yelling out to see if anyone was there. The secondary survey, where they would do detailed searching under desks and in closets, would have to come later, when there was more manpower available. In Farrell's experience, with the primary survey you find the survivors, with the secondary you locate the dead bodies.

At the 107th floor, Farrell entered the Windows on the World restaurant, a world-class establishment. It was an eerie scene. For a moment he figured he knew what it must have looked like the first couple of minutes after the volcano blew at Pompeii. Tables were elegantly set with fine eating utensils. Food sat, some of it untouched, some partially eaten. And over the whole there drifted a smoky haze that hung in the air like an ominous cloud.

Farrell had never been in either of the World Trade towers before, had never gone to the Windows on the World restaurant. He had always wanted to visit the towers and its famous eatery. Now that he'd finally gotten there, it had been in a most unusual way.

He looked around, but though he couldn't locate any Grey Poupon, Farrell did find two maintenance workers on that floor. He escorted them to the stairwell and directed them to the roof, first radioing Schierenback that the pair were coming. Once the two men got to the roof, Schierenback radioed back to Farrell that they had arrived.

Farrell continued his search. At the 98th floor he found four more people, this time office workers. Like the others, they were sent to the roof and Schierenback. To complicate his life, his police radio was now reporting that there was a major hole in the bottom of the towers. Questions were being raised as to the very stability of the building's structure. At the same time, one of the department's high-ranking chiefs found out Farrell and Schierenback had gained entry into the building from the roof level. He wanted an update on what kind of situation Farrell was facing on the roof, whether there was access to elevators from Farrell's location. Communications even wanted Farrell to go down to the 52nd floor and check to see if anyone was trapped inside an elevator there, what the weather conditions were at the roof level, and a half a dozen other questions. Once it was discovered by the brass and Communications that they actually had a couple of ESU officers inside the tower from the roof level, they started throwing job requests at Farrell like he had all of Seven Truck with him.

On top of which the chief demanded a phone call and the answers to all the information he'd requested, and *right now!* Except that on the floor Farrell was now on, the telephones were completely dead.

Farrell radioed back that he had fourteen civilians who needed evacuation. He decided he'd better head back to the roof, figuring a helicopter would be arriving soon to unload personnel and pick up some of the civilians.

He walked the twelve stories back up to the roof. Schierenback had nearly cleared the obstacles blocking the landing pad. He and Schierenback worked on a number of large searchlights that had to be removed before the helicopter would be able to land.

Farrell radioed to Semendinger in the 412 about the problem, and the helicopter came to a hover over the pad. Two more ESU officers, Joe Zogbi and Mike Curtin, rappeled to the roof. A few minutes later the lights were successfully taken down from their bases.

Semendinger watched as the two additional ESU officers slid down the line to the roof of the north tower. With them went a number of Scott packs and handheld lights. Over the air he had been informed that he would soon have some important cargo to deliver to the roof; five Otis elevator repairmen. An unknown number of men, women, and children were stuck in the tower's elevators, and the only people who would be able to retrieve them were the Otis technicians.

Except that Semendinger was worried about time. He had no way of knowing how long it would take for the ESU cops to clear enough of the antennas from the roof helipad to permit him to land the civilian workers. And the Otis repairmen sure couldn't rappel onto the place.

But then he got an idea.

Hovering over to the corner of the building, Semendinger placed the right skid of the 412 on the raised rim of the roof. His left skid dangled unsupported, 1500 feet above the ground. It took a great deal of concentration, but he found that he was able to safely balance the machine in that position. This meant that if he had to, he could have the five mechanics exit the helicopter from the right door, directly onto the roof. He slid away from the building. Because of the low cloud, the ground was only visible through his chin bubble as he descended once more to the LZ.

As the five elevator mechanics were loaded aboard the 412, Semendinger received a radio transmission from Farrell. The roof helipad had been cleared of obstacles and was ready for a landing.

Farrell watched as the big ship settled onto the now cleared pad. It seemed to him that a small army got out; an ESU lieutenant, two sergeants, and half a dozen officers emerged.

Farrell's first concern was getting Debbie Menut out of there. He walked up to Troche and explained that he had a pregnant woman on the roof. He asked if it would be okay to bring her to the ground.

Troche responded by saying, "By all means, bring her on board."

Farrell went over to Ms. Menut and said, "Your ride's here. It's time to leave." He asked her if she was nervous about flying in a helicopter and she replied, "No. Whatever is going to get me down."

Farrell walked her to the ship and handed her over to Troche, who helped her climb inside. Along with Ms. Menut, several other civilians also went aboard. Semendinger decided to depart with these people first. Since there was a landing pad—as well as the imminent arrival of a second department Bell 412 on the scene—there was no need to load the ship up with people.

Debbie Menut and the other passengers safely made it to the ground. Semendinger thought nothing of the act. A few others—very few, as it turns out—had a different view of the deed. In a much publicized criticism of the rescue, a New York City fire chief stated that removing Ms. Menut by helicopter had been dangerous and smacked of showmanship. It's hard to see how it would have been less dangerous to permit the woman to walk down from the roof of one of the World Trade towers to the ground. The woman would have had to make the hike in the dark, and in the process breathe in poisonous fumes and gases for two hours or so. Instead she was taken down to the street via a two-minute helicopter ride in clean air. But then everybody has to have an opinion.

A common decision was made to get as many rescue people onto the roof as possible. The logic was, it was far easier for the equipment-laden officers to walk down 110 flights of stairs than walk up them. A total of thirty rescue personnel would ultimately be transported to the northern tower by Semendinger and his 412 during the time he worked at the disaster scene.

All the while Semendinger's crew worked the disaster site in their lone Bell 412, other members of the unit were being rushed into service, to ready the department's second large twin-engine helicopter.

One of those first called was Tom McManus. He might be a New York City police sergeant with over twenty-five years on the job, as well as a pilot with the Aviation Unit with over 4000 flying hours, but at home he was simply either "Daddy" or "dear" to his five daughters and wife. McManus enjoys pointing out that in his house he is always surrounded by women. Even his dog is female.

On the day the madmen chose to bomb the World Trade towers, McManus was home with his nine- and twelve-year-olds—they were on their winter school break—as well as his wife. There was nothing special about the day, until he received a call from the Aviation Unit ordering him to get himself into work, "forthwith." From that point on, the day's pace rapidly picked up.

Less than half an hour later he pulled into Floyd Bennett Field. Driving up to the Aviation Unit hangar, he saw a single 412 on the flight line. He noted that unit members were busy putting the helicopter into Medevac configuration as well as placing rappeling gear and emergency rescue equipment aboard. McManus parked, hurried into the old building, and quickly got himself suited up.

On the way to the hangar, he passed Operations. One glance told him the officer at the desk had his hands full.

Not only were the telephones ringing off their hooks—mostly from the media calling—but the police radios were going nonstop. Up to that point the only information Mc-Manus possessed about what was going on was that there had been an explosion at the World Trade Center. As the probable magnitude of the disaster dawned on him, he felt a rush of adrenaline surge through his body and immediately made it out to his helicopter.

He chose for his copilot Detective/Pilot Matthew Rawley, and for crew chiefs, John Galligan, Nick Gregoriades, and Don Gromling. With 1500 pounds of Jet-A in the fuel tanks—enough for around three hours of operation—McManus departed for the LZ. By this time Semendinger had been working alone at the Twin Towers for nearly an hour.

Although he was now aware of the size of the ongoing rescue operation, the scene that he saw through his windscreen when he came around the tip of southern Manhattan still surprised McManus. He had expected the smoke billowing from the sides of the two towers, and the people waving white handkerchiefs from the windows they had broken open. Even the sight of hundreds of people streaming from the big buildings with faces blackened with smoke didn't seem out of place to him. But the spectacle of over five hundred emergency response vehicles on the street below—ambulances, police cars, fire department and ESU vehicles—was mind-boggling. This was indeed a major operation, the scope of which had never been seen before.

By the time McManus arrived at the scene, all the major bosses of the Aviation Unit had arrived and were either in the air in unit JetRangers or manning the temporary command center near the landing zone. The commanding officer, Captain Bill Wilkens, was there, as well as the operations lieutenant and a number of other unit sergeants.

Upon his arrival, McManus was ordered to ferry seven ESU cops and their equipment up to the roof of the northern tower. Still carrying a good load of fuel in his 412, McManus was concerned about the ability of the aircraft to take the heavy load. With the men on board, he slowly and deliberately lifted up on his power lever—the collective—as his copilot called off the percentages from his torque gauge.

Torque is the limiting factor in what his ship could lift. In the Bell 412 it's measured at the transmission; in some helicopters it's measured at the mast. Pull up just one percent beyond 100 percent and the transmission is in for an overhaul, with a resultant $400,000 repair bill.

McManus figured he'd better be real careful. As he cautiously added power, he could feel the skids first lighten, then break free of the ground. The torque gauge remained several percentage points below maximum. He gently nosed the machine forward, to use the assistance of the aerodynamic lifting capability of the helicopter to gain altitude, rather than pure engine power. It was close, but he managed to stay within the 412's limits.

As he ascended up the side of the northern tower, McManus eyed the smoke still billowing from hundreds of open windows. The sheer size of the buildings awed him. And so did the realization of how much responsibility he and the other members of the Aviation Unit would have in helping to remove the tens of thousands of people who remained essentially trapped inside the two buildings.

Coming up to roof level to make his first landing on the tower, a dozen thoughts—really fears—crowded into McManus's head. Would the antennas get in the way? What would he do if there was a sudden and significant wind change? The clouds were still low and still partially obscured the top of the tower. Like Semendinger before him, he wondered what he would do if they suddenly came down fifty feet.

McManus maneuvered the 412 to the ledge of the tower. The rotor blade clearance from the antennas surrounding the pad looked awfully close. But he had the advantage of knowing that Semendinger had successfully made the run several times. He could make it also.

He guided the big ship to the landing pad and let the ESU officers off. Although no one stood directly on the roof, he could see dozens of people huddled in a nearby stairwell, trying to stay out of the cold, and now trying to remain clear of the blast of downwash coming from the 412's blades.

As he would do on his twenty trips to both roofs, dozens

of civilians—some injured, others not—were put aboard his helicopter to be ferried back to the ground. But the first person he carried out as a Medevac was a lieutenant assigned to the Mounted Unit. McManus was informed by his crew chief that the man had suffered from significant smoke inhalation. He had worked his way up the full 110 stories, seeking out injured and needy civilians. Prior to coming onto the NYPD, the lieutenant had worked with the Port Authority police. Assigned to the tower, he'd used his knowledge of the buildings to save people's lives.

McManus noted the minute and second hands on his watch, and with the lieutenant in his helicopter, pulled up on the collective. If he brought the injured lieutenant down to the LZ, it would take an hour for the ambulance to make its way out of the mess the streets below had turned into. Instead, McManus decided on another option. A minute and a half later he touched down at the 34th Street heliport, adjacent to Bellevue Hospital. The way McManus figured it, that's what a helicopter was for.

When it was determined by the brass at temporary command headquarters that there would be an attempt to land on that roof, McManus chose to do it when his fuel and passenger load were light. It would be McManus who made the first landing atop the southern tower. But this time there would be no clearing of the dozens of antennas that stood in the way.

He first conducted a survey of the area in an attempt to pick out the most appropriate place to land. He wasn't happy with what he saw. The place was a veritable forest of antennas, assorted small towers, and microwave dishes. Many of the obstructions stood more than fifty feet above the surface of the landing pad. A blade strike during a landing attempt would likely ground his helicopter 1500 feet above the street, on the roof of the southern tower, with virtually no hope of repair until a new blade could be procured and brought up to the disabled machine. Which, if they were lucky, might just take a few days, not to mention costing the department something over a hundred thousand dollars.

He gently eased the big Bell 412 onto the pad. With barely

ten feet of clearance from the tip of his blades, McManus made the landing. He would make many more trips to that site before he was through, bringing up emergency workers, elevator repairmen, and taking injured and frightened civilians to the ground.

Farrell watched the second landing of the 412. Out of her came an ESU captain along with seven or eight ESU officers. Farrell went to the captain, took him down to the Windows on the World restaurant at the 107th floor, sat him down at a table and gave him a succinct report on what he'd seen so far.

The captain informed him that the plan was for elevator mechanics to be flown up to the roof to deal with the large numbers of people still trapped in many of the 120 elevators located in the Twin Towers.

The two men discussed their options. The problem was that between the two buildings, they had a combined number of 220 floors, their stairways, plus each one of their elevators to search.

The two men decided that a number of teams would be formed. There would be two elevator search teams, three stairwell search teams, two floor-to-floor search teams, and finally two response teams, who would respond to any calls for assistance from the other rescuers. They would each be made up of between three and four officers, led by a supervisor. And the elevator teams would have a number of elevator technicians assigned to them. Each of the teams would be responsible for sixty elevators. One team would handle the even floors, the other team the odd ones. The captain also made it clear that he wanted each and every elevator physically checked.

Farrell, assigned to the elevator detail, also learned that the buildings had their own elevator staff. These individuals were not only extremely knowledgeable about the mechanical specifics of the machines, but about their locations as well. Because the buildings were so large, only two elevators ran from the ground floor to the roof level. Most of the elevators ran for a limited number of floors only, and the number of floors they covered varied. One bank might take people to the fortieth floor, where they'd get off and go to another bank that took them up an additional twenty (or more) floors.

Farrell's team started at the highest level, where an elevator control/maintenance room was located. From there—as in each of these control rooms—markings on the exposed cables supporting the elevators could tell them on or between which floors each of the ten cars in that particular bank was located. The technicians—even without electricity—could also manually raise or lower the cars to the nearest floor level. The rescue team would then go down to where the elevators were situated and force the doors of the cars open, either to release the trapped occupants or verify that no one remained inside. Farrell would be doing the job for nearly twenty-four hours, until after four A.M.

Somewhere around the eightieth floor Farrell's team came upon their first occupied car. The three men had been trapped inside for over three hours and had taken in some smoke, but were otherwise unhurt. Farrell had one of his officers escort the trio to one of several triage centers which he knew had been set up on a lower floor.

Near the 60th floor, the team found a lone man in one of the cars. Thanking them profusely for rescuing him, he explained that he had felt the building rock just prior to entering the elevator. The car had jerked to a halt, and soon began to fill with smoke. The man thought for sure that he would die. Fortunately, after a while the smoke cleared. Then he realized he was hungry, so he began to eat the lunch he had just purchased. Once he started on the food, it occurred to him that if, as he believed, there had been a nuclear attack, he might be in the elevator for weeks. So he stopped eating his lunch and began to ration it.

At about the 56th floor, Farrell's team met members of the fire department—a lieutenant and two firemen—who had been working their way up the various levels, also checking elevators for victims of the bombing. The fire department team assured Farrell that they had checked all the elevators from that floor to the ground level and that they were clear.

Farrell thanked the fire officers, informed them that his

team had cleared all the cars above them and explained about the stairwell and floor search teams. He also told the firemen that his team would continue doing what they were doing until they completed their task.

When the firemen continued up the stairs and were out of earshot, one of the elevator mechanics suggested that since the firemen had checked all the banks of elevators below them, why didn't they just call it a day. Farrell explained that in the NYPD, when a ranking member of the service gives an order to do something, it's done. He had been directed to physically look into each and every elevator car assigned to him, and into each and every car he would look.

The elevator mechanics laughed. They couldn't understand the apparently inflexible position he took on the matter and were annoyed that they would have to perform what now appeared to be a meaningless task. That is, until they got to the bank of elevators three floors below and found and freed two people trapped inside one of the cars.

Detective John Fagan is chief pilot at the Aviation Unit. As such, he holds many responsibilities beyond that of pilot, his training role probably being the most demanding. Because he flies a large number of training flights, he is one of the most technically able pilots within the unit. When the disaster struck the Twin Towers, Fagan was among the first people called in.

With Semendinger in one Bell 412 and McManus in the unit's other, there was no urgent reason for Fagan to race to work. Still, he was the chief pilot, and the powers that be would certainly feel better with him in and ready to go.

When he arrived at Floyd Bennett Field, only a single JetRanger remained of the unit's fleet of six helicopters. But shortly after Fagan suited up, Semendinger returned in his 412.

The plan was for Semendinger's crew, who had been working for over four hours, to be relieved by fresh personnel; and when that new crew tired out, the "old" crew would relieve them. It was Fagan who took over the pilot-in-command seat of Semendinger's 412. As with many plans devised in the middle of an emergency, this one didn't work out as anticipated. Fagan and the others aboard his helicopter wouldn't be getting out of that particular aircraft for quite a while. With him would be Carlos Sanchez as copilot (later relieved by Detective Roy Alberti), and crew chiefs/mechanics Brian Hunt and Richard Troche. Troche, Semendinger's crew chief, although given an opportunity to take a break, chose to remain aboard the helicopter.

Fagan, with the advantage of knowing the kind of missions he would be involved in, had the 412 loaded up with only 900 pounds of fuel, a relatively light amount. It would be good enough for an hour's worth of flying. In terms of the short two-minute trips the 412s were performing from the roof of the towers to the LZ and back, and the large number of people being taken aboard the ships, the low fuel weight made sense. Anyway, he knew that when he got low, Jet-A was readily available from either the West 30th or East 34th Street heliports.

Once at the LZ, Fagan's first job was to bring elevator mechanics and Port Authority police officers up to the roof of the north tower. As with the other pilots who made the approach to the pad, the relatively small size of the landing area combined with the large number of antennas surrounding it concerned Fagan. Pilots refer to such missions as having a "high-puckor factor."

He took a deep breath and made the approach. Upon touching down on the roof landing area, he noticed that although a few of the antennas had had to be broken off at their bases to make clearance for the helicopter blades, a number of others had been designed with hinged bottoms. Those had only to be pushed over, and thus were not damaged in the operation, which Fagan thought made a great deal of sense if you were going to put antennas next to a helicopter landing pad.

By this time ESU personnel had control of the situation on top of the tower. Before Fagan's load of people disembarked, two Emergency Unit officers came up to the ship and escorted them off. Fagan figured that was a good idea. He knew that during periods of excitement a first-time helicopter passenger—which the elevator mechanics very likely

29

were—might experience the danger of coming into contact with the nearly invisible, whirling tail-rotor blades. It was always a factor to be concerned about.

In fact, during the remainder of the operation, Fagan never observed any "lost souls" wandering around the roof. There was always good control of personnel movement on the roof, by both ESU officers as well as members of the Aviation Unit.

Fagan saw that many of the Aviation Unit personnel—pilots and mechanics—who had come to the scene ostensibly to conduct flying missions, had found themselves placed in the role of rescuers. A number of unit members wound up deep inside the towers. One officer, John Galligan, rescued a second pregnant woman he found ten floors below the roof. He and the other officers carried her up the stairs in an office chair! She was eventually Medevacked out by Fagan.

Fagan continued his ferry flights into the afternoon, bringing personnel both up to and down from both towers, as well as performing Medevacs as necessary. As time progressed, one problem became clear—they were running out of daylight. The visibility had slowly improved during the day, but with the coming of night—with still no return of power to the buildings—it was becoming increasingly difficult to distinguish the location of the landing pad. And the surrounding antennas were becoming invisible with the approaching darkness.

Eventually, with Alberti at the controls during one of their runs, the rooftop pad dissolved into the shadows of the coming night. Fagan, not wanting to abort the mission, decided to try using the Nightsun attached to the belly of the 412. He turned on the multimillion candlepower searchlight, which did the trick. But its very brightness proved a disadvantage the nearer they came to the pad. Its intensity was also distracting to personnel working on the roof.

Hunt and Troche decided to use battery-powered lanterns which they found aboard the 412. They set one up at each of the four corners of the pad. In order to prevent the lights from being blown away by the helicopter's downwash, they placed some scuba lead weights—also found among the various items laying around the cabin—on top of each. These lanterns served as landing lights—albeit weak ones—until electricity was eventually restored to the tower.

It wasn't until after midnight that Fagan returned to the Aviation Unit base.

McManus worked until two A.M., heading over to the 30th Street heliport when he required fuel. Staying on the controls for so long became a tiring, almost tedious exercise for him. Flying a helicopter requires constant concentration, and he put in more than his share that day.

McManus's words express his thoughts better than any attempt at paraphrasing them: "Your heart really went out to the people who were victimized by this tragedy. It got to you. You could see your mother there, or your sister, or your children. It was a sad thing. An unnecessary sad thing. Unfortunately there are a lot of unnecessary sad things today. All you have to do is look around the world. And we're not immune."

After several hours of search and rescue, Farrell's team reached the sub-basement, 116 floors below the roof. With the primary survey for victims out of the way, someone in command decided to start up the secondary survey. They were looking for volunteers. Farrell and his team stood up and said they were ready to go. Assigned to search from the 70th to the 80th floors, they took one of the few functioning elevators, which got them to the 26th floor. Then they walked up fifty floors, conducted their search, and walked the fifty floors back down to the working elevator.

That day and into the night, Farrell calculated he trekked—up and down—more than 220 floors of the World Trade Center building he was assigned to.

The eleven-week-pregnant Ms. Menut and her coworkers weren't the only civilians removed from the roof that day. Thirty-four people were taken from the Twin Towers, five of them as Medevacs. The helicopters of the Aviation Unit were preparing to take over 200 people from the trade towers' two roofs when the mission was canceled, since electrical power was restored to the buildings and the elevators came back on-line.

As far as the pilots and crews were concerned, the mission went exactly as they had been trained to do it. To Semendinger it was clear that without a helicopter—especially a large twin-engine machine such as the big Bell—the operations performed would have proven far more difficult to accomplish. It would have taken the emergency response teams much longer to deal with the situation. Semendinger believes that without the benefit of the large police helicopters, there would have been a far greater loss of life than the six people who ultimately died.

CHAPTER 2

The Aviation Unit:
The Beginning Years

ONE OF THE AVIATION UNIT'S FIRST DOCUMENTED RESCUES
of note took place shortly after the unit was formed. In
December 1930 a Navy blimp, the *Akron,* went down several
miles off the shore of New Jersey's Beach Haven, close by
the border of New York City. Another blimp, the Navy's
J-3, was sent out to conduct rescue operations. With howling
winds and huge swells, *J-3* also went out of control and it
too crashed into the frigid Atlantic waters.

A department Savoia Marchetti—a badly underpowered
single-engine seaplane—flew out to the scene. Although the
ocean swells were so high that a landing would be extraordi-
narily risky, the pilot, seeing survivors of the blimp in the
water, put the plane down anyway, knowing that once on the
water, there would be no possibility of flying the aircraft off.

The victims of the crash managed to climb aboard the
floating seaplane. With no room for any of them inside the tiny
cockpit, they were forced to lie on her wings while the pilot
water-taxied the five miles to the nearest beach. Once the
hull touched sand, one of the sailors, eager to reach the
safety of land and not heedful of the danger of the whirling
propeller, made straight for shore. To save the man's life
the pilot threw out his arm, blocking the way but losing a
finger to the aircraft's propeller in the process.

For the bravery demonstrated by the department's crew,
the U.S. Congress wanted to award the police officers involved in the rescue the Congressional Medal of Honor, but
as the officers weren't in the military, such a presentation
was not possible.

In June of 1951 perhaps the world's first helicopter rescue by a police agency took place. A steeplejack, while working atop the church of St. John the Divine in upper Manhattan, fell from his scaffolding and onto a narrow parapet located hundreds of feet above the street. Severely injured—his back had been broken—there was no way to remove him from his precarious perch. Fire department ladder trucks couldn't reach nearly high enough, and there was no way he could be brought into the building and down the stairs in his injured condition.

The man lay on the ledge for two hours while Emergency Service rescue personnel tried to figure some way to get him down to ground level. Ultimately, and almost surely out of desperation, it was decided to try to get him to safety by a helicopter. Of course, the ledge where the man lay was far too narrow for the skids of the Aviation Unit Bell 47 to rest on. The helicopter was forced to touch down on the roof with one skid on the parapet and the other in the air, and to maintain that position while the gravely injured man was strapped onto the helicopter. Once that was done, the pilot flew down to nearby Riverside Park, where an ambulance was waiting and the victim was removed to a local hospital.

I had already been with the NYPD for fifteen years when I got the chance to join Aviation. I had just earned my Private Pilot license when a chance meeting with unit members informed me they were looking for a flying sergeant. The pilots told me that to be considered for the slot, I would need a Commercial Pilot license, which was both expensive and time-consuming to earn. It meant that I would have to add around two hundred hours of flight time to the eighty or so I already had so painfully—and at significant financial cost—acquired.

Undaunted (well, maybe a little daunted), I went out to my local airport, where I discovered that a young Air Force lieutenant had just purchased a small plane, a little Cessna 150 trainer. He had also just got himself transferred out of the area and couldn't take his airplane with him. I called him and arranged to lease the machine back from him for a modest hourly sum.

Next I went to my good friend, David Quam. Dave, a

four-thousand-hour seaplane pilot, the founder of the Seaplane Pilots Association, and a certified flight instructor,
agreed to train me. With Dave's help and some work on my
part, a year later I found myself sitting at the control's of a
$750,000 police helicopter.

After a promotion to lieutenant in 1985 and its mandated
transfer back to patrol, it took me until 1988 before I was
able to rejoin the Aviation Unit. Once there, I was quickly
trained to pilot our Huey and given an assignment as one
of the midnight tour pilots. In fact I was there because I'd
been checked out to fly the Huey. Even though it was a
thirty-year-old single-engine military surplus helicopter, the
old Huey was capable of flying over a hundred miles an
hour and could lift a great deal of weight. The machine's
strengths were needed, as we were a twenty-four-hour, "can
do" outfit.

Senior personnel avoided working midnights, and as I was
the junior lieutenant, I was the senior ranking officer on the
late shift as well as the only pilot qualified to fly the Huey.
Most nights, my other crew members consisted mostly of a
single, young mechanic—who would also act as the mission
crew chief—and a variety of newly assigned, equally young
pilots-in-training.

It was a serious responsibility. After all, the Aviation Unit
was the air arm of the largest municipal police force in the
world. My crew and I could well be called on to respond to
every emergency imaginable, from the horror of an airliner
crash to searching for an armed gunman, or getting involved
in car chases to responding to terribly injured persons in
need of swift helicopter evacuation to a hospital.

At around 0500 hours during one of my first early morning shifts, a Medevac was called in. There had been a fire
somewhere in Brooklyn. The smoke inhalation victim of that
fire was at the moment receiving medical attention from
emergency medical technicians. The EMTs decided that
their patient needed to be brought over to the hyperbaric
chamber—a device capable of infusing high pressure oxygen
into the human body, normally used to aid people suffering
from the bends, but invaluable in aiding smoke inhalation

cases—located out at the Bronx's City Island. The ambulance would meet my helicopter near the fire scene.

This was to be the first time I would act as pilot-in-command of a Medevac. My landing zone was to be an unfamiliar schoolyard in Brooklyn.

Pulling my crew together, we went out to the flight line. It was late winter and still dark out. I remember feeling very cold. Only moments earlier I had located the landing zone on my Hagstrom's city street map—flying around New York City meant such road maps were far more useful than any aeronautical chart—and wondered to myself how I was going to find my way around Brooklyn at night and fly the ship at the same time. Reminding my crew chief to undo the tie-down strap attached to the rotor—in the excitement of the moment he had forgotten that minor detail—I ran through the aircraft's systems in preparation for start-up.

Turbine-powered aircraft starts have to be carefully monitored. If fuel is introduced into the engine before the ship's electric starter brings the machine up to a certain minimum speed, the internal temperatures will rise to destructive levels. That requires a teardown of the engine, at a minimum, and the strong possibility of a repair job. Cost for such an error can be six figures.

And now I sat in the pilot-in-command seat. No two-thousand-hour instructor-pilot sat next to me to keep me out of trouble, only a young kid who had no idea how to work the helicopter we were in.

I was the pilot-in-command. I couldn't give that away, I couldn't delegate the job. Their lives, the life of the victim, and this mission was my sole responsibility. My crew trusted in me to get them back to base in time to go home that morning. I settled into the right seat, took a deep breath, and let my fingers begin to trip the dozen odd switches needed to bring the helicopter's big turbine to life.

Yelling "Clear!" I pressed the start button and more than two tons of fuel, men, and aluminum began to rock gently as the Huey's four hundred pounds of rotor blades slowly commenced to turn overhead. With a twist of my wrist I turned the throttle, introducing fuel into the engine. Now, with a muted roar, my big machine's heart began to beat in earnest.

Little more than a minute later—just long enough to let the helicopter's parts come up to their proper operating temperatures—I pulled up on the collective control and the Huey came off her dolly and headed north.

My copilot held the map in his lap and guided me to the LZ. Within five minutes of lift-off we saw the red and white flashing lights of a police radio car next to a school. I headed for them.

To my relief, dawn was just breaking. All around the school's playground—an area perhaps a hundred feet long by about seventy-five feet in width—I could see there was a fence a dozen feet high. Whoever designed the place clearly never gave any thought for helicopters landing there. The Huey is a long machine, and I had over thirty feet of tail bloom jutting out behind me, as well as nearly fifty-foot main rotor blades whirling overhead. This meant I had to come in slow, making sure both my tail and main rotors cleared the fence. If a blade struck something, the helicopter would whip around violently. And if that happened in such a confined area, there would be lots of other things we'd also hit, probably ripping the Huey and everyone inside to pieces.

I can't imagine what the people in the homes around the school thought was happening when the *whup whup* sound of the wide-bladed Huey disturbed their morning slumber. We flew around the perimeter of the area once, just to make sure there were no wires or other obstacles in the way of the landing approach. In the gray early morning light it appeared the way was clear for a landing. I slowed the helicopter down to around sixty miles an hour and lined her up with the empty playground. As I brought the machine over the fence, I had permitted her speed to lower to little more than a fast walk. Concerned about the tail rotor invisible behind me, I eased the Huey to the middle of the open space and let her gently come to rest on the concrete below.

I took a deep breath. At that moment all I cared about was that the helicopter had settled safely into the small yard. Looking around, I could see the four-story brick school building sitting to my left and the twelve-foot-high fence around my other three sides. Straight ahead, beyond the fence, were a number of fifty-foot trees. And it was in that direction that I ultimately would have to take off. This posed another problem for me to deal with. Getting into a landing zone is one thing. Filling a helicopter up with lots of additional and performance-robbing weight and then getting safely out again is another matter.

Within moments of our arrival, two large emergency medical technicians entered the yard. With them was their patient, unconscious on a rolling stretcher. The EMTs carried with them an assortment of heavy-looking oxygen bottles. My crew chief jumped out and helped the two technicians get the patient and their equipment aboard. A fourth person jumped in behind them. I assumed it was a relative of the victim, as having such additional passengers ride along with the victim was a common occurrence during Medevacs. I figured that in the two minutes it took to load everyone inside, my ship had taken on nearly a thousand additional pounds of weight.

So there I was, with a helicopter loaded down with people, nearly full of fuel, and with a fence and trees in the direction of my only practical way out. My only option was to first head straight up a hundred feet. Helicopter pilots—particularly single-engine helicopter pilots—don't like such maneuvers. Because in a single-engine ship the only thing holding you in the air while you're heading straight up is the turning blades of the machine, which are only turning because the engine is operating normally. If at some point during this maneuver, and before any meaningful forward speed has been attained, should the engine decide it was going to have a bad day, the pilot's day would soon get a lot worse. At least for as long as it took gravity to bring the helicopter smashing back to earth.

For reasons of safety, pilots much prefer to gather some forward airspeed before permitting the aircraft to gain any significant altitude. Should the ship's engine quit, the forward airspeed, as well as the momentum of the whirling rotor blades, would then permit a pilot to bring the helicopter back to earth for a safe emergency landing.

Flight at low altitudes with minimum forward airspeed was portrayed by a graph in the operating manual of every helicopter. It was called the shaded area and was to be avoided. Pilots referred to it simply as the "dead man's" zone.

I told my copilot to monitor my torque gauge. I would pull power up to the maximum allowed for the helicopter's transmission. If we kept on going up, okay. If we started to run out of power before clearing the obstacles, I would abort the takeoff and try again once we lightened the load.

Making sure all was clear around the machine, I started to lift up on the collective. As the power increased, my copilot began to read off torque percentages, which in the Huey maxed out at 47 percent.

"Thirty-nine percent . . ."

We broke ground.

"Forty-two percent . . ."

My eyes focused on the fence ahead. As we rose above it he continued, "Forty-four percent . . ."

We were clearing the tops of the trees just as he called, "Forty-five percent." I lowered the nose and began to let the ship slide forward. At a safe sixty miles an hour we cleared the obstacles, and at that moment I knew I loved the Huey. That old tub of an aircraft could get us out of anything. Together we were invincible.

Rising to an altitude of a thousand feet, we made our way to City Island. A police car and ambulance stood by next to a large baseball field close to the hyperbaric chamber. We dropped off the patient, and like most Medevacs I've ever known, never found out the person's name or how they fared. But we had done our job and had given her a chance. On the return to base I let my copilot fly the Huey the entire way back. It was all so uneventful.

Some of the dangers of the air are not concerns one would normally associate with flying. For example, during good weather, kites are a major problem for urban police helicopter pilots. Where these delightful ancient toys were once hoisted aloft using relatively weak string, the modern and now larger versions are attached to fifty-pound-test monofilament fishing line, often to an altitude of a thousand feet or more. This very strong material can (and has, to me!) wrapped itself around the relatively delicate and critical rotating mechanism of the helicopter—a machine that at the best of times is defined by its pilots as a group of dissimilar parts flying in close formation.

As the monofilament tightens, it can pull in on the aircraft's "push-pull" tubes, the devices that control the angle at which the blades meet the air. Once that occurs, the only thing left for the pilot to do is to sit back and enjoy the ride to the crash site.

During one otherwise routine patrol flight, I once was asked by LaGuardia air traffic controllers to investigate a kite that was reported to be in the way of aircraft on the approach path to their airport. My copilot and I located the culprit. As we came level with the kite our altimeter showed it was flying at over eight hundred feet above the ground, with her monofilament line tied off to a pipe atop a six story building in the Bronx, with no one in sight!

And there are other even more bizarre dangers. On one occasion, I recall an Aviation Unit lieutenant who went out alone for a Saturday afternoon's "beach patrol" flight. The unit operates from a hangar at Floyd Bennett Field, a former Navy base located in the southern part of Brooklyn. The field is surrounded by water; Jamaica Bay on one side, Gerritsen Inlet on the other, and the Atlantic Ocean a few miles to the south. Little more than twenty minutes after the aircraft had departed, the JetRanger returned to base. Once shut down by the lieutenant, he announced he had come back due to some unspecified mechanical problem. He told us he had heard a loud bang while cruising along the Rockaway beaches. Although detecting no anomalies in the gauges, he had immediately turned the aircraft around for Floyd Bennett Field.

Several mechanics and pilots began to look the helicopter over in search of the problem, until one officer noticed a gaping, irregularly shaped hole in the rear passenger compartment's Plexiglas window, in line with and less than a foot behind the pilot's head. Looking inside the cabin, all could see, sitting on the otherwise unoccupied bench seat, a six ounce silver metal fishing lure, hooks and all! And the lieutenant *swore* he had been flying no lower than three hundred feet. Right.

Birds were another source of potential trouble for Aviation Unit pilots. This was especially true when one of the city's garbage dump sites was in operation just a few miles from the Aviation Unit base. Literally tens of thousands of sea gulls inhabited the area. It was just a matter of time before the inevitable collision. There was an incident in which one of the large birds smashed through the windshield of a department JetRanger, striking the pilot in the chest. Although shaken and covered with bird innards, the officer safely landed the machine. Another time, while I was flying over Floyd Bennett Field at dusk, I heard a loud bang and felt a breeze. Not knowing what had happened, but realizing it was bad—you're not supposed to feel a breeze inside a helicopter—I immediately reduced my airspeed and set the ship up for a landing. As I did this, the pilot next to me monitored our engine gauges, looking for any rise in temperature. We both figured, correctly, that we had had a bird strike, and were concerned that the sea gull—since it wasn't in the cabin—might have been ingested into the engine's air intake. Were that to have occurred, within a very few moments there would have been an ominous silence when the engine died, followed by my helicopter heading for the ground at its autorotation rate of descent of nearly two thousand feet per minute. But once again luck was on my side. The bird had hit the helicopter facing head on, impaling itself on the metal thermometer probe affixed to the Plexiglas bubble. The impact of the animal had ripped the instrument out of the window, along with a substantial chunk of Plexi—hence the breeze—and bounced off the top of the helicopter, just missing the engine's air intake opening.

Sometimes the unit is called upon to assist other city departments. One such backup call took place right at Floyd Bennett Field. For many years a thriving military airport, in the early 1970s the base was turned over to the Federal Park Service, which had visions of the large field being used for public recreation. As with many such plans, the lofty goals met with the reality of limited funds, so the facility, for all practical purposes, now remains as little more than an unused airport that gives the appearance of having fallen on hard times. Its several-mile-long and hundred-foot-wide concrete runways crisscross what had once been neatly trimmed multiacre plots of grass, and which, after many years of lying fallow, are now inundated with an impenetrable growth of twelve-foot-high coastal grasses.

On that particular day, a section of the grassy part of the field had caught fire. For four hours the fire department worked to put out this stubborn grass and brush fire. Each time they thought they had it under control, the vagaries of the area's sea breezes would start it up anew. Finally, probably in sheer desperation, the supervising firemen came to the Aviation Unit and asked for some aerial help. Always wanting to assist their brother public safety department, a twin-engine Bell 412—the largest helicopter in the inventory, sort of a Huey with two engines—was hooked up to a "Bambi Bucket." How this device came to be known by that name I cannot imagine, but simply stated, it is a very sturdy soft-sided container that can both hold and release water.

The department's Bambi Bucket can carry up to 185 gallons of water. The 412 flew from atop its dolly and over to Dead Horse Bay, which is part of Jamaica Inlet, a little more than a mile away. Picking up its load of 1480 pounds of water, the big twin flew over the center of the intense fire and from a hundred feet dropped the entire load. With a *whoosh* and cloud of smoke the fire went out, much to the delight of those in the helicopter and to the presumed chagrin of the watching firemen as a rival city agency did their job for them.

The New York City Aviation Unit has pioneered in the field of airborne law enforcement in a number of ways. While initially equipped with fixed-wing aircraft—the only kind of flying machine that was practically available during its early years—it was the first police air arm to procure and utilize helicopters. In 1948 the first Bell 47 ever to be used in police service—its keys handed over by Larry Bell himself—was acquired by the department. The department's rotary-winged craft—a type of aircraft ultimately found to be uniquely suited to the task of law enforcement—were to eventually phase out the various fixed-wing ships the Aviation Unit had been using up till then.

By 1970 it was clear that piston-engined helicopters suffered far too many disadvantages over the newer turbine-powered (jet engine) ships—both in terms of power and reliability—to be considered for future purchase. Thus the first of many jet-powered helicopters the department was to acquire came in to the unit. The first sleek Bell 206 Jet-Ranger—as were its earlier piston-powered counterparts, the bubble-nosed and dragonfly-shaped Bell 47s—was a float-equipped utility ship.

The JetRangers, as fine an aircraft as they are, were found to be too light for much of the work the unit was called on to perform, particularly when it came to medical evacuations. During the money crunch of the mid-seventies the unit had to find a way to secure more powerful machines.

Fortunately, with the end of the Vietnam War, surplus Huey helicopters became available. A team of pilots and mechanics from Aviation went out to the Army aircraft graveyard in Arizona, and almost literally using no more than spit and wire, put together two Hueys from an assortment of junk in the yard. Except for the rattlesnake living in one of the ships, and the fact that on the way back to their home base at Floyd Bennett Field in New York one of the helicopters was nearly confiscated by the Mexican government—the pilot had made a wrong turn!—all involved survived.

For a decade these two surplus Hueys were the primary rescue aircraft the police department utilized, until the eventual procurement of twin-engined turbine-powered ships.

CHAPTER 3

Detective/Pilot Guenther (GEW) Rupprecht

Helicopter Down!

ONE OF THE GREAT THINGS ABOUT HELICOPTERS IS THAT THEY make such wonderful sightseeing platforms. The wide expanse of wraparound Plexiglas gives both pilot and passengers a view of the world unavailable in any other type of aircraft.

A spectacular sight—one enjoyed by thousands of tourists over the years—is the helicopter flight/tour that starts at Manhattan's East 34th Street Heliport. The heliport is located on the East River. The borough of Queens is situated opposite the heliport, across the wide river. The place is perfectly suited for flying passengers to and around the Statue of Liberty and Ellis Island. The people who partake in the adventure take home irreplaceable photos and memories. But on rare occasions those memories are of an adventure they'd rather forget.

It was a February day in 1990, and the Island Helicopter Bell LongRanger sat turning over at flight idle on the 34th Street bulkhead, having just been loaded with passengers. Among the excited and expectant people inside was a family of German tourists which included a thirteen-year-old boy.

The pilot turned the helicopters throttle to 100 percent power and pulled up on his collective for the takeoff. The heavily loaded LongRanger, parked with its tail pointed in the direction of the water, lifted off and hovered backward out of its parking place. Once clear of other helicopters and obstacles, the helicopter turned so that her nose faced toward the East River. The machine then began to move forward for takeoff. For some reason, the LongRanger's pilot didn't arm the emergency system the aircraft was equipped with. These floats are designed to fill large buoyant bags that are attached to each skid with high-pressure nitrogen gas when activated by the pilot. Once inflated, they would keep the machine afloat should it be on the water.

The LongRanger, instead of climbing out over the river and heading south to the Statue of Liberty, descended into the water and rolled over onto its back.

Detective/Pilot Guenther (GEW) Rupprecht remembers sitting around the luncheon table in the pilots' room when the unit's klaxon horn went off. The loudspeaker blared out the report that a helicopter was confirmed down off the 34th Street Heliport and in the East River. People were reported to be trapped inside.

Everyone headed for the flight line. Rupprecht, assigned for the day as the air/sea rescue pilot, took the right seat of the Bell 412. Bob Reveille flew as copilot, and mechanic Mark Cabibbo served as crew chief. Sergeant Steve Digregorio also climbed aboard, as did two wet-suited officers from the scuba unit.

Rupprecht's fingers flew among the switches and buttons as he went through the start-up procedure for the big Bell. Once he got the machine's engine temperatures up to normal he was ready to go. Meanwhile Reveille got on the police radio to the Special Operations Division dispatchers and continued to gather as much information as possible about the situation. Cabibbo already had done his part by getting the helicopter "unbuttoned" from the rotor tiedowns as well as the protective covers that had served to screen the machine's many openings from foreign objects and curious birds.

It was ten miles from Floyd Bennett Field to the East River heliport. As they flew along, Rupprecht's mind filled with all the possible scenarios he might be facing when he got there. Would people still be trapped inside the machine? Might the helicopter have already sunk to the bottom of the river? Would he and the rest of his rescue crew get there in time to do any good?

Flying over the Queens shoreline, he immediately attempted to locate the downed helicopter. All that was visible were a bunch of rubber dinghies in the water. He recognized department ESU Scuba personnel in the water. But what he wanted to locate most was the aircraft. Unaware that the East River's powerful current had carried the helicopter south and nearly over to the Queens/Brooklyn shoreline, it took him a moment to spot the gray machine's skids in the water.

From the moment the call came in, it had taken Rupprecht only eight minutes to reach the accident scene.

Two white sneakers stuck out between the fuselage and the skids. His worst fears were realized—someone still remained inside the aircraft. Coming to within a few feet of the water's surface, he called out to the crew chief, "I got somebody in the aircraft, get the diver in the water immediately!"

A moment later one of the men from Scuba jumped out.

With the scuba team now at the submerged helicopter, Rupprecht started to reposition his 412. It took only a few seconds for the scuba divers to free the young boy and bring him to the surface. He was a large youth, and the two divers worked hard to fit the rescue horse collar around him so he could be hoisted aboard the helicopter, which now hovered five or six feet above them.

Meanwhile, Rupprecht was unaware that a fire department boat was approaching rapidly from his rear. The vessel came close to pinning the divers between the downed helicopter and the fire boat, and nearly impacted the helicopter's rotor blades. To prevent a collision, Rupprecht was forced to move the 412 out of the way. The boy was hauled into a small rubber dingy attached to the fire boat.

At this point what had started out as a near perfect rescue mission fell apart. The youth in the water was perhaps two minutes by air from some of the finest medical facilities in the world. A well-equipped EMS triage ambulance was waiting on the Manhattan shore, across from the downed helicopter. New York City Medical Center and Bellevue Hospital sit adjacent to the 34th Street Heliport.

Instead of being transported to any one of those medical facilities, the boy was kept aboard the small dingy tied to the fire department boat while two firemen performed what appeared to Rupprecht to be CPR on him.

Rupprecht tried calling the vessel on the marine radio aboard his helicopter, to no avail. He had Special Operations Division try to contact the vessel through the fire department communications unit. There was no response.

In desperation Rupprecht contacted a Coast Guard cutter, which came up to the fire boat and took the child away from the firemen. From the time the helicopter had gone into the water until the time the young man first received quality medical attention was nearly one hour. It should have been ten minutes.

To this day Rupprecht cannot explain why the firemen had done what they had. Even if the firemen— for whatever reason—chose not to permit the helicopter to pull the youth aboard, why didn't they run the boy over in their dingy to the ambulance on the nearby shore instead of tying up to the big boat? Why hold on to this critically injured boy for such a protracted length of time?

Rupprecht was fuming. By the end of the day he wrote out a report that tore into the seeming incompetence of the fire department personnel at the scene. He could have saved the paper. There was a new mayor in City Hall. The last thing the mayor wanted was a controversy between his two primary public safety agencies.

The issue was permitted to quietly fade away.

And the thirteen-year-old boy? He died at Bellevue Hospital several days after the crash.

CHAPTER 4

Detective/Pilot John Fagan

Murder Suspect

DETECTIVE/PILOT JOHN FAGAN, WITH EIGHT YEARS IN AVIA-
tion, has the task of training the three dozen unit pilots.
Most of the time the training flights he conducts are routine
structured events. But every now and again something very
unstructured occurs.

It was February 22, 1988. Almost eight hours before
Fagan was to come in for his evening four P.M. to midnight
tour of duty, a family dispute had taken place in Brooklyn.
Such arguments happen with great frequency among the
tens of thousands of households in New York City. City
police officers, ill-prepared as they are to deal with the deep-
rooted social and economic problems that are the underlying
cause of much of the discord, must routinely handle these
incidents as part of their normal job.

The problem most cops have with managing these situations is the potential violence that can suddenly be generated
by them. Sometimes the violence is aimed at the officers,
but more often than not it stays within the family unit. The
handling of family violence is one of the most dangerous
tasks a patrol officer must contend with.

Hundreds of the city's two-thousand-plus yearly homicides
are generated by these disturbances.

*   *   *

48

Lydia Machado was afraid of her husband, William. She was so afraid of him that on the afternoon of February 22 she was scheduled to appear in Brooklyn Family Court to get a restraining order placed against him.

Lydia had moved out of the house and for several weeks had been staying at the home of her twenty-five-year-old brother, Eddie Morales.

It was nine A.M. on the twenty-second when William came to the Morales residence in the Bushwick section of Brooklyn. It was a tough area, and William wasn't making a social call. Armed with a knife, he forced Lydia into his van. Her brother tried to intervene. With his sister already in the car, Eddie grabbed onto the driver's side door handle as the vehicle pulled away from the curb. It was a mistake. As the van speed away, William pushed Eddie off the rapidly moving vehicle.

Eddie was killed.

For the next seven hours Lydia would remain a captive in William's van.

Fagan knows that it couldn't have been much later than three P.M. when he and Officer Bob Reveille went up for a routine training flight. A few minutes after they were airborne, Aviation Unit base radioed their helicopter, a Bell 206B JetRanger. From the scant information given, Fagan wasn't sure what the situation they were needed for was all about. It was clear from the transmission that there had been a homicide, and detectives from the 83rd Precinct were looking for a brown van. But where the van might be located at the moment seemed somewhat vague.

Fagan headed for the place he was first told to look, a Brooklyn location, aware of the fact that in not much more than a half hour the winter sun would be going down. Before they got to the first destination, they received another call from the base, this one telling them to head over to the Forest Park Golf course in Queens. It was explained to them that detectives from the 83rd Precinct had had previous dealings with Mr. Machado and believed he hung out in that heavily wooded park area a good deal of the time.

Fagan made a 180-degree turn in the direction of the golf

course. Between the waning light and the uncertainty as to where he and Reveille should search, he had little hope of actually finding the wanted vehicle.

Fagan flew over the Interboro Parkway, located near where the crime was committed and had an exit right at Forest Park. Soon, he and Reveille were directly over the Queens golf course and the extensive acreage of connecting parklands and cemeteries which that section of the borough consisted of. From over the Interboro he began to fly low, following the roads leading into and away from the large wooded site. Not seeing the van on any of them, he opted to work his way from parking lot to parking lot, if for no reason than that he figured the exercise would be good training for Reveille.

In one of the lots, Fagan spotted a van fitting the description of the murderer's vehicle. He pointed it out to Reveille. Part of the information they had was the wanted van's license plate number. The place their suspect van was sitting was surrounded by woods and sufficiently far away from residences that Fagan felt comfortable getting down low to try and read the numbers on its plate.

But before either Fagan or Reveille could make out the numbers, the van began to drive away. At the time, Fagan believed the vehicle's movement was simply a coincidence. Nonetheless, he once again climbed to a safer altitude and continued to follow the van, which was now heading toward Brooklyn. He also requested that a Highway unit be notified to stop the van. Until Highway got on the scene, he and Reveille would continue to call out the vehicle's location as it headed west.

Fagan told Reveille to get out their Hagstrom city road map. Reveille opened up the ten-by-thirteen-inch size book and began to search for the place over which they were now flying. It was a tough job. The writing in the big atlas was small, and finding the street names in a moving helicopter as dusk approached proved to be a difficult task for Fagan's copilot.

After traveling a few miles on the Interboro Parkway, the van exited near the Brooklyn border, but then turned around and, following a service road, returned to the Interboro. Once he came upon the next entrance he again got on that roadway and continued on toward Brooklyn.

The maneuver made no sense to Fagan—unless the driver was (naively) trying to confuse the helicopter flying above him. The van driver's actions heightened Fagan's suspicions, and the pilot radioed Communications once again, asking where the requested ground units were. Had Fagan checked his watch, he would have seen he was making his request during the change of shift time for Highway.

Finally, now that the van was in Brooklyn, the vehicle exited the main road and made its way down a number of side streets. To Fagan it appeared that the driver was aimlessly wandering about the borough. Every few streets the van would make a turn, square the block, or double back in the direction he had been driving.

And all the while, Fagan and Reveille were calling out the location of the vehicle over their radio and hoping that a Highway car would soon arrive. Because by this time there was little doubt in Fagan's mind that they had the right van. But the pilot also had another problem to contend with. The rapid changing of streets and the necessary gyrations of the helicopter made reading the Hagstrom map impossible for Reveille. Fagan now had to fly low enough for him and his copilot to read street signs. And that was below the tops of many of the three-story buildings they were passing. Way too low for Fagan's comfort.

Suddenly the van headed back in the direction of the Interboro, with Fagan now sticking firmly on its tail. Should the van get onto the highway, the pilot was fearful that they'd wind up back at the heavily wooded Forest Park area. A thought crossed Fagan's mind. The person they were looking for was wanted for a homicide and kidnapping. If that indeed was the man in the van—which Fagan no longer doubted—and the victim was still alive and with him, should he and Reveille lose sight of the vehicle once it got to the extensive park grounds, what would the killer's reaction be in regard to his captive?

Fagan again called out the van's location in the hope that responding ground units would soon get there.

Just before the vehicle came up to the entrance to the Interboro, Fagan spotted a two-officer Highway unit coming off that very roadway. As Fagan continued calling out the suspect vehicle's location, the ground unit made a beeline for the van. With red lights flashing, the suspect was pulled over. He was taken out of the van at gun point, his victim physically unharmed.

Less than a minutes later Fagan was amused to see the location swarming with heavily armed Emergency Service Unit personnel as well as local precinct officers. Better late than never, he figured.

CHAPTER 5

Captain Joseph Mottle
Detective/Pilot Guenther (GEW)
Rupprecht
Police Officer/Pilot Herman Velez

The Crash of Avianca Flight 052

CAPTAIN JOE MOTTLE PULLED UP TO THE COMMANDING OFFIcer's parking spot at the New York City Police Department's Brooklyn-based Aviation Unit, located at Floyd Bennett Field. It was Thursday, January 25, 1990. He was scheduled to work a ten-A.M.-to-six-P.M. tour that day, but as was his habit he arrived a full hour earlier.

Mottle entered a side door to the unit's old hangar—Aviation had been housed there since the mid-1930s. He walked past the dozens of photos tacked up on the wall, which spanned the more than sixty-year history of the place, without giving them a glance, and stepped into the cramped office used for telephone and radio communications—including ground-to-air as well as police department frequencies—then signed his name in the Command log. He noted that one of the tour's pilots had jotted down the current weather forecast. It was lousy. But Mottle already figured that out on the ride in from his home on Long Island. The clouds were so low you could practically reach up and touch

53

their bases. It was also raining. Mottle figured it would be a good day to do some paperwork.

Before slipping into his uniform, he wandered out to the hangar bay, saying hello as he passed by his administrative lieutenant and a few of the other unit members.

Normally, at least two helicopters remained on the flight line at all times, twenty-four hours a day, seven days a week, every day of the year. But today the poor weather had all the aircraft inside. Maintenance personnel were taking advantage of the lull in flying to deal with the never-ending task of keeping these terribly complex flying machines airworthy and safe.

Of the six aircraft in the large hangar, two stood apart from the others by virtue of their size. They were the unit's Bell 412s. Large twin-engine derivatives of the military's Huey, they were the bread and butter helicopters of the unit. With them, the most serious missions would be undertaken by Aviation's crews. Besides which, each of the 412s had redundant navigation and communication gear to permit safe flight under instrument conditions. All unit aircraft had A.U. numbers; the JetRangers were A.U. 1 and A.U. 2, the Bolkow 105 was A.U. 5, and the two 412s were A.U. 12 and A.U. 14 respectively. A.U. 14 even had weather radar mounted in its nose. Each of these large machines could lift a couple of tons if required and would be put into service for virtually any rescue mission attempted by the unit.

Arrayed around the two 412s, sitting high on their rectangular-shaped four-wheeled dollies—so that small powerful tugs would move them in and out of the unit hangar—were the rest of the unit's complement of helicopters. There were two JetRangers, a Bolkow 105 "light" twin, and a Bell 222 sitting in the far corner. The 222 was a beautiful shark-shaped aircraft, its form made famous by the television show "Air Wolf," which used a 222 as its "star." Regrettably, the real-life 222 in the Aviation Unit inventory wasn't quite as spectacular a machine. In fact its two Lycoming LTS-101 engines had proven to be very delicate indeed. No matter how gently handled by the unit's pilots, cracks would form in the helicopter engines' compressor sections, frequently grounding the machine. Because the 222 flew so infrequently, the mechanics had given the helicopter the nickname of "hangar queen" for the long periods of time she remained on the ground for maintenance. They also figured the 222 had earned that title, considering how much this "royal" machine had cost the city to buy.

Mottle looked at the various helicopters through the eyes of the person most responsible for them and the crews that flew in them. He had been around the Aviation Unit for quite a few years, first as a sergeant, then a lieutenant, and now as its commanding officer, and he was capable of flying every ship in the inventory. Nonetheless, he had found that each additional step up the administrative ladder brought with it added burdens and obligations. With twenty-twenty hindsight he had discovered that as a sergeant he'd enjoyed a great deal more job and personal freedom than as a lieutenant, and belatedly discovered that as a captain he had almost no leeway in his actions. He was held accountable for what the unit did or did not do by those above him in Special Operations Division, as well as at the highest levels of the police department. His was probably the most visible unit the department had. And at times it proved to be most difficult explaining to nonaviation-minded ranking officers that only a helicopter or two was available for any given mission. This was most often due to required maintenance being performed on the machines, or because of some unexpected delay in securing a critical part for a helicopter that was otherwise flyable.

But today just about everything—except the 222, and that had long ago been discounted as a viable piece of emergency response equipment—was airworthy and ready for a mission. For the moment it was just one less bit of pressure on Mottle.

While he might admit that he had a tough job, it was still one he loved.

After a last look around the hangar, he wandered back to his office to change into his captain's uniform. He was cheered by the knowledge that the next morning—only a few hours after this tour of duty ended—he would be heading out to Colorado for a long-planned skiing vacation. Maybe the poor weather outside was a blessing in disguise.

He could use a full day set aside solely to deal with administrative tasks before he left for his week's leave.

The Boeing 707, first put into production in the mid-1950s, remains a fine aircraft. Although nearly forty years old, the venerable four-engine jet is still a common sight at many of the airports of the world. It is less commonly observed, perhaps, in the United States. It is somewhat curious that the aircraft is no longer used very much in the country that designed and built it. There are a number of reasons for this. It's not that the jet can't still fly 6000 miles at Mach .9. It certainly can. But there are problems revolving around cost of fuel per passenger mile—of little consequence in the days of cheap jet fuel, but now, with airline deregulation, a matter of major concern—as well as the level of pollutants and noise the older-style engines on the 707 series put out.

The Boeing is still a perfectly safe and businesslike flying machine, it's just that newer, more modern planes now fly the old routes. Anyway, the 727, 737, and 747 series of jets are offshoots of the earlier aircraft, so if one chose, one could argue that the basic design is still alive, well, and flying.

One of the foreign carriers where these aircraft continue in service is with Avianca Airlines, the national airline of Colombia. The 707 involved in this incident was first flown by Pan American in 1967. Ten years later the jet was sold to Avianca.

It would be that particular Boeing 707, one given the designation of Flight 052 on that foggy night in January 1990, that the members of the New York City Police Department Aviation Unit would come to know most intimately.

The 707 had first departed Bogota, Colombia, then made an intermediate stop in Medellin, a part of the world which has, regrettably, become synonymous with cocaine trafficking. On the ground the aircraft was refueled in preparation for its more than 2400-mile trip to John F. Kennedy Airport in Queens, New York. It was to be a routine flight. That particular aircraft and her crew had made many similar trips, and there was no reason to believe the flight of Avianca 052 would end in any way different from the others.

Flight 052 was being flown using a version of the Boeing referred to as a 707-321B, which could carry up to 195 passengers. The range of this model is nearly three times greater than required for the trip this particular 707 was going to make. The captain planned on a four hour, forty minute flight en route, plus thirty minutes for any holds the ground controllers might place on his aircraft, plus thirty minutes if he had to fly to an alternate airport, plus nearly another thirty minutes for additional reserve. A total of an hour and a half of extra fuel.

This added up to nearly 74,000 pounds of jet fuel. The dispatcher in Medellin had the 707 loaded with 78,000 pounds. On top of which the captain added another 2000 pounds. The fuel load totaled 80,000 pounds. After all, Avianca Flight 052 was being flown in a 707 that had been built in 1967. The aircraft had nearly 62,000 hours on her, with well over 22,000 flights to her credit, and the captain conservatively calculated that she burned around ten percent more fuel than the book said she did.

The flight engineer wrote down that they carried 82,000 pounds of jet fuel. That was 2000 pounds more than the amount that should have been indicated, but was most likely due to what the engineer read from his fuel gauges. The gauges had a plus or minus three percent accuracy margin, so the data he had before him was well within acceptable parameters. And, at any rate, there was at least 6000 more pounds of fuel aboard Avianca Flight 052 than the thirsty jet would need for the trip. A solid thirty additional minutes on top of the normal reserves, just in case. And thirty minutes in a 707 doing Mach .9 means the jet can travel a lot of miles in that short period of time. Which can be a real lifesaver, if it has someplace to go to.

It was seven P.M. by the time Mottle left the office. After signing out, he headed in the direction of his home in Nassau County on Long Island. But first he had to stop in at the 107th Precinct in Fresh Meadows, Queens, so he could interview a lieutenant working there who was interested in an administrative job about to open in the Aviation Unit.

The interview took an hour to complete. Before leaving the precinct, Mottle called home and spoke to his wife. A registered nurse, she had just gotten home herself. She suggested he pick up some Chinese food on the way in. He did. It was 8:15 P.M., and as he left for the restaurant, he noted that the weather was still miserable. He was sure it would be a lot better in Colorado.

The crew of Flight 052 hadn't expected any difficulty landing at JFK. The initial weather forecast was for one to one and a half miles of visibility, with a ceiling of between 400 and 800 feet.

But as the four-engined Boeing approached its destination airport, the situation was not as expected. The weather had taken a dramatic turn for the worse, all up and down the eastern seaboard. This meant that the air traffic control system was beginning to bog down with delayed arrivals and departures. The poor visibility was causing commercial jetliners to execute a large number of "missed approaches." This meant that aircraft would attempt to land at their destination airport but the pilot would fail to see the runway through the low visibility conditions at an altitude that would permit the pilot to land. This required the ship to climb and fly a predetermined course, to try again. Or, if that were not deemed desirable by the captain, the aircraft could fly to its alternate airport, theoretically a destination far enough removed from the local weather situation that whatever conditions were causing the problem would not affect the other location. The system generally worked very well.

The crew's first delay was encountered over Virginia, where they were told to "hold." That is, they were essentially directed to fly a standard racetrack-shaped pattern over a fixed position on the ground—a radio beam told them where exactly—until released to proceed to their next destination. That could be to either an airport or to another hold.

They flew in circles over Virginia for nineteen minutes until they were released. And their next destination would be another hold.

Flight 052 left its second hold, which had lasted for nearly thirty minutes, over Atlantic City, New Jersey, and flew off to yet another delay. At 8:18 P.M. the crew found themselves boring holes in the sky forty miles south of JFK. By this time all the "extra" fuel that had been conservatively placed aboard the aircraft was gone. Six thousand pounds of jet fuel can only be stretched so far when an aircraft burns over 11,500 pounds an hour in order to maintain cruise speed.

This last hold kept the jet using up her precious fuel and going nowhere for almost half an hour. And time was running out for the crew and passengers of Flight 052.

While still in the holding pattern, at 8:44 P.M. the first officer contacted the ground controllers and stated that his flight "needed priority." He informed the controller that the aircraft no longer had sufficient fuel to reach its alternate airport, in this case, Boston's Logan. He told the controller that Avianca Flight 052 only had enough fuel to hold for five additional minutes. For whatever reason, at that point no one on the ground picked up on the urgency of the situation the crew faced.

At 8:46 P.M. controllers directed Flight 052 to leave the hold and enter the traffic stream landing at JFK. Ten minutes later the ground controllers relayed a wind-shear alert to the aircraft they were handling. As if in some bad dream, the crew of Flight 052 found that on top of their now nearly empty fuel tanks, they had to contend with weather that continued to deteriorate.

It took two minutes for Flight 052 to make a 360-degree spacing turn, as they were directed to do by the ground controllers. At 9:11 P.M. the aircraft finally began its approach to the airport.

Flight 052 was at last headed for the runway. The captain called for gear down, but was advised by his first officer to wait. The first officer was concerned that with the meager amount of fuel remaining in their tanks, the lowered gear— which also meant they'd have to fly at a lower airspeed— would have them flying with the nose of their 707 at a deck angle so high that they might starve their fuel pumps. The captain agreed and held off putting the gear down.

But the gear had to come down eventually, and as they closed in on the airfield, it became necessary to fly the aircraft at a relatively slow approach airspeed. This, with a wind on their nose that blew at seventy miles an hour. While it was true that the closer they got to the ground there would be a reduction in the wind force on their nose—wind speed decreases at lower altitudes—it also meant they would have to compensate for the extreme airspeed fluctuations with more power, and hence consume more fuel.

The approach to the airport was a turbulent one. The captain fought with the controls in an attempt to stabilize his descent and center the needles on his navigation gauges. Try as he might to dominate the flight path, the big jet was making the needles jump from one side of the gauges to the other.

When only two and one-half miles from the airport, the 707 hit wind shear, a dangerous condition for aircraft where rapidly moving air comes together from different directions at the same time. In three-tenths of a mile the aircraft dropped four hundred feet of altitude. In the cockpit the sound of the ground-proximity warning cried out in its chilling whoop-whoop call. The captain asked—whether of the other crew members or God, it's hard to say—"Where is the runway? I don't see it! I don't see it!"

Looking outside from his left-seat window of the jet, all the captain could make out was a gray wall of fog. He called for the jet's landing gear to be raised, added power to the 707's engines, and climbed away from the airport.

Herman Velez already had fifteen years with the New York City Police Department when he finally won his transfer to the Aviation Unit. On January 25, 1990, he had hardly been there a year. Still in training as a police pilot, his primary job since he'd been assigned to Aviation had been in the parts' room.

He wanted the sky, yet he found that most of the day he was buried in the bowels of the parts' trailer. In hundreds of bins and on dozens of steel shelves, the tens of thousands of bits and pieces of machinery that make up helicopters were partially his responsibility. It might be an important job, but it was pretty boring, and certainly wasn't what he'd had in mind when he joined the unit.

On top of that, there was only so much ordering and filing

of parts that a person can do in one day before going nuts. The only thing that made his hour-plus commute from his Bronx home worthwhile was the flying. And the weather on that Thursday was so crummy, nobody had gone up.

Velez recalls sitting around the Command log area that evening, chewing the fat with the other members of the unit. It was a small room, set off only a few feet from the entrance to the Aviation Unit and adjacent to the commanding officer's office. Located away from the hubbub and noise of the hangar and pilots' room, it was a good place for incoming calls to be received, log entries made, and other clerical tasks to be performed. The base's aviation and police radios were also housed inside the room.

The whole tour had been one in which everyone couldn't wait until it was over. A few of the pilots were discussing the idea of taking "lost time" and getting the hell out of there. That is, they would put in a slip for the remaining hours of the shift, the time to be subtracted from either vacation or comp time. The consensus was that anything beat sitting around the office just waiting for the end of the tour.

You can taste fear. It's something that's palpable. It's a thing. And the crew of Flight 052 knew all its manifestations on that January night in 1990.

The captain called to his first officer, "Tell them we are in emergency." He repeated the sentence again.

The officer replied, "I already told him." But that wasn't really true. The first officer had only informed the ground controllers that their aircraft couldn't make it to their alternate airport, a statement apparently never picked up by the controllers. He had never used the word emergency. And that was a very important omission. For when a crew member of an aircraft declares an emergency, those in air traffic control do whatever is necessary to bring that airplane to a safe landing at an airport. Routings are changed, other flights are held at bay, even runways not in use are freed up. But they have to hear that word.

Approach Control, unaware of the desperate situation

that now existed with Flight 052, said, "Climb and maintain three thousand."

The captain—in Spanish, since all cockpit conversation went on in that language; the first officer spoke in English to the ground people—told the first officer, "Tell him we don't have fuel."

The first officer transmitted, "Maintain three thousand and we're running out of fuel, sir."

Approach replied with, "Okay, fly heading 080."

The captain asked his first officer, "Did you already tell him that we don't have fuel?"

To which the first officer replied, "Yes sir, I already told him. . . ."

Approach cut the man's answer off with the words, "Avianca 052 heavy, I'm gonna bring you about fifteen miles northeast and then turn you back onto the approach. Is that fine with you and your fuel?"

The first officer replied, "I guess so, thank you very much."

Of course that wasn't fine. They were flying on fumes. Had someone in the cockpit only transmitted, "No, we are out of fuel and declaring an emergency, we require an immediate turn to the airport to land now!" that is precisely what the controller would have assisted the crew in doing. But when the ground controller hears "I guess so, thank you very much," when he asks if his last directions were "fine," unless that controller is a mind reader, it's hard to fault that person for the consequences.

From his earlier questioning words and with his next query, "What did he say?" it would seem that the captain was not monitoring the radio frequency.

The second officer answered, "The guy is mad."

It would appear that everyone in the cockpit of Flight 052 knew how desperate a situation they were now in. They simply hadn't gotten the point across to the people on the ground.

The captain was once more "flying the gauges." He said, "I'm going to follow this"—needle on the gauge—"as if my life depended on it."

At 9:30 P.M. the first officer replied to a request from

Approach Control that they climb to 3000 feet with, "Negative, sir, we just running out of fuel, we ... okay, three thousand now, okay."

At 9:31 P.M. the controller transmitted, "You're number two for the approach. I just have to give you enough room so you make it without having to come out again." He didn't know it, but there was little point in the conversation. Flight 052 was soon to become a glider.

The 707 began a turn to the left, to intercept the proper course needed to make the landing. Now well out over Long Island and to the east of Kennedy Airport, the engines began to die, one by one.

It was 9:32 P.M.

The first officer called out to Approach, "We just lost two engines, we need priority please." The word priority has no meaning in such a situation. The term emergency has meaning, but in the circumstances the crew of Flight 052 faced at that moment, it really didn't matter all that much.

Approach Control calmly replied, "Avianca 052, turn left heading 250, you're fifteen miles from the outer marker, maintain two thousand until established on the localizer, cleared for ILS 22 left. . . ."

The crew of Avianca Flight 052 found themselves over fifteen miles from the airport, at an altitude of 3000 feet, with all their engines silent. And nothing visible from inside the cockpit but fog.

Shortly after 9:30 P.M. the telephone sitting next to the Command log rang. One of the pilots picked up the telephone. It was LaGuardia Airport. A Boeing 707 had gone off their radar. They had no idea what happened to the aircraft. And by the way, this was no freighter flight. Nearly two hundred people were reported to be aboard that jet.

While that officer was talking to LaGuardia, another telephone rang. A pilot picked up the handset and was told by someone working at the Kennedy Terminal Control Area (TCA) that the plane had gone down somewhere over Cove Neck, on the north shore of Long Island.

The next few minutes were a cacophony of ringing telephones and radio communications. Nassau County Aviation called, asking for assistance, and the Federal Aviation Administration called looking for someone to send up a helicopter to see what the hell was going on. Other controllers at Kennedy and LaGuardia towers rang the unit, wanting to know what was happening. Operations called after receiving a number of calls about the presumably downed aircraft, wanting to know what the Aviation Unit could do about it. Ditto with the Communications Unit. And then the New York media began to call, wanting to know everything about anything.

And everybody who called asking for information or help was talking to a bunch of pilots and mechanics who had no more idea than anybody else what had happened to that 707.

It only took a few moments for the magnitude of the potential disaster to sink in to the various members of the unit standing around Operations. They literally began to run into action. Although there were serious reservations among the pilots about the weather's flyability, reports were gotten of the various local conditions, and all available helicopters were taken to the flight line. The machines were set up in Medevac configuration and filled with fuel.

Now what was needed was for someone with the right rank to make a decision.

Both Mottle and his wife were tired after their long day and hoped for an early bedtime so they would be fit to catch the commercial flight out to the ski slopes the next morning. They had just completed eating their won ton soup and were about to start on the chicken and broccoli when, at about 9:40 P.M., the telephone rang. It was from Lieutenant Tom Innis, acting commanding officer of the Nassau County Police Aviation Unit. He told Mottle that they had reports from Kennedy that there was a plane down somewhere on the north shore of Nassau County, near Oyster Bay. At the moment, they weren't even sure if it was down on land or in the water.

Innis asked Mottle if the New York City Police Aviation Unit could help him, as his unit was totally weathered in due to the thick fog.

Mottle told Innis to stay on the line, and using a second

telephone, rang the NYPD Operations Unit, which was responsible for all major decisions during nonbusiness hours. The call was picked up by the duty lieutenant, and as Mottle spoke to the man, he discovered that Operations already had the NYPD's chief of department, Robert Johnston, on the telephone. Mottle began to realize that a lot of people already knew about the reported plane crash which he had only just found out about.

Mottle could hear the chief of department talking to the lieutenant at Operations, saying that if Nassau County requested the NYPD to help, the department would go, but short of that, the department would hold at the city line.

Mottle informed the lieutenant that he already had the Nassau County Aviation Unit's commanding officer on the line and that they were asking for assistance. Johnston responded simply with, "It's a go."

After hanging up with Operations, Mottle spoke to Innis. He told him the Aviation Unit would give it its best shot and do whatever they could do. But one pilot to another, it was clear they would likely be severely limited by the weather. Innis let Mottle know that he'd be heading out to the crash site by police car, to which Mottle replied that he hoped he would see him out there in a little while.

Mottle called in to Aviation. Sergeant George Kohler picked up the telephone and was told by Mottle that Operations had given them the okay to attempt the mission. Kohler was told to ready every flyable helicopter in the fleet and fill them with crews. He was also told to make sure Scuba would be along. If that aircraft was in Long Island Sound, sure as God made little green apples they'd need trained personnel in the water. And lastly he told Kohler to leave one pilot seat empty on a 412. Mottle intended to be at the Aviation Unit base in a few minutes.

Mottle, still dressed in his tie and suit, kissed his wife good-bye and jumped into his car, a 1986 Audi. The Audi—with only 40,000 miles on the odometer—was a treat Mottle had recently permitted himself. He would find that his little car would be pushed to the limit that night. And maybe a bit beyond.

It was 10:15 P.M.

Mottle's home was thirty-two road miles from his unit. He pressed down on his car's accelerator and, once on the highway, soon found he was traveling at between ninety and 110 miles an hour. The weather was still rain and fog. As he headed in to work, he noticed that one of the nearby high-rise buildings was obscured in the thick gray mist from the fifth floor up. He figured that made for a ceiling of less than two-hundred feet above the ground. Flying around in a city with buildings three and four times that height would be perilous. Mottle wondered how his helicopters were going to make it to the crash site; indeed, if they should even attempt such a flight in this poor weather.

Even so, as he drove, he tried to reason out the best possible route to try and make the attempt. Passing other cars as if they were standing still, the only signal device Mottle had with him to let other drivers on the road know he was on an emergency run was a small red rotating light with a magnetic base. He plugged its cable into his cigarette lighter, aware that the damn thing would be viewed as little more than a toy in a city where drivers only reluctantly pulled aside for siren-sounding ambulances and air-horn-blaring fire trucks.

Halfway to the unit, a New York City Police Department Highway car pulled up alongside the Audi with its little red light rotating bravely on the roof. Mottle rolled down the window and yelled, "I'm the C.O. of Aviation."

The Highway officer gave Mottle a thumbs up, pulled ahead, and while maintaining speeds in excess of 110 miles an hour, escorted Mottle to the unit's front door. Mottle never caught the man's name and to this day doesn't know who he was.

Getting out of his Audi twenty minutes after leaving home, Mottle could smell that something underneath the car was very hot. But at that moment he had no time to deal with the problem. He saw four helicopters sitting on the flight line, ready to go. Running into the building, he checked the Command log. Detective/Pilot Richard Siracusano had already done weather checks for the north, south, and middle of Long Island. He also had the presence of mind to notify the air traffic controllers at both Kennedy and LaGuardia Airports of the situation and the likely need for their assistance in getting the unit helicopters to the crash site. In addition he had photostated both Hagstrom city maps and Terminal Control Area aviation maps for the mission, highlighting all the major obstructions on them that he knew about.

Mottle had already directed Kohler to assign Siracusano to his helicopter. An experienced National Guard pilot, Siracusano was a flight leader in the military, and as his unit flew from a Long Island base, knew the area from the air probably better than anyone else in Aviation.

Mottle, still in shirt and tie but now having gotten into his blue nylon flight jacket, his baseball-cap-style pilot's hat on his head, called all the crews together. He told the assembled members that while this was an important mission—people out there needed their help—safety came first. If any pilot felt he was getting into trouble because of the bad weather and poor visibility, he was to put his helicopter down in the first open spot he saw. In short, nobody was to push themselves beyond their limits. The last thing Mottle wanted was one of the machines under his command needlessly turned into a ball of scrap aluminum. That wouldn't do anybody any good.

It was around 10:30 P.M. and Detective Guenther Rupprecht was just pulling into an empty parking spot at the Aviation Unit. He was surprised to see the hangar doors wide open and members of the unit scurrying about in flurry of activity. Aware that this was not how midnight tours usually started off, he called out to the first person who came close to him and, still seated in his car, asked what was going on.

Without stopping to explain, an officer answered, "There's a plane down," and kept on going.

Rupprecht at first thought the man was joking. He parked and went inside. Looking around, he saw that there were too many people involved in too much activity for the guy's answer to have been made in jest. And anyway, nobody seemed to be smiling. Rupprecht went to his locker and suited up.

With ten years in Aviation, and over twenty-five "on the job," Rupprecht was one of the senior members of the unit. An experienced Bell 412 pilot, he immediately headed for one of the two big twins.

He jumped into the various jobs being performed by the other members of the unit, pulling off the machine's inlet covers, removing the rotor tie-down strap, and jumped inside the aircraft to prepare the helicopter for the impending mission. From the early information available, it appeared likely that the downed airliner was in the water. So beside the normal lifesaving equipment tossed into the belly of the 412, Rupprecht and the others made sure a good deal of water-related rescue gear—life rafts and preservers—along with extra line, was placed aboard.

When the C.O. got to the Aviation Unit base, things began to happen quickly. Once Mottle came through the door, he began calling out that "It was a go," and commanding crew assignments on the run.

On the flight line the four helicopters prepared for the mission were already turning over; two 412s, a JetRanger, and the Bolkow 105. Veléz, not yet a pilot, feared he would be odd man out. Yet, if there was a 707 down, it would be a disaster of major proportions and every able officer would be needed. He approached Sergeant George Kohler's Bell 412 and tentatively asked the sergeant if he could be of some assistance. Velez was aware that the sergeant already had a full crew. Detective/Pilot Guenther Rupprecht sat in the right seat, mechanic Nick Gregoriades was crew chief, and in the back sat two officers from the scuba unit.

Kohler told him to get on board.

With Mottle settled in the right-hand pilot-in-command seat, Siracusano sat beside him and would act as his copilot. Police Officer/Mechanic Bruce Adams was their crew chief, and in the rear of the helicopter two members of the scuba unit were belted in. Three other helicopters sat on their respective dollies, their blades whirling and their crews waiting for the order to go.

Mottle sat in the cockpit and briefly looked around. The

responsibility for the lives of the dozen or so officers who sat in the aircraft, machines worth a total of ten million dollars, now rested on his shoulders. Should he make the wrong decision, there would be hell to pay.

He decided he had but one option and that was to give the mission a try. The problem was, Mottle was concerned with what he saw. The ceiling above him was somewhere between seventy-five and eighty feet. Now that he had the Bell 412 running, as he attempted to gain altitude he discovered that he had hardly come off the dolly when he was bumping up against the immutable layer of opaque cloud.

He let out a sigh and contacted the Terminal Control Area, radioing, "Kennedy, this is Aviation Number Twelve. Flight of four out of Floyd Bennett requesting clearance westbound, at or below five hundred feet." He quietly mused that the standard jargon of requesting "at or below five hundred feet" was little more than a joke with the weather conditions he was about to fly in.

Kennedy replied, "Aviation Twelve is cleared to the west."

The plan Mottle had decided on was that instead of heading out over the city, to take the most direct route to the crash site—with all the construction cranes, towers, and the hundreds of apartment buildings obscured in the low cloud—he would head west, out over the water and away from the area of poor visibility. There, he would attempt to follow the New York City shoreline as it curved around Brooklyn, continue toward Queens and on to the downed 707 in adjacent Nassau County.

Mottle, piloting the lead 412, moved out toward Coney Island, due west of their station. In a few minutes, even though the helicopters were no longer technically under Kennedy's control, the personnel working the tower continued to keep track of the four machines, hoping to be able to assist them in their mission. The Aviation Unit helicopters would be receiving radar coverage from either Kennedy or LaGuardia for a good part of that night. Unit members and the controllers from those two facilities knew each other well. The unit's base was situated directly within the area of Kennedy's responsibility. A helicopter couldn't even lift off from its dolly without first asking Kennedy's permission. The relationship between the pilots and the controllers was excellent, and Mottle knew that in this sort of emergency the New York City area controllers would extend themselves to the maximum for the Aviation Unit.

To his surprise, Mottle found that after traveling a few miles along the south Brooklyn shoreline, he could clearly see the island of Manhattan as if through a looking glass. It immediately became apparent that the dense fog only covered a portion of the city. Nonetheless, what it did cover was both formidable in size and dimension—the line ran from Coney Island to beyond LaGuardia Airport, in a sheet of impenetrable fog 500 feet thick. Yet, to the north and west the ceiling and visibility was unlimited. But unfortunately they weren't heading in those directions.

The four machines quickly made it around the western Brooklyn shoreline, and as they neared the Williamsburg Bridge were handed over to the LaGuardia controllers, who remained with them as they flew along the Queens/East River border. As they passed by LaGuardia, Mottle could see the airport tower clearly, but the field itself was invisible under fog. The tower looked to him like a mushroom jutting out of fresh soil.

LaGuardia informed Mottle that although the sky was clear to the west, conditions east of LaGuardia were reported to be an indefinite hundred- to 150-foot ceiling, with the top of the fog showing at about 500 feet. Above the 500-foot level there was a break to about 1500 feet, where the clouds from which the rain was coming would be found. It wasn't good news.

Now that they were for the moment flying over the top of the fog, Mottle observed holes in the gray blanket where ground lighting could be seen. It looked to him like he was over some kind of enormous Swiss cheese.

After traveling a few miles beyond LaGuardia, Mottle saw that the holes in the fog were closed up. The ground below, for as far as he could see, was solidly in the soup. He decided to take the opportunity while he still had sight of the ground under him and get below the main layer of fog and head to the crash site at a hundred or so feet above the surface. If he waited until he got directly over the crash site, he would likely have to descend down through the fog. That would be a virtually impossible thing to do safely. He and the other pilots would have no way of knowing what objects were under or in front of them as they came closer to the earth.

He turned to Siracusano and suggested the four helicopters would be safer following the north shoreline of Long Island to the accident scene. His copilot disagreed. Siracusano informed him that all of the north shoreline was ragged. It would take them a very long time to get to the downed aircraft if they followed that route. And second, he told Mottle that once they were over the water by the shoreline, there would be little or no ground lighting to use for reference. At least over land they'd have streetlights, cars, and homes to know which end was up.

Mottle briefly considered Siracusano's opinion. The other man made good sense, and Mottle took his advice. The four helicopters took the land route.

Still making their way eastward, Mottle found that although his altimeter showed the bottom of the fog layer now remained at a fairly constant 100 to 150 feet, the land under the fog rose and fell. By necessity, to keep out of the fog the four helicopters were flying from telephone pole to telephone pole. By any reasonable standard the visibility conditions he and his crews found themselves in were unflyable. Except that somewhere out there people would die if those helicopters didn't show up.

The four aircraft were flying nose to tail in a loose formation, the helicopters bringing up the rear using the white nightlight on the tail of the helicopter to their front to maintain visual contact. Formation flying wasn't practiced very much at the Aviation Unit; there was little call for the skill. And such flying would never take place under such horrible conditions of poor visibility.

Velez, seated in the rear of the 412, could only watch the lights of the city pass by underneath as the helicopter he was in moved beyond LaGuardia Airport. Up to that point the flight had been uneventful. By traveling first in a westerly heading, then making the turn to Long Island as close as possible to the north shore, the pilots had managed to keep the machines out of the soup. But it was obvious to Velez that the relatively clear flying wasn't going to last much longer.

Through his headset he heard a voice command, "Slow down and get lower!" Even from his station by a side window the initial impact of going from visible flying conditions to the dark murk of a cloud was extremely disorienting. He figured it must be a hell of a lot harder on the pilots. And the weather was forcing the helicopters, now flying in a long line and trying to maintain their relative positions, to move in and out of the fog.

After a few minutes of cruising in the poor visibility, Velez saw a blur come up and pass them on the left side. It was the Bolkow 105. Kohler called out to the helicopter over the radio, "Slow down! You're gonna kill someone!"

The light twin immediately decelerated and broke off to the left. Velez watched as the other helicopter then fell back and into its position in line. Fortunately, that was the lone incident that took place during the night that came close to being a tragedy for the Aviation Unit.

Velez, a bit shaken by the incident, still figured he'd rather be where he sat than shuffling parts back at the base.

The flight of four kept on going.

As the helicopters approached Oyster Bay, Mottle could see flashing lights in the distance. He already had a good idea where he was, as he had just flown over the home of his sister-in-law. Now nearly on top of the crash site, Mottle was astounded at what he saw. Every street leading into the area was filled with emergency vehicles; police cars, fire trucks, ambulances, each with its flashing light on. There must have been nearly a hundred clogging the roads. And more were coming. It looked like the Long Island Expressway, a road notorious for its traffic jams, on a bad rush-hour morning. The dilemma that Mottle wondered about was how any of the vehicles below would be able to extricate themselves from the congested roadways.

Directly over the crash site hovered a Nassau County police helicopter, its Nightsun searchlight illuminating the ground below. Speaking with the Nassau County pilot over the aviation radio, Mottle was told that at the moment there was no safe place for the helicopters to put down near the wreckage. As the pilot and Mottle discussed the situation, Mottle could see helicopters flying all over the place. At once he became fearful that the lack of control over which helicopter was flying where held the very real potential for his worst fears materializing: a midair collision. He immediately ordered all four machines to find a place to set down until some plan could be formulated.

Mottle headed north and put his 412 down on a beach a half mile from the downed jetliner, to wait for further directions from Nassau County. By then it was half past midnight.

After working his way to the general area where the crash site was supposed to be, Rupprecht was glad to see the lights of emergency vehicles across a bay just under the nose of his helicopter. He wasn't sure exactly how they had gotten there, but at least they were in the right place.

As they flew over the crash site, Velez could hear conflicting reports come over the radio. Someone transmitted that there were no survivors. A moment later that same voice came over the frequency with, "There are people all over the place! Keep the ships coming in!"

Nassau contacted Mottle and told him they'd found a spot for the helicopters to land at the crash site to enable them to evacuate victims. Mottle radioed the information to the other helicopters. The Nassau County police JetRanger with its Nightsun would put itself directly over the accident site. There he would act as the center of the wheel, lighting up the crash site and ensuring the other aircraft maintained proper separation. Mottle would go in first, followed by the light twin Bolkow, which in turn would be followed by the other 412. And he informed everyone that they would fly a left-hand traffic pattern. He wasn't about to have another near miss, as had happened when they'd first come onto the scene.

Seeing the Nassau County Police Department Long-Ranger depart the landing zone, Mottle made his approach.

It was a tough spot, right in the backyard of someone's home. Mottle later found out it was the residence of the father of the famous tennis player John McEnroe. To make the situation even more difficult, Mottle had to be careful his tail rotor didn't hit obstructions on the ground, the most notable a nearby swing set. It was apparent, even from where Mottle sat, that this was no inexpensive children's toy put together using cheap metal-tube construction. This model was fabricated from four-by-four legs of lumber that looked to Mottle as if they were either bolted or cemented into the ground.

As they were settling down to land, Mottle mentioned the problem over the intercom. Officer Bruce Adams, a Vietnam War veteran helicopter mechanic and Mottle's crew chief, got the message. Adams jumped out of the 412. He would be sure to take care of that little matter before Mottle got back to pick up his next group of injured.

Mottle kept the 412 running while one of the crash casualties was brought to his ship. He still had a great deal of fuel aboard, as well as the two-man scuba team and his crew chief. Because of the difficult landing site, he knew he would have to come straight up for sixty feet to clear tall trees surrounding the landing zone before he could move forward. He had to get rid of as much weight as possible.

Calling out to Adams to lighten the machine, the scuba officers were put out, as were life rafts and any other excess gear. Even the unused seats—although they only weighed a relatively few pounds each—were removed by the crew chief. Adams would also be staying behind, as Mottle decided he needed someone on board who would be able to guide him to the Nassau County medical facility they'd be heading for. So he traded his crew chief for a Nassau County police officer who was standing nearby.

The first injured person was put on the 412. It's an image that Mottle won't forget. A woman lay in a stretcher. She looked into his eyes, not saying a word. No sound came from her, even though the bones of her legs were jutting out through the flesh.

Once the helicopter was loaded with four crash victims, Mottle pulled power and lifted the machine into the air. The gauges showed he was just at redline. As he cleared the treetops he found he had only a few feet more to go before he would be into the base of the fog layer. He realized that if the fog settled any lower to the ground, there'd be no more flying possible from that site.

The Nassau County police officer guided Mottle to the hospital. Not being a pilot, he gave his directions as if he were sitting in a car. "At the light make a right. At the next fork in the road make a left," and so on.

Overhead, Mottle looked up to see a perfect white ceiling, as beautiful as it would be deadly to enter. Should a helicopter fly up into the dense fog, in a few moments the machine would likely go out of control, unless the pilot immediately transitioned to the aircraft's attitude instruments. In the distance Mottle saw the medical center. There was just one more obstacle in the way, a railroad trestle. Maneuvering around it, he continued on and at the hospital flew down a driveway. It took him well below the surface of the roadway, to where the emergency room entrance was located.

The Nassau County LongRanger that had departed the crash scene a few minutes before he did was still there. The other pilot, aware that Mottle had to get in, moved over enough to permit the much larger 412 to land. It was a tight fit, with Mottle's rotor blades spinning above the LongRanger's whirling blades, but it worked. It wouldn't be the last time such a tight maneuver would be necessary that night.

After Mottle's patients were removed, the 412 was loaded up with emergency medical equipment. There were bottles of plasma, bandages, splints, oxygen, drugs, blankets, and innumerable other items stuffed into the cabin.

Pulling power once more, Mottle lifted the big 412 up and headed back for another pickup. As he made his approach in to the backyard landing site, from the corner of his eye he noticed four big NYPD Emergency Service guys lugging the heavy swing set into the woods. Mottle later learned that after he had let Adams out, the mechanic had gone down to the crash site. When he got there, he found four ESU cops working on the wreckage of Flight 052 and explained to them his problem. They had all returned to the backyard and, using their chain saws, cut the swing set off at the base of each of its four legs, then hauled it into the woods.

Mottle smiled, shook his head and landed the helicopter.

Rupprecht counted eight aircraft working the crash site. Suffolk County police had their twin Bolkow, another Bolkow was there from a private helicopter ambulance service, Nassau police had its Bell LongRangers, and of course the NYPD had its four machines.

At first it was chaos in the air. Nobody knew in which direction to make turns, how or when to approach the scene. Then a pilot from the Nassau County Police Aviation Unit got to the landing zone with a portable radio and straightened the mess out.

Whoever the pilot was, Rupprecht figures the guy saved everybody's bacon that night.

The ground controller called for another 412. Rupprecht pulled power and climbed out from his temporary parking place in an empty lot. As he came around for the approach to the LZ, he took a moment, and for the first time he and the rest of the people aboard their helicopter had a chance to see the downed jet.

The Avianca Flight 052 was sitting upright on sloping ground. Resting nose high, it looked like the machine had been pancaked in. He was surprised by how little damage there appeared to have been done to the surrounding area. The nose of the jet had made contact with a home's porch, separated and rolled a short distance away from the rest of the wreckage. Rupprecht didn't know it at the time, but the aircraft's captain, first and second officers had been killed in the impact.

Little more than a few treetops had been broken off as the big jet made its silent approach to the earth. And there was no sign of fire. Without any fuel in her tanks, a fire would have been most unlikely.

Rupprecht set up for a landing in the McEnroe backyard.

When Velez's 412 landed at the backyard LZ, he was asked to give a hand to the other emergency response people working on the ground. There were, after all, a lot of people who needed help out there at the moment. Velez and the two officers from the scuba unit got off the helicopter. Velez stepped back and watched as the big Bell departed from the area. He was now ground crew.

All around him he saw people in different uniforms. There were Emergency Medical Services personnel, firemen from dozens of different departments—he'd read their town names on the back of their jackets to find out where they were from—police from various Long Island communities, from Nassau County, and the New York City Police Department. There were people in the area that were in uniforms he'd never seen before, and to this day has no idea to what agencies they belonged.

The first problem Velez and the other members of the "ground crew" had to deal with was people—presumably neighbors—who were trying to get into the area of the landing zone with video cameras. It would appear that either everyone visualized themselves as having the opportunity of a lifetime to make some money selling their home videos to one of the popular television "crash and burn" shows, or else they couldn't resist the chance to get some exciting tape of the action. Whatever the motive, it was clear to the emergency professionals on the scene that having hordes of people running around the badly injured crash victims taking home videos wasn't going to improve the situation. In addition the whirling tail rotor blades of the landing and departing helicopters were both invisible and lethal.

Before Velez and the other officers could deal with the injured, they had to first chase those people away. He and a number of other officers suggested to the interlopers that unless they vacated the area they would be placed under arrest for interfering with the rescue operation. The threat of spending the rest of the night in jail did the trick and the offenders left.

Victims were being lined up in areas named Triage 1, Triage 2, and Triage 3. The crash victims being brought to where Velez was working had not gotten there by chance. Once removed from the wreckage of the Avianca jet, they had been stabilized, treated as appropriate, and classified as to their immediate medical needs.

Velez isn't an EMT. He wasn't certain what the medical terminology he was hearing the medical technicians use meant, he only knew what he was told: that the patients lying around in the stretchers for airlifting to local hospitals were there because if they didn't get medical attention quickly, they were very likely to die.

It was ironic that although Velez had been brought to the scene almost as an afterthought, he had one skill that few others there possessed. He was fluent in Spanish, in the middle of dozens of crash victims from a Spanish carrier, many of whose victims spoke nothing but that language.

One of the first patients Velez dealt with was a young child. As she lay on a stretcher, the seven- or eight-year-old blond girl kept calling for her mother in Spanish. Velez, in her native tongue, calmed her down and told her she was going to a hospital and would soon be with her mother.

Another man, in a cast from his midsection down to both his legs, was fearful for the rest of his family. Velez soothed the man as he helped load him onto a helicopter. He told him that what was happening at the moment was the hardest part, and that he was being taken to a hospital and everything would be okay.

The other person he specifically recalls was a little girl, a child who only spoke Spanish and whom Velez comforted. When he first saw her, she seemed very quiet. More quiet that even the shock of the accident might account for. A man in a blue medical smock, with gray hair pulled back into a ponytail, and incongruously wearing an Aviation Unit cap—given to him by unit mechanic Nick Gregoriades to enable the man to move unchallenged around the triage area—began to examine the child.

Rupprecht was to later learn the man's name was R. Geoffrey Broderick, and he did a prodigious amount of rescue work that night. Rupprecht believes he probably saved the little girl's life. Although Broderick spoke no Spanish, and the child no English, the medically trained man had one major advantage over all the other people caring for the crash victims. He was a veterinarian. He was used to patients who were in pain and were injured but couldn't use words to describe their plight. And Broderick saw that something was going dramatically wrong with the little girl.

He jumped into the 412 and examined the child. He discovered that the IV was not functioning properly. Broderick relocated the IV and would continue to monitor the child on the flight to North Shore Hospital. As it turned out, he would be staying with Rupprecht and the Bell 412 for a good part of the night.

Four of the crash victims were put aboard Rupprecht's helicopter. He later found out one of the injured men turned out to be a "mule." When X-rayed for internal injuries, a large quantity of drugs was discovered, wrapped in condoms, inside his body, swallowed by him before he boarded the flight.

Rupprecht sat at his controls and watched as his helicopter was loaded up with the four patients. The process only took five minutes. The 412 can hold six people on stretchers, but the two on the top would have been so close to the roof of the cabin, and thus almost impossible to work on, that in their immediate situation the space was unusable.

He also recognized that there were three crew members on board as well as Broderick. That was eight souls in a helicopter already heavily laden with fuel. Rupprecht found himself worrying about the tall trees at the end of the open backyard.

When they were ready to fly, Rupprecht prepared to pull up on the power lever while Kohler called off the numbers showing on the torque gauge. Helicopters are strange machines. The internal twisting forces are so great that in their pilot's hands is the capability to severely damage critical parts of the craft if too much power is demanded of their engines.

It was to be a maximum-performance takeoff. The only safe way to leave the relatively confined space they were in at their heavy weight was to see if the helicopter could make it to an altitude just above the trees. If there was enough power available to do that, they'd have it made. If not, Rupprecht would slowly lower the collective and permit the Bell to once more settle back to the ground. They'd remove some weight—it might have to be a patient—and try again.

As the noise of her twin engines increased, Rupprecht could feel the machine get light on her skids. Once he was free of the ground, he continued to gently pull up on the collective. Kohler read off the percentage of power he was using; 85 percent—light on the skids, 90 percent—slowly climbing, 95 percent—still going up, 98 percent—everything seemed to be functioning normally, 100 percent—maximum power as the helicopter cleared the top of the trees. Rupprecht lowered the nose, permitting the airspeed to build up. Once he reached sixty miles an hour, he turned the helicopter in the general direction of North Shore Hospital. Piece of cake.

Velez looked up from aiding an injured victim and saw that a number of NYPD Emergency Service vehicles had just driven in. On their roofs were large lights. Up to that point the place where the helicopters were landing was dark. It was difficult and dangerous to work in the inadequate light, and Velez was aware of how demanding it was for the pilots to land in the confined area of the poorly lit backyard. He went over to the ESU lieutenant on the scene and asked it they could set up the lights for the landing helicopters. A few moments later the ESU units were arranged around the LZ, and from that point on lighting was no longer a problem.

As Rupprecht started off in the direction of North Shore Hospital, he used the instructions read to him over the air by a Nassau County officer from the man's portable aviation radio. They sounded like directions from a local gas station attendant; follow Route 106 to the Long Island Expressway, make a right to exit 33, take the service road to the first light, make a right, and half a mile farther down the street they'd find the hospital.

Right.

The situation that almost immediately caused Rupprecht a problem was that by the time he got to the end of Route 106, the fog had forced his helicopter down to somewhere around a hundred feet above the ground. Flying that low meant, in order for him to avoid the fog-cloaked water towers, utility and light poles, he had to stay directly over the roadway.

He managed to get to the Long Island Expressway and became part of the traffic flow, albeit with his vehicle riding a bit higher over the roadway than was the norm. Things at first seemed to be going smoothly, when, while they were traveling along at about seventy miles an hour, he discovered that power lines were strung across the highway between exits 37 and 38.

He pulled power and jumped over them, in the process putting himself in the soup for a very long moment until he felt he had gone past the danger, then he once more permitted the helicopter to settle closer to the road.

Just as Rupprecht popped out of the cloud and leveled out beyond the danger area, the man with the portable got on the air. He matter-of-factly transmitted, "Oh, by the way, look out for the power lines between thirty-seven and thirty-eight."

Thanks a lot, Rupprecht thought.

Mottle, who would make four runs to and from local hospitals that night, figures it happened during his third drop-off of a crash victim. By now he had been up for nearly twenty-four hours. Bone weary and hungry, he was going on adrenaline. Ready to leave Nassau County Medical, he pulled up on his collective and began to gain altitude. The cloud cover was still little more than a hundred feet over the ground, and, instead of nosing the helicopter over when he cleared obstacles around him, Mottle found he had lifted himself right into the base of the white ceiling. His reflexes, his mind, his reaction to being in an opaque cloud—nothing was working right. He got vertigo. He saw the gauges in front of his eyes, and for that instant they no longer had any meaning for him. It was as if his thousands of flight hours experience had suddenly vanished. At that moment he found himself as helpless as a baby.

All he recalls is the voice of Siracusano calmly calling out, "I've got the controls." The next moment they were below the base of the clouds with Siracusano casually saying,

"You've got it," handing the controls of the 412 back over to Mottle.

Mottle then returned to the crash site to pick up another victim. Just like nothing had happened.

It was close to six A.M. and Velez figured things were beginning to wind down. The number of crash victims being brought to the triage area had slowed to a trickle. It had been a long night. The weather was consistently lousy throughout, with intermittent rain and a raw temperature just above freezing. And of course there was the fog. That hadn't changed at all.

Velez heard the sound of a large helicopter making its approach. As it came in over the trees, he could make out the Aviation Unit number 12 on the big Bell 412's tail. It was the machine piloted by Mottle and Siracusano.

He helped place a patient lying on a stretcher aboard the aircraft. Seeing that there was nobody else in sight who needed Medevacking out of the area, Velez climbed aboard Mottle's helicopter for the ride home.

The local Nassau County hospitals were now filled to capacity with the crash victims. Thus, the 412 headed to Fort Totten, located just over the Nassau County border in northern Queens. The flight took only a few minutes, and once they landed at Fort Totten, a waiting ambulance relieved them of their patient for transport to a New York City hospital. At first the flight back to the Aviation Unit was uneventful. But once they made a left at LaGuardia and headed across Queens, the fog closed in on them. The helicopter descended to barely two hundred feet above the ground. Looking out the window, Velez could just about make out the streetlights below.

Once over Flatbush Avenue in Brooklyn, the pilot took the helicopter down to the top of the lamp poles. The machine inched its way down the avenue, the pilot knowing that so long as the aircraft stayed over the roadway, there was nothing they'd impact into. Except maybe power lines.

It seemed like it took forever, but eventually Velez saw that their helicopter, still on Flatbush Avenue, was exactly at the spot opposite where their hangar sat, separated only by a chain-link fence. The distance was little more than a quarter of a mile, but the intense lights fitted around the hangar were hardly more than faint glowing things obscured by the thick ground-covering cloud.

Still, as he figured before, it was a hell of a lot better than being in the parts' room.

Rupprecht got off the expressway at exit 33 as advised. Using the supplied directions, and after dodging the now routine power lines and light poles that were in the way, he found North Shore Hospital. Making a steep approach to its helicopter landing pad, he saw a full medical team was waiting outside for their arrival.

Rupprecht suggested to the crew chief to load up on medical supplies and bring the stuff back to the accident scene. Soon the cabin of the Bell 412 looked like a medical supply warehouse.

Before departing the hospital, Kohler punched in their location on the Loran navigation unit. Originally designed for water navigation, the machine receives signals from low frequency radio transmitters located around various parts of the country. Once it was told where it was, the device would enable them to return to within a few feet of where they now sat. Rupprecht figured it would enable him to fly back and forth between the crash site and the hospital. He would be able to fly at a higher altitude because he wouldn't need to see the local roads. This would be both a lot faster and safer.

When Rupprecht got back to the crash site, and while his 412 sat turning over at flight idle waiting for the completion of the loading of the next four patients, some idiot standing off to the side turned a bright video light right at the helicopter. Rupprecht figured it was one of the "junior" newsmen who had been chased away earlier and who now saw the chance to get their fifteen minutes of fame on the television show "Rescue 911." Not only was the light blinding Rupprecht, but it destroyed what night vision he had built up over the last several hours.

Rupprecht flipped on the bright spotlight mounted in the

412's underbelly and aimed it at the offender. A few seconds later the guy got the idea. The light went out and he took his camera elsewhere.

Rupprecht just shook his head and thought to himself, What a moron.

Rupprecht's 412 needed fuel. He knew that the closest airport to the crash site was five miles due south at the Grumman aircraft testing facility situated in Bethpage, Long Island, so he decided to try for it. What he didn't know was that one of the Aviation Unit helicopters, the Bolkow 105, was already sitting there, unable to get out due to the dense fog.

Rupprecht later heard that the 105, also in need of jet fuel, had gone looking for the same airport. What they found was that the conditions of visibility got worse the closer they came to it. At one point, completely confused as to their location but confident the airport was nearby, the 105 crew landed in an empty—at two A.M., not a surprise—supermarket parking lot, trying to get their bearings. The pilot spotted a civilian walking down the street—one can only wonder at what his thoughts were when he saw a helicopter parked by his local Waldbaum's—and asked for directions. The passerby told them the airport was just beyond the lot and over a fence. They followed his directions and discovered he was quite correct. But once at the airport, the limited visibility made further travel impossible, so they were stuck.

Rupprecht flew over the field, learned from the Bolkow crew of their plight, and changed course for LaGuardia.

After refueling, Rupprecht and Kohler returned to the LZ, ready to pick up more crash victims. It was nearly dawn, and by that time the last of the really desperately injured people had been removed. There was one other helicopter sharing the space with him, a light twin from Suffolk County.

It was clear to Rupprecht that the weather was getting worse. Visibility had long before deteriorated beyond the bounds of rational and reasonably safe flying. With nobody's life in peril, Rupprecht shut down the 412. If another patient needed to be flown out, or if one of the emergency people got hurt and needed to be airlifted to a hospital, he was ready, willing, and able to hit the starter button and make the run. But for the moment he and everyone else in that helicopter would just sit tight.

The Salvation Army eventually brought a canteen truck to the triage site. It was a van with a simple kitchen inside, the kind whose side opened up for dispensing meals to people. Rupprecht and the others were famished. They got in line for whatever food was being served.

The Salvation Army served bowls of beef stew to whoever wanted some. Rupprecht noticed the stuff came out of gallon cans and had the unlikely label of Pocahontas Beef Stew. It might be a strange name to give a stew, but Rupprecht sure thought it tasted great.

Mottle led the three helicopters back to the Aviation Unit base. Once the machines were safely on their dollies, he ordered them all placed in the hangar. Each of them would need a close inspection after the hard work they'd been put through.

When the helicopters were inside the well-lit hangar, Mottle saw that the top of his 412, normally white, looked as if someone had made a poor attempt to paint it red. His helicopter as well as the other machines were all thickly lathered with human blood. When the 707 had impacted in the trees, many of its passengers had been ripped apart. The helicopters' whirling blades had disturbed the leaves of the trees where the blood and small body parts had come to rest, and had deposited them on the ships. They had also blown bloodsoaked bandages about, with the same result.

Mottle ordered the machines to be washed immediately.

It was 7:30 A.M. and Rupprecht and Kohler had yet to return in their 412. Mottle called him on the radio, determined that there was no more work to be done by helicopters at the crash site, and ordered him home.

Mottle recalls standing near the flight line, anticipating the imminent arrival of the final helicopter out there and beginning to physically tremble. He wasn't sure whether it was the long period of sleeplessness, the release of tension, or an irrational and undue fear that now, at the very last moment, something might go wrong.

But nothing went wrong, and Rupprecht and Kohler landed safely in their bloodstreaked 412, just as all the others had.

Rupprecht and Kohler brought the last Aviation Unit helicopter to the base. They had waited for first light, permitting the dense gray fog to luminesce into a thick bright haze. It helped.

After landing the 412 on the dolly at Floyd Bennett Field, Rupprecht remembers finishing up whatever paperwork he had to do, changing into civilian clothes, and heading home. After all, the next shift he was scheduled to work was coming up at midnight.

Mottle, with all the helicopters now in the hangar, went back to his office and typed out a short report on the night's events. He reflected on the terrible weather, the coordination of the four crews and machines, the number of people rescued. He attempted to explain the drama of the night in the dry wording required of a police report. The narration ended with the words that this was probably the finest day in the history of the Aviation Unit.

Getting into his Audi—he still wanted to make that Colorado ski trip!—he started her up. Something felt and smelled strange on the trip home. He soon found out that the hundred-mile-an-hour dash to work the evening before had burned out his transmission. It cost him three thousand dollars to replace it.

Aftermath

The rescue mission of the victims of Flight 052 is to date the largest number of accident victims ever recorded removed from such a situation by helicopter. One hundred seventy people had been aboard that flight; nine crew members, the remainder passengers. Forty-seven victims were taken from the area by air. Of that number, the four helicopters of the New York City Police Department Aviation Unit carried out twenty-two of the injured.

The accolades came shortly after the successful mission.

There was the 1990 Helicopter Heroism Award from the Aviation/Space Writers Association, an Award for Heroism from the Federal Aviation Administration, as well as other civilian and governmental honors. And, of course, department medals for bravery and valor.

Thirteen medals were awarded to the members of the NYPD Aviation Unit by their own agency. There had almost been twelve. Velez, since he was not officially assigned as part of any of the helicopter crews, was left out when the department recognition first came down. It took significant effort by the unit's members to get Velez a Commendation, an award somewhat lower than the Honorable Mention given the other twelve members who participated in the rescue. Even though Velez performed the same job and faced the same dangers.

Which again demonstrated that for a police officer life is rarely fair, just, or logical.

BOOK TWO

Maryland State Police
Aviation Division

CHAPTER 6

Corporal Observer/Medic Louis Saffran, Jr. (ret.)

Stolen Army Huey and the White House

IT WAS A SATURDAY NIGHT INTO SUNDAY MORNING tour in February 1974. Corporal Louis Saffran, Jr., paramedic and the ranking shift member of Maryland State Police Helicopter 2, figured it was going to be just another quiet and peaceful winter weekend evening. His pilot, Don Sewell, a "slick sleeve" trooper with " 'Nam" flying experience, agreed with him as the pair sat around their Andrews Air Force Base pilots' lounge and chewed the fat. Both men were in one of the several State Police offices connected to Hangar 12, located on the Navy side of the sprawling military complex.

What they didn't know was that a very upset young man was preparing to liven up their morning, as well as that of the Secret Service, the White House Security Forces, and virtually all the ranking members of the United States Armed Forces stationed in the Baltimore/Washington, D.C., area.

It was shortly after midnight when the unit's telephone rang. Saffran picked it up. It was Andrews' control tower. The tower had just received a call from Baltimore-Washington International. An unidentified aircraft flying without navigation lights had just flown into an area of positive control airspace. Such airspace requires permission prior to a pilot

91

entering the area, and continuous communication with ground controllers while there. This particular aircraft wasn't responding to radio calls and was heading in the direction of the capital. So, if the crew wouldn't mind . . .

Saffran and Sewell didn't mind. Both men were experienced troopers, and Sewell was a veteran combat pilot. This would be a piece of cake. No, they didn't mind a bit.

Both men put on their gear and got aboard their nearly new—with only seventy-five hours on the machine—Bell 206 JetRanger. Two minutes later they were airborne, looking for somebody flying around without lights who either couldn't—or didn't want to—talk to anybody.

Vectored to the target by ground control's radar, within twenty minutes they spotted the aircraft. Since the Huey was flying without any of its lights showing, the troopers needed a lit background in order to see the aircraft. Therefore it was necessary for the JetRanger to deliberately approach the other aircraft from above.

Even though the target ship was painted the dark mud-brown color that the Army likes to slap on their Hueys, Saffran and Sewell spotted it easily against the bright ground lighting of Washington, D.C. But because they had come in from the other helicopter's front, and their JetRanger was flying with running lights on, the larger military ship also spotted them. The other pilot turned away from the 206 and started to follow the route of a major highway underneath, flying low and heading deeper into the capital city.

Saffran and Sewell followed behind the Huey. They knew immediately they had a couple of problems. The first was how were they to determine if this was simply a military exercise gone awry. It certainly was a possibility. The area was filled with Army, Air Force, Marine, and Navy flying units. Maybe the pilot was in trouble, perhaps having suffered a complete electrical failure. That would mean no lights, along with no operating navigation gear. He might just be a little lost and looking for a safe place to put the aircraft down.

Maybe.

It didn't take long for the troopers to receive an answer from their radioed query about legitimate military activity in the area. Everything from everyone who was up flying at the moment was accounted for. Well, perhaps not exactly everything. An Army Huey was missing from the flight line at Fort Meade.

Saffran and Sewell had a major concern. Military Hueys were combat aircraft. They could carry an impressive array of missiles, machine guns, rocket and grenade launchers. Was "their" Huey so armed? And what were the intentions of its pilot? As the larger helicopter now headed toward the center of some of the United States government's most prized and revered buildings, Saffran grew even more worried.

Saffran wanted to be cautious, but he also knew he couldn't simply observe. So long as the Huey was flying around the city, it was causing havoc with local airports. Aircraft couldn't be permitted to depart or land while this freewheeling and unpredictable helicopter was aloft.

Saffran didn't know what was going to happen, but he was taking no chances. He called up Baltimore-Washington International and asked them to notify the White House security people. After all, you just never know about these things.

Saffran watched as the Huey came to the Washington Monument. The big helicopter hovered over its pinnacle, doing what pilots refer to as rudder turns. The Huey began to slowly pirouette in the air like some giant weather vane; first facing its nose north, then northeast, east, southeast, south—all the way around the points of the compass. Then it started to perform its little dance once more, this time in the opposite direction; pointing north, northwest, west, and on and on.

Saffran was familiar with this basic training maneuver, normally a test of skill and coordination of the pilot. But the drill was not usually done 556 feet in the air, directly over one of the nation's greatest monuments.

All at once Saffran could see that the Huey had stopped its antics and was now facing their JetRanger, itself hovering less than a thousand feet away. A moment later it became clear that whoever was in the military helicopter did not want company, as the Huey charged at the troopers' machine.

The JetRanger moved away from the other ship quickly. Although the 8000-pound Huey had an engine nearly three times more powerful than that of the 3000-pound JetRanger, the two aircraft began an aerial dance that later would be described by Saffran as something that could only be called a dogfight.

The Huey lunged after the smaller helicopter. Sewell brought the JetRanger hard around and pulled up hard on the collective. The JetRanger was both faster and more agile than the Huey. Sewell kept turning inside the other aircraft, keeping it in sight while maintaining a safe distance from the crazed pilot's maneuvers. When the Huey would straighten out its flight path, Sewell would again close in on his prey. And once again the Huey would turn into the JetRanger to repeat his futile attempts at intercepting the State Police aircraft.

After several minutes of chasing after the JetRanger in an attempt to scare it away—or perhaps to do something far worse—the Huey pilot gave up the pursuit and settled once more into a hover, this time between the national monument and the White house. To their surprise, as the troopers watched, the military ship lit up with its external and internal lighting. Watching the now brightly illuminated helicopter, Sewell commented to Saffran that by this time the pilot had to be low on fuel, and both men silently hoped the ship would just settle to the grass and the adventure would be over. Because if it continued, neither Saffran nor Sewell had the faintest idea how they could bring the other helicopter's antics to an end.

The troopers decided to come to a hover next to the Huey. Perhaps they could somehow communicate with the pilot. But as they came up alongside the other ship, the Huey dashed away and made for the large building directly ahead. It was the White House. And by the reckless way the Huey was being flown, it looked to Saffran and Sewell it might well be the pilot's intent to smash his aircraft into the building.

Saffran and Sewell followed close behind.

It only took a minute for the Huey's short flight, but now

the two lawmen were faced with the possibility of the rogue military ship on the White House lawn. At that point the troopers felt they had to place their JetRanger between the Huey and the President's home.

The troopers discussed their options. If the two ships came into contact, the Huey's four hundred pounds of whirling rotor blades would—quite literally—cut their aircraft, along with them, in half. But on the other hand, they weren't about to let some madman destroy the White House. Both men were mature individuals, with families and careers, with lives to look forward to—they took a deep breath and prepared to make what appeared to be an unavoidable sacrifice.

Just a moment before their JetRanger started toward the Huey, Saffran heard a fusillade of gunfire ring out from around them. From behind trees and shrubs he could see bright bursts of light as the White House security personnel opened up on the other helicopter. Almost at once the Huey dropped to the ground and bounced on its skids, its main rotor still turning over.

Landing the State Police helicopter, Saffran saw the door of the Huey open and the pilot jump clear of the machine. The man then ran directly for the White House. The trooper wasn't sure what to do next. Did the guy have a bomb? Why the hell else would he head for the White House? Somewhere in the darkness Saffran was aware there was an army of people with guns, all aimed at the intruder. To step out of the helicopter now would put him right in the cross fire of the security personnel's weapons. But the direction the man was heading would put him within arm's reach of Saffran.

Call it bravery, call it cop instinct, call it guts. Whatever it was, Saffran had it. He wasn't going to let whoever had been in that Huey get to the White House. Saffran jumped from the JetRanger and tackled the man. Wrestling on the ground with someone any normal person would have every reason to believe was a homicidal lunatic, Saffran never even took his gun from his holster. What seemed to the trooper like an eternity went by—in reality perhaps it was five or six seconds—when a dozen of the White House security staff piled on top both of them, ultimately relieving the trooper of his burden.

It was only later, after a personal thank you from President Nixon at the White House, the awarding of medals, promotions, and commendations, that Saffran and Sewell learned from Army sources that the pilot of the Huey had every intention of killing himself that night, and by smashing his helicopter into a major government building.

The pilot of that Huey had been a dangerously suicidal private first class who, after having recently flunked out of the Army's flight training program, had just received a "Dear John" letter from his girl. As Saffran later said, "His string just kinda popped."

If you ask Lou Saffran about that early morning back in February of 1974, he'll say something about having had a couple of close ones before and plenty of close ones after, but none quite so near to the edge as with that crazed Huey pilot on the White House lawn.

Baby Born in JetRanger

Medevacs might be thought of as the "meat and potatoes" job of the Maryland State police's flying troopers. And Saffran had performed over a thousand such flights in his long career. But as in any profession, what starts out to be some "routine" task sometimes turns out to be more "routine" than others.

Saffran and trooper Pilot Paul Jones were contacted on the SysCom hot line—Systems Communications, a centralized radio room relaying information and requests from all Maryland countywide fire boards. An interhospital flight was required for a woman experiencing a troubled birth. It would be a simple early morning flight from St. Mary's County Hospital to Johns Hopkins, forty minutes by air but two and a half hours by ambulance.

Saffran was glad to see that the expectant mother, Shelby Anderson, was quite calm when put aboard the JetRanger. And, as there would be plenty of time until the baby was due—the woman wasn't going to deliver until later that morning—Saffran propped her up so she could look out the window, to watch the lights below and enjoy the flight. She had informed him it was the first time she'd been on a helicopter.

As the JetRanger approached the Fort Meade area, both troopers were surprised when Mrs. Anderson strained at her litter's safety straps and screamed out that she was about to give birth. Saffran started to argue with her, after all, hadn't that doctor back at St. Mary's assured him such an event wouldn't take place until many hours later, and certainly not aboard his helicopter. Mrs. Anderson replied she didn't care what the doctor had said, her baby was being born right now!

One look at the grimace on the woman's face told Saffran that he had picked the wrong moment to begin such a debate. He suggested to Mrs. Anderson that he could verify her concerns but that to do so would require that they become very well-acquainted.

Getting on the intercom to his pilot, Saffran asked the other man to turn on the map light and point it in the direction of Mrs. Anderson's groin area. Saffran twisted around in his seat—the patient's head lies toward the rear in a JetRanger—and lifted the sheet Mrs. Anderson was covered with. He could see that the baby was in fact crowning, and relayed that information to the pilot.

Over the medical frequency the pilot informed SysCom that the helicopter had to divert to University Hospital, which had a shock trauma unit, and wanted staff to be waiting for them when they set down. And they wanted an isolette—a portable incubator with its own heater and oxygen—to be standing by. Mrs. Anderson had had two previous miscarriages, both taking place at first-rate hospitals with skilled medical personnel in attendance, and now Saffran was about to deliver a three-month-premature baby in a most inappropriate and difficult place.

Saffran recalls that while the actual delivery of the baby went fine—it was a task he had performed a number of times in the past—the mother didn't appear to be doing as well, at least emotionally. After he placed the baby, with its umbilical cord still attached, on the mother's stomach and covered the newborn, Mrs. Anderson appeared to be very upset. She said to the trooper, "I'm going to lose another one."

Saffran stimulated the tiny infant—the boy was hardly more than two pounds in weight—and reassured the mother that the baby seemed to be doing all right at the moment.

Turning up the cabin heat to maximum, the helicopter landed at university and waited on the roof for the staff to relieve them of their precious cargoes.

Although Robert, Mrs. Anderson's firstborn—she's now the mother of two—remained in the hospital for the first eight months of his life, he is a fine and healthy child. Saffran and the Anderson family continue to remain in touch. And, as Mrs. Anderson still likes to point out, it took the skill of a Maryland State Trooper, in the cabin of a small helicopter, to successfully deliver her first baby.

Aerial Rescue at the Naval Academy

What do you do when you have to rescue someone who's suspended from a guy wire eight hundred feet above the ground? If you have a choice, you call a helicopter. And that's exactly what happened on a hot summer's day at Annapolis when a worker's safety harness malfunctioned while he was atop a radio tower.

On that August afternoon Saffran was part of the crew of a Sikorsky H-34. The ship was of Korean War vintage and was powered by a conventional reciprocating engine. Beside the two pilots, Mike Wenrich and Milton Stewart, Observer/Medic Ralph Smith was also aboard the helicopter with Saffran.

During the late afternoon the Anne Arundel County Fire Board called out for assistance from the Maryland State Police. A technician working on one of the Navy's tall low-frequency radio towers—the ones used for communication with submarines—had had an accident. He had fallen from his work perch and now was trapped, suspended from a cable high above the ground, unable to shimmy up or down the hundreds of feet necessary to gain access to a ladder and safety. He'd been hanging up in the air for the entire morning before anyone even noticed he was in trouble. It wasn't until his fellow workers discovered him missing and started searching the installation for the man that they discovered him dangling from his backup safety harness high in the antenna.

Approaching the area, the crew of the Sikorsky could see they faced a major dilemma. The tower was supported by an array of dozens of strong metal guy wires, which radiated out from the tall structure in a 360-degree arc. The victim hung from a spot near the upper two-thirds of this array. There was only one way a rescue could be executed. One of the airborne troopers would have to be lowered down through the wires by the helicopter's hoist and grab hold of the man.

To Saffran it looked like they were hovering over an enormous spiderweb. And whoever was going to go down to do the rescue had better not get himself tangled up in the wires, or that person would become part of the problem.

Ralph Smith and Saffran flipped a coin to see who would go down in the harness to get hold of the victim. Smith "won" the toss and opted to make the rescue, while it would be Saffran who operated the hoist and directed the pilot.

To a layman, the operation would seem plain enough. Just lower the trooper down between the wires while the pilot hovered over the same spot. But as with much else in life, it just isn't that simple. The biggest problem for a pilot is the difficulty in maintaining a constant position. He's flying an aircraft that wants to drift. Air currents, blade movement, and his own unconscious control inputs are all elements working against him keeping the machine over any one spot above the ground. There is no instrument aboard a helicopter that can tell a pilot if he's moving from a desired station at any position. The best that can be done is for the person at the helicopter's controls to keep the machine's nose on a particular spot on the horizon and at the same time attempt a glance out the side window for any object in the distance that might be used for a reference. And, if there's a crew chief, to listen to his directions.

It is tense, hard, mental and physical work. Exhausting to the mind and body. Particularly so when two hundred pounds of man and hoist wire is swinging underneath the belly of the helicopter, acting like a big pendulum.

Saffran helped hook Smith into the rescue harness, a series of wide nylon straps fastened with heavy metal clasps. Saffran reached outside the open door of the helicopter and took hold of the winch's metal cable, grabbing onto the metal hook at its end. In his other hand he held the electric switch which let out and pulled in the cable. He pressed on the release button. The winch whined and he slowly pulled the cable end into the cabin. He hooked the end to Smith's harness.

Smith was lowered between the cables. Grabbing hold of a wire several feet under the hapless technician, the trooper tried to shimmy his way up to the man in order to place the rescue collar he had brought with him around the victim. The pilot attempted to lower the machine so as to give Smith enough slack in the cable to enable him to work. But as the pilot reduced power, the big helicopter began to drift away from the men below. The hoist cable caught on one of the guy wires, causing tremendous tension to be placed on the hoist line. Saffran—Smith was without any means of communication—called out corrections to the pilot, watching in horror as the hoist cable, now tangled in the wires, had more and more pressure put on it. All at once what Saffran feared happened. The hoist wire Ralph Smith was dangling from came loose from the antenna's guy wire. Under tremendous strain, it caused the unfortunate trooper to be propelled—almost like he was shot from a cannon—high into the air. For a moment it appeared to Saffran that the man and cable, like some giant rubber band being snapped in the hands of a mischievous child, might come back around and foul itself on the helicopter, possibly even reaching the rotor blades. Smith's body arched upward to within only a few feet of the big Sikorsky, then fell back down between the wires, and now began to sway in a wide arc under the helicopter.

Through careful control inputs (and some luck), the pilot managed to stabilize the wildly swinging Smith. But the troopers' initial problem was still there, the man on the antenna.

Once more Saffran directed the pilot to lower Smith back in among the snaking wires. This time Smith was able to attach the rescue collar around the victim, whom Smith was pleased to see remained calm. He explained to the man, who was now badly dehydrated from the ordeal of staying out in the hot sun for almost four hours, that the hoist couldn't carry both of them up at the same time. The trooper would have to return alone to the helicopter so that the cable could once more be lowered to the victim. Smith gave the man a knife and instructed him to cut his safety harness away from the guy wire once he had securely hooked the end of the cable up to the rescue collar.

Saffran saw Smith wave, indicating he should be hoisted aboard the helicopter. Saffran pressed on the take-up button and the slow process of winding the cable back into the winch began. It took five minutes for Smith to get back into the aircraft. He told Saffran the instructions he had given the victim. Saffran once more lowered the cable.

Saffran wondered what they would do if the victim attached the end of the cable to himself and for some reason could not or did not cut his harness loose from the wires. What if the machine drifted as it did before, with the man still attached to both the antenna and the aircraft? Saffran decided he didn't want to consider those possibilities.

But the victim did as he was told, and this time the helicopter didn't drift enough to cause a problem. The man was successfully hoisted aboard the aircraft. He had been out in the hot sun for so long—hanging from his harness unseen by passersby for half the day—he was in shock and suffering from second degree burns. But considering what might have happened to him, he was very happy to be aboard the chopper.

Crew Killed in Medevac Attempt While Flying into Fog

Pilots hate fog. That silent gray mist that, as Carl Sandburg wrote, "comes on cat's paws," holds a deceptive lethality for aviators. Only experience and training can protect fliers from the trouble fog can cause. And sometimes even that's not enough.

Saffran and his pilot were working a three-to-eleven P.M. shift. Both men had done some flying during the evening, but found the weather to be marginal. Saffran and his pilot had been checking the temperature/dew point spread—the closer the two numbers were to each other, the greater the likelihood for visible moisture to be in the air—since they'd started work. The numbers had been getting closer as the night progressed. On top of that, the weather forecast called for dense fog to come rolling in off of the Chesapeake Bay.

Toward the end of their shift a call came in for the troopers to do a Medevac. It was a pickup at Easton Hospital, located across the bay. The victim of a drug overdose needed the transport.

Saffran and his pilot discussed their options. The flight, normally a routine task, would require that they fly over water, in the dark, at the same time as dense fog would be obscuring everything under them. Their horizon would likely be obliterated as well. Even on a clear evening, when a light aircraft goes from a ground area that is well lit and overflies a large body of water, the effect is disorienting. On a starless night it was like flying into a black velvet sack. The pilot would have to fly by reference to his attitude and navigation instruments; to watch and scan the little three-inch artificial horizon, airspeed indicator, altimeter, and rate of climb indicator for signs they weren't flying straight and level. And anyway, from the sound of the reported weather, Easton might damn well be fogged in by the time they got there, adding yet another unpleasant possibility to the equation.

No, Saffran and his pilot decided, they would opt to do what they rarely ever did. They would decline this Medevac.

The crew of the shift that was to relieve Saffran and his pilot walked in shortly afterward. The observer/medic was a trooper named Nole, his pilot a trooper named Russ.

Russ checked the sheet and asked about the Easton pickup. True, the weather was lousy, but Russ knew the eastern shore like the back of his hand. And any pilot will tell you that how familiar a pilot is to a given area does make a big difference in what a person should or should not attempt.

The relieving pilot gave a call to weather. It was still garbage out there. And the fog was coming. But what the hell, Russ was an experienced pilot, flying helicopters for the National Guard as well as the State Police. Maybe he and Nole would go up, take a look at how bad it was, and if worse came to worse, they could abort en route and return to the hangar.

As Saffran and the other trooper left for home, the new crew took off for the mission. It was bad out, but they pressed on. Russ was on instruments as he flew over the water, working to keep the helicopter level, navigating by the ship's electronic equipment, and communicating with the ground; what pilots might refer to as a "high workload" environment. But they were going to save a life, and that meant something significant to the two troopers. Even if it was someone who had decided to wreck his life with drugs, who were they to decide on right or wrong, good and evil?

It must have been very dark up there as they headed into Easton, the glow of the JetRanger's instrument panel the only visible light in the world the two men could see. And it would have been real nice if someone had bothered to call up those two men and tell them that the person they were sticking their necks out to save had passed away sometime earlier at the hospital. But nobody thought to call Nole and Russ, just a couple of guys drilling their way through the opaque midnight air.

Russ, his hands at the controls, gentle put the necessary pressure on the cyclic stick between his knees so as to keep the sensitive flying machine in level flight. He pressed in on the control stick's red transmit switch as he approached the invisible shoreline. The State Police are here, get ready with our Medevac patient.

Except there was no Medevac patient to be picked up.

Some invisible voice, sitting safe behind a crash-proof desk, must have said something like, "Thanks anyway, guys. Sorry about that. I guess we forgot to tell you."

What happened next nobody will ever know for sure, but every helicopter pilot who has flown over water, or in fog, or with no horizon for reference, knows in their hearts what happened.

Russ had landing on his mind. He was worried about getting down through the murk to do his pickup. But now there was no pickup. All his mental preparation, the tight gut, the cold sweating, it was all for naught. Now he had to do a 180-degree turn, back around into the jet-black velvet sack.

Nice gentle standard-rate turn. A standard rate turn, about fifteen degrees to the right, that's what was called for. Yeah, but a standard-rate turn would take a whole minute to come back around to where he wanted to go. That's a long time when you've just sweated out a useless trip on the gauges. So, just maybe he went to a twenty-degree turn, to speed things up a bit. No big deal. As Russ came back over the water, whatever lights he might have had under him and off the nose of his helicopter disappeared. It's a surreal feeling, impossible to truly understand unless experienced. Maybe he looked out through the windshield, to see what was out there. Just for a couple of seconds. A peek. Maybe he figured he could catch sight of the horizon, maybe the fog hadn't gotten all the way back home yet. Maybe he wouldn't have to sweat bullets on instruments all the way back to the hangar.

Russ and Nole never even heard the crash. The remains of their ship were found on shore, the helicopter's nose facing in the direction of their base.

And all for a dead junkie.

Death of Newly Trained Observer and Pilot

A crew member, newly transferred to the Maryland State Police Airborne Division, doesn't just hop aboard an aircraft and start to perform their job. Whether they are pilot or crew, there is a structured, regimented training program that must first be successfully completed before they are "cut loose" to accomplish the unit's various missions.

Lou Saffran did his share of training newly assigned personnel in his twenty-odd years with the airborne unit. Mostly it was to give the new guy the better part of two months of "do this, don't do that," how to communicate on the VHF aircraft radio, how to set up the helicopter for the Medevac configuration, and above all else to keep everyone away from the tail rotor. There was a whole new language to learn, about weight and balance, over torquing the machine, hot starts and foreign object damage to the engine—the overhaul of which, depending on what was found inside, could go for the better part of a hundred thousand dollars.

Saffran never considered teaching new people such a bad deal. After over seven thousand hours in the air, he suspected he had a few things of value to say on the subject, and anyway, there were always one or two bits of information that someone in the business for a long time forgets but really should remember. So, Saffran figured, the process was a good review for himself as well.

Parkerson, the new observer/medic Saffran was training, had already been in the State Police for a number of years. He wasn't a pilot, but like Saffran, loved to fly. He had wanted in on the airborne unit for quite some time before an open slot was available.

Saffran was scheduled to work with Parkerson as well as his steady partner and pilot, Charles Rathel, on a three-to-eleven shift. But Saffran got a call the day before. He was overdue for finishing up his mandatory in-service police officer training—you may be flying around all day in a jet turbine-powered helicopter, but after all is said and done, you're still a cop. He was told to come in on the A.M. and take care of his last day of training. Saffran could let the new guy—who was just about at the end of his instruction period anyway—work the whole shift alone with Rathel.

So Saffran went in for his in-service, and when three o'clock rolled around, Parkerson and Rathel showed up at Andrews Air Force Base, where Parkerson was given the news that he was "cut loose." That is, he would be permitted to perform his job unsupervised by a trainer.

I can only speculate on what ran through Parkerson's thoughts when he was told he would finally be allowed to do the work he so badly wanted to be involved in. It had to be a good feeling.

So it was that the two troopers—a senior pilot and a green observer/medic—went off for the routine late afternoon traffic flight. It was a clear day, a good day. A nice day to be flying.

The two made their way up Route 1. No major traffic problems, nothing much to do but enjoy the sensation of flight.

It was by an open field off the side of the highway that Rathel decided to practice a few autorotations.

Now, with helicopters, as with virtually any aircraft, when an engine fails, the machine just doesn't fall out of the sky. A light fixed-wing craft will travel around ten feet forward for every foot of altitude lost. Stated a more meaningful way, someone in a civilian single-engine aircraft who has engine failure at 10,000 feet will be able to travel close to twenty miles in search of a safe landing spot before they touch.

Helicopters are a little different. When a JetRanger-size machine has engine failure, the pilot has to do several things at once, and do them quickly, to salvage the situation. First he must "dump the collective," that is, lower the lever to his left, which controls power, in order to maximize the amount of energy that will remain in the whirling rotor blades overhead as the helicopter heads for the earth at between 1500 and 2000 feet per minute. Not to reduce collective quickly enough might also mean the rotor-blade speed will fall below a certain value and the blades lose their rigidity. That would be a wholly lethal combination, as the blades would start to flap and the ship would soon be out of control.

Still, to a new pilot it seems there is much to do and damn little time to do it; dump the collective, maintain airspeed—too much and you go down too fast, too little and you have no energy reserve left in the blades to recover at the bottom—watch your rotor RPM—no less than 100 percent, no more than 107 percent, or they're overspeeding—and all the while be looking for a nice safe place to gently put your helicopter down in, without turning it into three-quarters of a million dollars' worth of scrap aluminum.

While the technique takes many hours to master, autorotations are routinely practiced by professional pilots. Because, to a helicopter pilot, it's something that once mastered could truly save his or her life.

Rathel checked around his airspace. He confirmed that he and Parkerson were alone up there. He would probably have informed the paramedic about what he intended to do. To a new man, a practice autorotation would be a blur of fast-moving helicopter heading straight for the ground.

So Rathel twisted his throttle closed, watched as his "needles split," the rotor RPM staying at the 100 percent mark while the engine speed bled down to around 60 percent. He then lowered his collective and the JetRanger headed for the ground.

Saffran got home from his in-service training when the telephone rang. It was work. They wanted him to know, before he heard it on the radio or saw it on the TV: Rathel and Parkerson. They had been doing practice autos. Probably came too close to a treetop. Looks like they clipped the branches. The machine landed on its side and burned.

Sometimes death can be a very difficult thing for the living to accept. Saffran flew into a rage. He just knew, if he had been there, it wouldn't have happened. He and Rathel worked as a team, each one watching out for the other. Saffran would have spotted the tree before his partner got too close, he would have prevented the accident. He just knew he could have.

Could've, would've, should've. If only they would issue crystal balls at headquarters, then nobody would ever have to die.

Severed Airway

Trooper Paul Jones flew the JetRanger around the landing zone just one more time to check for obstacles. There were already fire department and rescue vehicles at the scene, and satisfied all was well, he and Saffran headed for the ground to pick up the victim of a motorcycle accident.

After touching down, Saffran jumped from the helicopter and walked over to the fire department medic. In the ambulance he could see a young man—he was nineteen—resting on his stomach, propped up on his elbows. The medic explained that it was the only position the victim was comfortable in. The man's off-road motorcycle had taken him through some barbed wire, hit him in the throat, and caused a small puncture wound.

Saffran looked back over to the JetRanger. If he put the man inside the helicopter the way he was lying in the ambulance, if something went wrong medically there would be no way for him to work on the victim. No, it was clear to Saffran that comfortable or not, the young patient would have to lie on his back for the trip to the hospital.

As gently as possible the victim was placed on the JetRanger's litter. The helicopter took off, and although Saffran had immediately started the man on pure oxygen, by the time they had reached 800 feet, the victim was turning blue from lack of air. What was to be a routine transport was quickly turning into a medical emergency of the first order. The pilot did a 180 turn and landed once again by the rescue vehicles.

On the ground Saffran jumped out and he and the other medics virtually yanked the young man from the stretcher and put an esophageal obturator airway tube down his throat. This opened up his airway enough for color to come back to the victim's lips and face. The situation seemed to be under control for the moment.

Once more the man was placed on the litter. Saffran knew there was more to the injury than they could see, but damn little could be done for the man in a farmer's field. He needed serious medical attention, and the quickest way to get it was by flying him out.

Again the helicopter took off, heading for Baltimore Trauma Center. Saffran kept on pumping pure oxygen into the victim, and it appeared to the trooper that the EOA was doing its job.

As they approached the outskirts of Baltimore, the supply

of oxygen in the JetRanger ran out. Saffran began to vigorously pump on the "Ambu" bag—the plastic sack that was connected to the oxygen mask—attempting to keep air going into the man's lungs. It was a losing battle. Saffran told the pilot to get on the horn and let the medical people below know their victim wasn't going to make it if they continued on to their destination hospital, and that they would have to make a landing at Greater Baltimore Hospital Center instead. He also told the pilot to tell them to have a doctor, gurney, support staff, and oxygen waiting for them below when they landed. Especially the oxygen.

Setting down at Greater Baltimore, the JetRanger crew could see that the medical staff had taken their request seriously. Everything went smoothly as the victim was hurriedly placed on the waiting gurney and oxygen administered. The physician was told that although it looked like a relatively minor injury, there must be some sort of airway blockage. Saffran urged the doctor to have the victim taken immediately in for emergency surgery.

Rushing the victim into the operating room, the first thing the doctor did was to perform a tracheotomy. Saffran had been wrong. There was no blockage in the airway. There had been no airway to block—it having been severed by the impact of the barbed wire. The doctor told the trooper that the only thing that had kept the man alive had been the trooper's insertion of the EOA.

Just another Medevac, another life saved. Another routine flight.

CHAPTER 7

Trooper/Pilot James Watson

Loss of Pilot and Female Medic/Observer

IT WAS AROUND 10:30 P.M. AND JIM WATSON AND HIS OBSERV-er/medic were just about set to end their evening shift at the Frederick section. Nothing much had happened that night, and Watson briefed the oncoming pilot, Greg May, as much. May had been flying choppers for the unit for about a year and had served as a medic/observer before that. With May that night was Carey Poetzman, a young woman who was married to a Maryland trooper and who had worked in the air division as an observer/medic for a number of years.

Watson kidded Poetzman about her new frizzy hairstyle, telling her she looked like she had stuck her finger in an electric socket. She showed him photos of a log house she and her husband were building.

Before he left, Watson told May that although the weather was flyable at the moment, in a few hours it was supposed to go down to the ground.

That morning Watson woke up well before dawn. He looked at his alarm clock, noted it was 4:05 A.M., and went back to sleep. There was no reason for him to be up at that hour, but every now and again it'd happen.

As was the custom in the Watson household, early Sunday

everyone headed out for church. It was a slow ride that day, as a thick fog blanketed the area.

Coming back to his home from church, he entered his house to a ringing telephone. Watson picked up the receiver. It was his mother. She was crying and hysterical. Once he calmed her down, she finally explained that on the radio news they were reporting that the State Police helicopter from Frederick was missing from last night.

After he had assured his mother that everything was fine, Watson called his section. The trooper on the other end told him that May and Poetzman went out on a Medevac at around 3:30 A.M. that morning and hadn't been seen since dropping off their patient at the trauma center in Baltimore. Which meant that somewhere between Frederick airport and the hospital, a fifty-mile distance, the helicopter had gone down. And at the moment—in that heavy fog—there was no way air operations could be initiated to look for the two troopers.

Watson headed into work, driving along the roads he speculated was the route of travel May and Poetzman would have likely flown. Halfway to work his State Police radio broadcast that the missing helicopter had been located. Both pilot and observer were dead.

The whole story later came out. A person suffering from a self-inflicted gunshot wound desperately needed transport to the trauma center. The weather was getting bad quickly, but a person's life hung in the balance. Both May and Poetzman decided to take the flight. They didn't have to do it, nobody ordered them out; they chose to do it.

After picking up the victim, en route to the hospital May had to ask Baltimore Center for some vectors to the medical facility, as he was losing contact with the ground. As any pilot knows, the only thing worse than flying in fog is flying in fog at night.

Once the crew had landed at the trauma center, the medical team that met the helicopter reported that both the pilot and observer/medic seemed to be rushed. Clearly they were fearful about being able to get back to their station. Sure, they could have just shut the machine down where they were. But then their relief crew in the morning would have had to drive an hour to the hospital, then everyone would have had to play musical cars. In short, it would have meant a hassle all the way around. May and Poetzman probably figured, we got here, we can get back.

Once the patient was out of the machine, Poetzman got back in, May pulled up on the collective, and off they went.

Five miles away from the trauma center, May flew into cloud. Following the procedure taught at that time—now pilots are told to fly straight ahead and climb—he made a U-turn, a 180 to bring him out of the soup. But May was a low-time pilot, with only around three hundred hours in JetRangers. Maybe he didn't believe his attitude instruments. Maybe he just looked away for a few seconds. Whatever happened inside that helicopter, no one will ever know, except that the pilot made a descending turn and the two troopers flew into trees. They were both killed instantly.

Now, Watson was quick to point out that he doesn't believe in premonitions or psychic phenomena or anything like that. Only, after the incident, it just seemed kind of strange. He was told that the clock in the JetRanger's wreckage had stopped at 4:05 A.M., the same time he'd woken the morning of the crash.

What is there left to say about two brave law officers who are killed trying to save a life? Pilots "what if" such situations mercilessly. They should have turned down the job, they shouldn't have tried to fly in worsening weather, they shouldn't have ...

But if every police pilot decided to stay in the hangar when there was some "weather" outside, not much flying would get done. Sometimes a cop does what a cop has to do. Most of the time it works out okay. Most of the time.

CHAPTER 8

Trooper/Pilot William Force

Up, Up and Away

WILLIAM FORCE STILL FLIES HELICOPTERS AS A MARINE IN A local reserve unit. Among the aircraft he pilots is the Sikorsky CH-53, an 88-foot-long monster that grosses out at 42,000 pounds. On one occasion the Marines, wanting to do a little flag waving, sent Force and his crew, in a CH-53, out to Marysville, Ohio, to an annual hot-air balloon and air show.

Once out there, Force remembers seeing ads on the local TV. The advertising proclaimed that Marysville was the home of Scotts Lawn Care Company, and was "the town that watches the grass grow." A nice quiet little town, he decided.

On early Sunday morning of the show, Force walked around the balloons as they were preparing to launch, wondering aloud if anyone was interested in having a Marine helicopter pilot/Maryland State Trooper come along as ballast. Force managed to find one balloonist, someone who was going to instruct a student pilot in the fine art of ballooning and who needed an additional ground-crew person—their one man, Tiny (he wasn't), wasn't sufficient to the task. So Force traded the services of his helicopter's crew chief for a ride.

As they lifted off, Force recalls asking the two pilots the naive question, "Where we going?" The answer, of course, is that a balloon goes wherever the air currents take it. In retrospect, Force isn't surprised that the two balloonists, in response to his query, simply looked at him as if he had stepped down from Mars. And anyway, Force really didn't care. It was a beautiful day, all the other balloons were coming up, and it was a glorious sight to behold.

Force noticed, as they moved silently over the green farmland below, that the two pilots carried Bic lighters in their hands. At the time he didn't consider the significance of the lighters, but before his little ride was over, he'd have a much better understanding of the fact that when flying in hot-air balloons, something or someone had to supply the heat.

A hot-air balloon is not a responsive craft. To gain altitude it takes a seven-second burn of the on-board propane gas burner for the balloon to react. Force watched with interest as the pilot instructor put his student through some balloon training. Force quickly learned that there are only three things you can practice doing in a balloon; going level, going up, or going down. And the trooper watched as the student began to practice the last of the exercises, the descent phase.

Moving over a cornfield, Force saw that a highway ran perpendicular to their flight path. And, although still some distance away, directly ahead sat a parked white station wagon, with Dad, Mom, and the kids standing alongside, waving to all the balloons.

Ballooning, by its very nature, isn't a loud sport. But Force noticed that it had become even quieter than before, as the flame from the propane burner had gone out. He then found out what the two Bic lighters were for, as both pilots madly began to flick their Bics in an attempt to get a relight, which wasn't happening.

Much to Force's dismay, he noted that their rate of descent was increasing rapidly. Compounding the problem was the added dilemma of the white station wagon, which appeared to be sitting precisely on top of that piece of ground where the balloon was about to land (rapidly). The balloon pilot, now that it was obvious they weren't going to gain height in time, moved to the front of the basket and frantically gestured at the man below to move the car.

Just prior to hitting the ground, it seemed to Force that

several things happened at once. The bad news was, the pilots got the burner lit just a few seconds before impact, which didn't really help the situation all that much. The good news was that the man in the station wagon had managed to move the car a few feet down the road and the balloon missed crashing into it.

Once they made ground contact, Force found himself, along with his two companions, dragged across several lanes of interstate highway, over the median, and fully across the opposite lanes of traffic just before heading back into the air—the entire event taking the seven seconds needed for the balloon to respond to the reheat. Force, during the unintentional ride, wanted to jump from the gondola. But he found that he couldn't get out due to the speed of the balloon. During the seven-second adventure he did, however, manage to tear his flight suit, his shoulder got banged up, the basket he was riding in was damaged on the impact side, and the balloon's altimeter and radio were destroyed, as was a bunch of other stuff that was breakable inside the basket. It was about that time that Force decided he wasn't having any fun at all. Otherwise, considering everything, Force figured it had been a real good landing.

Back in the air the balloon's pilot/instructor critiqued the descent as having come down a bit too fast and told the student pilot he shouldn't let the balloon cool so rapidly in the future, and to keep a better eye on the flame. Meanwhile, Force noticed that he was bleeding, but nobody around him was paying him any mind anyway.

They continued to fly along until the pilot spotted Tiny and Force's crew chief, the pair sitting in a farmer's soybean field which lay ahead of them. The pilot dropped a long line from the basket to the ground, and Tiny (all 400 pounds of him) and Force's crew chief grabbed hold of it. As Force recalls, the pair of ground crewmen gave every appearance of water-skiing through the field as they tried to slow the forward movement of the balloon. On top of which, Tiny had parked their pickup truck smack in the middle of whoever's property they were on, tearing up a good amount of soybeans in the process.

Finally, with no additional excitement and much to

Force's relief, the flight came to an end. The balloon was down, quickly tied to the bumper of the pickup truck, with all hands on the ground. It was then that Force saw the farmer heading their way. And he was clearly upset. Five people, one pickup truck, and a hot air balloon were now sitting in the middle of his working soybean field, not to mention the assorted furrows made in the young growth by Tiny's attempts at stopping the moving balloon.

Irate farmers were apparently a routine matter for balloonists to have to deal with. Force saw that, fortunately, the balloon people had a solution to that problem. Out of the truck comes a bottle of champagne, a Polaroid camera, and a photo of the balloon along with a certificate—in suitably flowery lettering—which in glowing terms informs the world that on this date farmer Jones had the great good fortune to have his farm picked by their balloon as a place to land. Before the farmer has had a chance to say much, they stick the farmer and his family in the balloon—still tethered to the truck's bumper, lucky him—and run it up in the air. Now that the farmer is suitably impressed, they reel him and his family down, take a picture of him and the family in the balloon, give everyone a drink of bubbly, shake his hand, and then everybody quickly piles into the truck and leaves.

As they headed off the field, Force wondered if the reason a bottle of champagne is uncorked after each balloon flight is because their landings were always so eventful.

CHAPTER 9

Trooper Observer/Medic Steve Proctor

A Typical Night

IT WAS A LATE JUNE SATURDAY NIGHT. TROOPER FIRST CLASS
Steve Proctor and his pilot, also a trooper first class, Vern
Daley, were working a four-to-midnight duty shift. That day
they were assigned to the Norwood section, and as was his
habit, Proctor had arrived early to work.

The temperature was ninety-five degrees with high humid-
ity. Uncomfortable even in light civilian clothes, the two
airborne unit officers wore heavy Nomex flight suits and
gloves—fireproof lifesavers in the event of a crash, but miserable in that kind of heat. They also had to wear their
Beretta 9mm service pistols in shoulder holsters, along with
heavy military-style boots, and, when flying, "brain buckets," their military-type safety helmets.

Daley started on his preflight on his Aerospatiale Dauphin—a large twin-engine helicopter. Proctor, after signing
for and hanging around his neck the narcotics key—for access to the narcotics locker—taken from the observer/medic
he was relieving, began his check through of the helicopter's
on-board medical gear. He hurried through the list of required equipment; defibrilator battery, oxygen in the on-
board system—enough for at least one and a half and as
much as several hours of use, depending on the nature of
the injury of the victims it was used for—and went through
the rest of what remained of the complex and technical medical equipment his flying ambulance held.

At 1550 hours, technically ten minutes before the start of their shift, a call came in for a child struck by a car while riding on a bicycle. The accident took place in Hartford County, in a small rural town named Belair. As Daley started up the helicopter, Proctor buckled himself in, grousing to himself that he hadn't quite finished his inventory of their on-board medical equipment.

The helicopter soon came upon the scene, and, after the pilot checked over the landing zone, put the machine down a block from where the accident took place. Proctor jumped out and headed for the injured child. It was a twelve-year-old girl, rather large for her age. He figured her to weigh around 150 pounds, and from the looks of her leg, she had a fractured femur. The bleeding was bad, and the bone, although not breaking skin, was pushing out at a nasty angle.

Proctor immobilized his patient, inserted lactated ringers, a solution of water and electrolytes used to treat shock, put her on oxygen and splinted the badly damaged leg.

Working with the ground-based medical emergency team, the child—screaming in terrible pain—was put aboard the helicopter. Once in the air, Proctor contacted a physician on the Trauma Line at the Shock Trauma unit in Baltimore, and relayed the nature of the problem. All the while he measured the young girl's cardiac rhythm, took her pulse and blood pressure readings, and did a complete secondary survey.

The trip to the hospital was uneventful, as was the landing on the six-story-high helipad of the hospital. A trauma team was already standing by: a trauma nurse, an anesthesiologist, and two trauma technicians. After turning over his patient to the team and retrieving the helicopter's stretcher, Proctor went back up to the roof. The air temperature hadn't cooled since he started working, and he found himself drenched in sweat.

On the helipad, from a bunker located there for the purpose, he restocked the supplies he used on the previous mission. As he picked and chose the items he needed, a telephone near the bunker rang. It was SysCom asking if the crew was available to head out to another accident up by Lock Raven Dam, in Baltimore County. There had been a motorcycle accident ten miles and, by helicopter, barely ten minutes away.

It was 1635 hours, 4:35 P.M. Proctor and Daley had been on duty only an hour and a half and they were already heading out on the second run of the night.

Once over the scene, Proctor saw that fire department personnel were already there. As was often the case, when other emergency unit members know a Medevac helicopter is on the way, and with the best of intentions, they mark out what they believe to be a suitable landing zone. Often it's not. Proctor and Daley took one look at the small parking lot below, a lone car sitting in its middle and the place surrounded by fifty-foot-high trees, and realized there was no way they would safely be able to use that site.

From the advantage of a viewpoint several hundred feet above that enjoyed by the fire department personnel, the two troopers noted a far better landing zone, an open field less than a quarter mile away. Proctor relayed that they would be putting down at the other spot—which also happened to be closer to the accident scene.

Shortly after setting the JetRanger on to the ground, the ambulance, with the victim inside, pulled up to the helicopter. It would be the first of two motorcycle accidents they would have that night. Here the rider had taken a sharp turn a little too fast and lost control of his bike, hitting his head on the guardrail. His helmet had been totally destroyed, and Proctor saw that the man still had a substantial head injury. The victim also stated he remembered nothing of the incident. Nonetheless, he was alive. Proctor had seen a good number of head injuries generated by motorcycle accidents. Maryland had just reinstated their helmet law—and without a helmet, Proctor knew that a rider had little or no chance of surviving such a mishap.

Proctor set the patient up in the helicopter with the routine IV and oxygen. He and Daley flew the man back to the very same trauma center they had just flown from. They dropped the patient off and headed back to their base.

On the ground, Proctor set about to first clean up the

helicopter from their two runs, then he got down to completing the paperwork involved on the jobs. The form was called a run sheet, a detailed two-page breakdown of patient information. He estimated each Medevac took a minimum of thirty minutes of clerical work afterward. While the observer/medic works on that material, the pilot refuels the aircraft, does a postflight check of the helicopter, and brings his flight and maintenance logs up to date.

About fifteen minutes into working on their necessary but unexciting tasks, the third call of the evening came in. A child fell into a swimming pool and had suffered a head injury. The location was only seven miles from the hangar. They fired the helicopter up and within a few minutes were circling over the location. As they looked about for a suitable landing site, a ground unit advised them that the child had in fact suffered only a minor injury and told them they could put their helicopter back in service.

Once more returning to their base, they no sooner shut the machine down and entered the hangar when the telephone rang. They had a transport, from Prince Georges Doctors Hospital to D.C. Children's Hospital, the pediatric trauma center in Washington, D.C., located within view of the nation's capitol.

This patient was a six-year-old child who had been struck by a car. The youngster was unconscious and not breathing. This job would be what Proctor would consider their first "serious" (life-threatening) case for the evening. It was 1730 hours, 5:30 P.M.

Landing behind a fire station near where their patient had been brought, Proctor was taken by the fire department's ambulance to the emergency room, where the victim lay. The trooper examined the unconscious child and saw that he had a rock-hard abdomen—a sign that blood had found its way into that part of the body. The victim was also diaphoretic (sweaty), in shock, had a pulse rate of 160, and suffered a major depressed skull fracture.

Once Proctor was assured his patient had a clear airway (Proctor intubated—inserted a hollow plastic tube down the throat of the victim and hooked him up to a respirator), the medical team, which included a medical technician from the fire station where they had landed, returned to the helicopter for the six-minute flight to D.C. Children's Hospital. Had the child been taken by ambulance, the ride—in the heavy urban rush-hour traffic—would have taken close to an hour.

At D.C. Children's the patient was removed and the helicopter shut down. As with most of the injured Proctor dealt with, once they disappeared into a hospital, he never saw or heard of them again. Inside, the machine "was a fairly substantial mess," as Proctor put it, and with today's concern for AIDS infection, blood and body fluids are cleaned up as soon as possible. Also, airborne Medevac teams love to shut down at D.C. Children's because of their very nice pilots' lounge. Inside is a stocked refrigerator just for the helicopter crews, filled with bowls of some of the best tasting home-made chili found anywhere. And fresh coffee sits perking for anyone who wants a cup.

So Proctor found himself involved with the usual division of duty. He cleaned up blood while his pilot and the "kid-napped" fire department medical tech went to get some chili!

Just about the time Proctor completed his cleaning job, around 2000 hours, eight P.M., a call came in from SysCom. Up in Poolesville there was a serious motorcycle accident Could they go? And if so, how long would it take them to get there?

Indeed, they could and did go. It took less than fifteen minutes to get over the accident location. As it was a rural area, with hospitals in the region spread out quite thinly, the helicopter arrived just a minute or two after the ground units got to the scene.

Approaching to land, Proctor noted a furrow dug into a nearby cornfield. At the end of the nearly hundred-foot-long swath lay a motorcycle, its rider prone nearby. Across the road from the field the trooper observed a dead deer and from that information pretty much figured out what the situation had been.

Once down, Proctor ran from the helicopter to where the patient was lying. The man had been in the cornfield, unseen for two hours, until a passerby found him. The rider had not been wearing a helmet, and the trooper could smell the heavy odor of alcohol around the victim.

He was a beefy man, and wore the cut-off leather jacket and other bits of gear most often associated with motorcycle gang members. As Proctor did a survey of the man, the victim—the man, not the deer—stated he could remember nothing about the accident. During the check, Proctor found a large bowie knife concealed inside the man's pants and relieved him of the weapon.

The rider was immobilized for transport and taken to Suburban Hospital, just north of Washington, D.C. It has a tight landing zone, situated in the middle of the hospital's parking lot. When a Medevac comes in, the hospital security staff has to make sure that no vehicles either enter or leave the place until the helicopter departs.

After unloading the injured motorcycle rider at Suburban, it was decided they had time to return the medical technician back to the fire station from where he first came. As luck would have it, as they headed in that direction a new call came in; a pedestrian was struck right in front of the very same fire department building they were flying to! Fate had seen to it that another child lay critically injured on Good Luck Road, the same ill-named street—Proctor figured the name signified that you had to have good luck to make it safely across—where the other child only a few hours earlier had been struck by a car.

Upon landing in the parking lot of the fire station, they found that their newest patient was a four-year-old who had suffered two fractured legs and had blood seeping into his abdominal cavity.

Their destination hospital was again D.C. Children's. Before lifting off, the child's mother, hysterical and not in good control of herself, asked to be permitted to go with her child. On occasion, if the parent had their act together, Proctor would permit such a ride along. But he decided, with the risk of dealing with a potentially confrontational parent in the confines of a helicopter while it was in flight, it was not going to be one of those times. He comforted the woman, told her he'd do whatever was necessary for her child and that she would be brought to the hospital by ambulance.

Leaving the fire department EMT at the fire station, the helicopter made the seven-minute flight to Children's Hospital. Both en route and at the hospital, Proctor saw to his young ward's welfare. Once the child was safely in the emergency room, Proctor handed a patient report to the hospital staff and completed whatever paperwork was necessary to get the job done. Coming up to the pilots' lounge, he met Daley, who, Proctor saw, was indulging himself with another bowl of chili.

The pair worked their way back to the hangar. Once again it was necessary to clean and refuel the helicopter. Before the troopers had much time to relax, a call came in for a search. Their machine was equipped with FLIR—Forward Looking Infra Red. Through this system, via a video console aboard the aircraft, images would be made visible solely due to differences in their temperature. Whether it was light or dark out, but most often during the coolness of night, the machine could see things the unaided human eye would never be able to make out. It could show the warm engine of a recently driven car, its hood shining brightly among the other vehicles parked in the middle of a large lot. Or it could be used for locating lost people in a forest or at sea. And, frequently, it was used for finding people who were trying not to be found. One case that Proctor recalled was their locating a fugitive who had secreted himself under a log near a lake. The man had only the top of his head showing, but it created a sufficiently distinct spot of light on the FLIR screen for Proctor to walk the ground personnel right up to where the man was hiding.

In this case the police up in Hartford County had discovered the dead body of a cab driver stuffed in the trunk of his own vehicle earlier in the day. They had been working the case since that morning, and now believed they had two suspects surrounded in a nearby wooded area.

After about ten minutes into the mission, with a perimeter just established and the helicopter now beginning a productive search pattern, the troopers were called away on a Medevac. The unit's mission was medical, and it was their mandate to break off any non life-threatening police task when a medical call came in. They immediately terminated their part of the search and made for the new assignment.

Their seventh assignment of the evening was a shooting at a housing development in Annapolis, the Maryland state capital. Landing in a school ball field right where the incident had occurred, Proctor found himself working on a twenty-year-old male who had taken two .38 slugs into his body. One round, which was embedded in his arm, wasn't so serious, but the other, deep inside his abdomen, was. The young man was in severe shock, with heavy abdominal bleeding.

A helicopter landing in the small neighborhood was a major event; shootings, on the other hand, were all too common. People appeared from nowhere to examine the machine. While Proctor was working to save the life of the victim, members of the fire company at the scene did their best to ensure that the locals didn't inadvertently damage the helicopter.

Proctor placed MAST (Medical Anti-Shock Trousers) trousers on the man. The device had been invented in Vietnam. It was designed to be inflated once placed on a person. The air pressure would force blood from the lower extremities up to the heart/lung and brain area, where it was vitally needed in cases of shock. With the antishock trousers in place and inflated, they took off for the Shock Trauma Center in Baltimore.

It was to be the last Medevac of the night. Proctor took time out to clean up blood from inside the helicopter as it sat on the pad at Shock Trauma. The two troopers finally got back to their hangar at around half past midnight, where Proctor tidied the machine up some more and made a stab at finishing his paperwork.

The troopers were off duty at 1:30 A.M. Proctor admitted that it was a rough night, especially with all those injured kids. Proctor will tell you that he doesn't really care for pediatric stuff; he doesn't like to see kids in pain.

Once home, he treated himself to a beer and a half hour in his hot tub. Proctor had decided that the tub was the best investment he'd made in a long time. Especially after a night like he'd just had.

A White-Water Canoe Trip

It was early summer, and the weather had been so bad during their previous week of duty that Observer/Medic Steve Proctor and his pilot, Bart Gotchall, hadn't flown very many missions. But no sooner had the skies cleared when a call came in regarding some canoeists who were in distress out on the Potomac River, near Harpers Ferry. It was a popular rural picnic and recreation area.

Even before the JetRanger lifted off, Proctor figured he had some idea of the problem. The Potomac had many faces. At times a gently flowing body of water, there were sections—depending on season and weather—that could rival the ferocity of Colorado rapids. Its proximity to the Maryland–Washington, D.C., area made the river a popular diversion, and sometimes people got in a bit over their heads. Proctor knew that each year there were as many as ten drownings in the river. There was good reason their helicopter carried a fifty-foot length of rope and a Billy Pugh rescue net. The Billy Pugh was made up of intertwined nylon ropes and had a flat bottom about four feet across which let a person stand upright during rescue. The net was designed for pulling people in distress from rivers and lakes.

What the troopers were expecting to deal with was a single victim standing on top of a rock. Yet, as they approached the area of Harpers Ferry, Proctor saw more and more debris floating downstream. There were coolers, paper plates, and upside-down canoes. The last thing they thought they'd see was the sight before them: a small army of people clinging to overturned canoes, tree limbs, and on rocks jutting from the water.

Proctor took a quick count and figured there were at least a dozen people out on the river, all members of a supervised canoe trip. Their JetRanger was never designed to deal with a situation such as they now faced. The troopers could see fire rescue units on the shore. But it was clear from the white water below that there was no way the people on shore could get their boats into that raging torrent. And it was equally clear that the people stranded mid-river were impossibly out of reach of any ropes thrown by the ground-based rescuers who stood helplessly watching the scene from the banks of the river.

The two troopers did what they had to do; as the pilot put in a call for another helicopter, Proctor rigged up the Billy Pugh net.

Methodically, the two men rescued person after person. They'd lower the person the net, which was shaped like a six-foot-tall, upside-down ice cream cone with a flat bottom. The victim would get aboard and then be safely lifted to the shore.

The drill became routine after a while; Proctor, from the rear seat, would give the pilot the guidance needed to place the Billy Pugh by someone in the water. One by one the potential drowning victims got into the Billy Pugh net, were lifted up and over any obstacles between them and land, and were deposited safely to shore. The maneuver was trickier than it sounded, as they had to avoid injuring people by dragging them over the rocks and the trees that formed a line along the shore.

Proctor began to feel they had the procedure down pat as victim after victim was plucked from the river. It took some time but nearly everyone had been saved. Proctor saw that there were only three people remaining in the water. The next canoeist, a man, was standing on a hunk of concrete by a nearby dam. He climbed into the rescue net without difficulty. Proctor gave the pilot the signal to gain altitude when he saw that their rescue line was tangled with a bent piece of steel jutting from the dam wall.

He called out to the pilot to lower the machine and frantically worked to free the line. If the line had tangled mid-river, Proctor would have had the pilot descend to a hover and free the rope by hand. But it was wrapped around a piece of steel protruding halfway up a dam wall. The helicopter couldn't go any lower than the top of the thirty-foot-high dam. All the while, the victim was hanging over the water, supported in space by the piece of steel.

Proctor wasn't having any success in detaching the stubborn rope. He figured he had two options; free the line or cut it. If he cut it, the man in the Billy Pugh net would fall into the fast-moving water. Entangled in the net, he'd surely drown. If the line wasn't cut, the helicopter could remain hovering until it ran out of fuel in an hour. Before that happened he'd either have to cut the line or they'd all die.

Proctor had the pilot move the machine up and down, first over to one side, then over to another. All the while, Proctor played on the line like some giant banjo string, uncertain which way it was hooked or how to free it. As Proctor worked, it seemed to him that his options were running out. Just about the time the trooper decided he'd have to cut the line, one of his random tugs broke it free. With much relief the victim was taken to shore, and the rest of the rescue went as smoothly as those before. But for a few minutes Proctor knew they had come awfully close to losing one.

Once everyone was out of the water and the rescue completed, the troopers landed on the shore to find out how it all had happened. It was then that one of the victims mentioned the person who had been in charge of the canoe trip. The group was sponsored by the Park Service. Its leader, an experienced twenty-one-year-old woman who had been doing this sort of thing for several summers, had been in the lead canoe. Coming around a bend in the river, she was surprised by the violence of the water and thrown from her canoe. The rest of the party—all inexperienced people—didn't last long without her guidance. Proctor was told that she was still somewhere out there.

The troopers now set out to find the woman. Hovering low over the river, they located her body. It had lodged itself under a rock. Using the strong wind created by the helicopter's rotor wash to try and free her, the pair wanted badly to bring her to shore. But it was no use. The body, now turned on its back, remained just out of reach. Proctor looked into the young person's face and asked himself whether they should have gone for her first. That the troopers hadn't even been told she was out there until everyone else had been saved didn't lessen Proctor's pain at having lost her.

It was a record helicopter water rescue for Maryland, and perhaps the country. Once back at their Frederick Airport base, Proctor and his pilot found their telephones ringing off the hook. This was a major news story, but without first clearing with headquarters what they could say about the event, the pair couldn't comment to the media.

They were instructed to do a field report on the incident. For a Maryland State Trooper, getting into a shootout with bank robbers was preferable to writing up one of those reports. The detail it required was painstakingly laid out for them in the rule book and had to be followed, even to the point of mandating a rigid format; so many inches from the left margin, so many from the top, etc. It was a job for a professional secretary, not a working street cop. And Proctor and his partner had no secretary.

The first version they handed in was rejected. Someone didn't like how the events were described. They redid it. It was rejected again. And again, and again. After several weeks of failed attempts at getting the action down on paper the way someone else wanted it to read, the two troopers informed their critics that if their report wasn't satisfactory the way it was written, their critics could write it themselves!

Proctor guesses that someone must have thought the final version submitted was okay, as both men received a Superintendent's Commendation for their actions that day.

A By-the-Book Kind of Guy

Proctor was flying out of the Frederick section, a rural area in north-central Maryland. On the day in question, Proctor can't recall any one particular or unusual event, except for the case that might well have cost him his position as an observer/medic and which almost certainly saved a young woman's life.

The call that came in was of a kind the flying troopers received often; a bad car accident. It was a head-on collision, with several patients involved. A woman in her early twenties who was the driver of one of the vehicles was in particularly bad shape.

By the time their helicopter arrived at the scene, the woman had been extricated from the wreckage and was in the back of an ambulance. Unconscious, she had suffered a serious head injury, with one dilated pupil—meaning there was a brain injury on the opposite side—and had multiple rib fractures. And, Proctor could see, she wasn't breathing well.

He immediately started on airway care. It was a basic rule of emergency medical treatment; regardless of the other injuries a person might have, if air getting to the patient's lungs was a problem, it had to be dealt with first. Proctor intubated the woman in an attempt to force air down into her lungs to help her breathe.

But he soon realized he had an even more serious dilemma on his hands. Touching the patient's skin, he felt a sensation he described later as a crunchy feeling, like Rice Krispies. He was aware that it meant only one thing: oxygen was escaping from one of her lungs and getting between the layers of skin. There was no doubt in his mind, this victim was suffering from a tension pneumothorax. In plain English, there was a hole in one of her lungs, and the more air he pumped into her to try and keep her alive, the greater the air pressure he was creating inside the chest cavity as that oxygen escaped from the opening in the lung. With the added pressure, the other lung as well as her heart were rapidly being collapsed. In effect, if he stopped ventilating the woman, she would die from lack of oxygen, and if he continued, she would suffocate when her lungs collapsed from the increased air pressure in her chest.

The solution, in theory, is simple. Create a way for the excess air pressure to escape. In practice, though, this meant putting a small hole in the woman's chest. Oxygen would get into her lungs to keep her alive, but no excess pressure would be built up. Proctor knew full well that he had no lawful authority to perform such a sophisticated medical maneuver. For him to save this woman's life would be to jeopardize his position in the air unit, and perhaps within the state police. Not to take action, and permit the woman to die, would result in no action being taken against him. After all, he would just be going by-the-book.

Proctor knew the woman was in big trouble. She had no breath signs on that side of her chest where the collapsed lung was. Breath signs on the other side were being lost very quickly. She was in shock, MAST trousers had been put on her and an IV inserted. Her blood pressure was deteriorating, her oxygen saturation was lousy, and Proctor knew she wasn't going to live much longer.

The procedure he had to use is called a plural decompression, a couple of ten dollar words that meant sticking a needle into somebody's chest. And Maryland, which was very strict with its protocols for paramedics, said Proctor couldn't do that. There was a book; for each medical emergency there was a procedure. Deviate from the protocol and you risk being decertified as a paramedic. It meant Proctor would be out of the division, a position he had worked very hard to get and which he dearly loved.

Proctor called the local trauma center, Washington County Hospital. The woman physician on the other end listened to his description of the situation. Now she put her medical license on the line—a physician is legally not allowed to tell a medical technician to perform a procedure outside of that technician's protocol—and directed Proctor to perform the plural decompression.

By this time both sides of the victim's chest had filled with oxygen. Proctor picked up a regular IV needle, the only tool he had to do the job. Just before starting the procedure, he recalls turning to the medical technician standing next to him in the ambulance and saying, "Well, I really didn't want to be a paramedic anymore anyway."

He very carefully began to insert the two-inch needle into the correct anatomical area—an error in where the needle was positioned could severely injure or even kill the patient. As soon as the needle entered the chest, he heard an immediate rush of air as it escaped, under pressure, from inside the woman.

Almost instantly her color improved, she began to breathe without difficulty, her oxygen saturation went from 70 percent to 98 percent as her one good lung did its job, her pupils got smaller and her blood pressure began to rise.

Proctor eventually inserted two needles into the woman's chest. He left them there during the helicopter transport to the hospital, Washington County.

Once at the hospital, and after the patient was turned over to the personnel there, Proctor had a talk with the doctor who had given him the authority to perform the "illegal" procedure. She assured him that they had both done the right thing and that she would back him up if any flack came his way.

When he got back to the Fredericksburg hangar, Proctor now had to initiate a Protocol Error Procedure form. The form was intended to be completed when a paramedic made some error, most often involving the incorrect administration of some drug. The situation Proctor now found himself faced with was having to generate a document informing everyone involved—his agency, the emergency room physician to whom the patient was transported to, Proctor's medical supervisor (a lieutenant), as well as his medical director, a physician who oversees all the medical aspects of the program and who was also the Assistant State Emergency Medical Services Director of an error he made, when in fact what he did was—from an ethical, moral, and medical perspective—absolutely correct. It just wasn't the right thing to do according to the rules.

Fortunately for Proctor, the division's newly hired medical director, Dr. Doug Floecare, turned out to be a very progressive individual. And he apparently recognized the dilemma of "save the patient, lose the certification" which Proctor and the other paramedics of the Air Division faced. As a direct result of Proctor's incident as well as several other similar ones, he changed the protocol so that kind of situation would in the future be rationally dealt with.

Today the rules read that if a paramedic knows that a patient is in need of some extraordinary treatment, the technician can call a physician, get the authorization, and save the patient. The act is no longer considered an error, but instead is called an Extraordinary Care Protocol, certainly a more accurate representation of the function Proctor and the other members of the Maryland State Police paramedics would be performing under those unique circumstances.

The decision of the paramedic when extraordinary care is given is still subject to review, but not in a negative light. So long as it was a reasonable decision and the job was done correctly, fine. And as far as Proctor and the other paramedics are concerned, that kind of review is never a problem.

BOOK THREE

*Georgia State Patrol
Aviation Section*

CHAPTER 10

Captain Michael Chumley
Sergeant Mike Ferros

The Beginning

CAPTAIN MICHAEL CHUMLEY, NOW COMMANDING OFFICER OF the Georgia State Patrol's Aviation Section, probably never thought he'd ever see either that rank or position when he started working in the unit as a trooper in July 1974, the month and year of the Aviation Section's inception. Until then there had been no aircraft of any sort—with any Georgia state or local law enforcement agency. The idea was to put together an airborne resource available to assist rural enforcement agencies. Once the advantage such an active air arm gave to ground units was seen, the unit soon outgrew its humble beginnings.

What had started as a five-person unit, with four pilots and a commander—its total inventory a military surplus Cessna 172 fixed-wing aircraft (a T-41) and later a surplus Bell 47—is now nine turbine-powered helicopters and six fixed-wing aircraft. There are currently thirteen pilots and three observers assigned to the State Patrol's Aviation Section. They could use more fliers, but their requirement that new members have, as a minimum, two years experience as a trooper plus an unrestricted fixed-wing Commercial Pilot license, keeps the unit lean and mean manpowerwise.

Although the Aviation Section still flies on traffic patrols and performs other routine duties as required, the majority of its flight hours are dedicated to dealing with major crimes. The unit is part of the Georgia governor's drug task force, along with the Georgia Bureau of Investigation, the Department of Natural Resources, and the state's National Guard. Which means these flying troopers work a large number of narcotics interdiction missions, which in turn results in each of them putting in many hundreds of flight hours per year.

It can be a dangerous sort of work. Over the last few years, three of their helicopters have been hit by bullets while working narcotics enforcement. The Plexiglas bubble on a Bell 47 was shot out, a tail boom on a Bell 206 Jet-Ranger was struck by ground fire, and their Hughes 500 turbine helicopter took several hits as well.

Although only twenty years young, the air arm of the Georgia State Patrol has seen a good deal of action. And Mike Chumley was there to have either witnessed or been a part of it all.

Every organization ever put together has its list of "first persons"; a first mayor, a first governor, a first president, and, in the case of the Georgia State Patrol Aviation Section, a first pilot.

Sergeant Mike (not Michael, it's Mike) Ferros has put twenty-eight years in the patrol. Back in the early seventies, when the aviation unit was only the germ of an idea being discussed by those in authority, he was the only certified pilot also working as a trooper with the Georgia State Patrol. Because he was virtually their sole source of aviation knowledge, he was looked upon as a valuable resource by the management people.

Once the decision was made to start up an air arm for the state, it was necessary to search for an aircraft they could afford to procure. Money for the unit was desperately short in the early days—not that it's all that bountiful now. Fortunately for the patrol at the time, they wished to begin the unit shortly after the Vietnam War era, during which the federal government was allowing other governmental bodies access to surplus military equipment. This excess material included both fixed and rotary-winged aircraft.

So Ferros and another patrol officer went out to Davis-

Moffet Air Force Base, located in Tucson Arizona. Here, in the vast dry desert land of the Southwest, thousands of assorted aircraft are flown in, go through a preservation process and are stored either for future use, stripped down to their air frames, or surplused off.

The aircraft Ferros desired was probably the lightest and least expensive model flying in the military's inventory, the T-41. A trainer, it is the military version of the Cessna aircraft company's ubiquitous high-wing, four-passenger Model 172. The most obvious difference between a T-41 and a Model 172 is that instead of using the normal civilian-category 150-horsepower engine, the aircraft is powered by a 210-horsepower variation.

The aircraft was prepared to be flown out of Davis-Moffet by Ferros and a member of the Georgia Bureau of Investigation. At that period in the life of the aviation unit, it was the intention of the brass to use pilots from both law-enforcement units to operate the machines. Both law officers—each of them were licensed pilots—flew the green-and-orange-colored aircraft back to Georgia. Once there, the program was continued, still operating on a shoestring budget, with Ferros having the aircraft refurbished at the Americus Georgia Technical and Vocational School. This was done for the cost of parts alone. He later had it painted the proper Georgia State Patrol colors in Ashburn, again at a "community service" fee.

Now that they finally had an aircraft, the next question that arose was, "Now what do we do?" The Georgia Bureau of Investigation had the answer. Fuel thefts.

It seemed that a larceny scheme resulting in substantial losses of money was being perpetrated against a major power company. The generators that were used to create electricity for the area were run by large diesel engines. These machines consumed substantial quantities of diesel fuel, which came to the generation sites via truck delivery tankers. The heavy hoses that were used to unload the "product" from the trucks to their holding tanks themselves held many gallons of diesel fuel. By shutting the valve from the fuel truck to the hose, this product was trapped inside and was able to be later drained from the hose without registering on the truck's fuel-flow meter.

Thus, drivers would unload the prescribed quantity of fuel at their stops, then move on to other locations and sell the confined fuel that remained within the hose after the off-loading process. The hoses were large, and the quantity of stolen fuel the thieves were selling was substantial.

The investigation had been stymied by the fact that because so much of Georgia was rural, tailing the trucks by land vehicles proved to be almost impossible. When one of the drivers suspected there was someone following him, that individual would simply perform his job in the proper manner, negating the usefulness of the surveillance.

But when people think of being followed, they don't imagine a need to look up. Ferros took the patrol's "new" aircraft and went flying. During times of both day and night, he and members of the Georgia Bureau of Investigation conducted a joint investigation.

At this period in his flying career, Ferros was a pilot of very limited flight experience, with barely five hundred hours of time in the air—he now has over six thousand hours. Most of those early hours had been in training, first for his private license, then the commercial, and finally for the instrument rating. The ink on his certificate, Ferros likes to point out, had just barely had time to dry.

A pilot with low hours is very much like an automobile driver who has just passed his or her driver's test. Such individuals are competent enough to meet a mandated minimum standard, but still have a long way to go before it can be said they are truly skilled on the road. Pilots like to say that a person with a new rating is only in possession of a license to learn.

So there was Ferros, flying around the mountains of Georgia at night, in the overcast, keeping one eye on moving fuel trucks, one eye on mountain peaks, and one eye on his aircraft's gauges. All the while, he had to maintain communication with patrol ground units. It was a true learning experience for the trooper.

Yet despite initial difficulties, Ferros kept at it and the investigation was ultimately brought to a successful conclusion. There were a number of arrests made, and those who had advocated the use of aircraft for law enforcement in Georgia felt vindicated by the results.

While this was the first practical demonstration of the patrol's new air arm, it has turned out to be just the beginning of this productive unit's enviable record. And Mike Ferros still remembers that first assignment very well, because you always remember the first time you accomplish something really important.

CHAPTER 11

Sergeant Mike Ferros

Have a Nice Flight, Governor?

DURING THE MID-1970s GOVERNOR GEORGE BUSBEE WAS IN office in Georgia. THE governor was a pilot, and the Aviation section found he used their services frequently.

One evening, Ferros was flying the governor in a Bell 47 to an engagement north of Atlanta. The trip to the speechmaking event had been uneventful and completed in good summer weather. Flying back later that evening, Ferros could see that the fair weather clouds that had formed during the day were beginning to build up into small thunderstorms. Still, visibility was good and the pilot wasn't concerned about dodging the small cells.

The area the trooper and governor were flying over was quite rural. And while the jagged tops of the several-thousand-foot-high mountains they were traveling over might be referred to as mere hills in the western part of the United States, the fact was that the terrain moving under them would have been most inhospitable in the event they had to make any sort of unscheduled landing.

It's quite true that when pilots fly in the dark they tend to be more careful about things. Night flying is somewhat more dangerous than daytime flight, and Ferros admits that he might have been scanning the instruments a bit more often than usual as they moved over the heavily forested mountainous terrain. Where a minor noise or potential problem in the daytime might be shrugged off, in the evening it's paid attention to. Certainly, when something goes wrong in an aircraft, and the only things visible to all those inside the aircraft is just a black void below, it's enough to get people's awareness.

During one of his scans of the instruments, Ferros saw that his oil pressure gauge needle had dropped to the zero mark. Ferros immediately grew tense. He knew this was not a good thing for the gauge to be indicating. As any experienced pilot will attest, without oil pressure, a reciprocating engine will scize in a very few minutes. Quickly cross-scanning the other instruments on the panel, he saw that the oil temperature gauge still read in the green, as did the cylinder head temperature gauge.

Those readings meant that either the pressure gauge was faulty or the other gauges just hadn't yet had time to catch up with the first instrument.

The governor, seeing the look of concern on Ferros's face, asked the pilot what the problem was. Ferros quickly explained the situation, which the governor confirmed by a look at the gauge. Both men knew that the most desirable course of action would be to land. But in the dark, over the kind of rough ground they were over, that would have been impossible.

Noting that none of the other instruments showed indication of an oil pressure problem, and that the Bell 47's engine sounded and felt normal, the men decided to continue on. While Ferros flew the machine, the governor carefully monitored the panel's gently glowing gauges for any further sign of an impending engine failure.

The remainder of the flight back seemed to the two as if it took forever. But fortunately it ended safely, with the Bell 47 landing exactly where it was supposed to, at the governor's mansion. Ferros took a deep sigh of relief when he finally pulled that engine's mixture control and let the blades of the machine wind down.

When the unit's mechanics later checked over the helicopter, they discovered that the problem had been a defective oil pressure relief-valve spring. But for an hour or so the two pilots, Mike Ferros and the governor of Georgia, knew what the expression "white knuckle time" was all about.

A Minor Flap

One of the first types of aircraft the Georgia State Patrol acquired after the T-41 were a number of military surplus Helio-Couriers. These had been used extensively throughout the Vietnam War period, and were known for their Short Take-Off and Landing (STOL) characteristics. An experienced pilot in the type could land in as little as several hundred feet of open space, and the machine needed only a few hundred feet of runway (or dirt road) to take off from.

The craft had been designed for specialized uses and was well-suited to the needs of the State Patrol.

One day Ferros was flying one of the unit's Helios out of the Albany, Georgia, airport. It was to be a routine flight, and as he taxied out to the active runway, he ran through his checklist. One of the items he went over was the airplane's mechanical flaps. As in any aircraft with these devices—and most fixed-wing planes have them—they are made up of the rearmost inboard section of the wing, which, when moved downward, increases both the lifting capability of the airplane's wing and its drag, or resistance to the air. This accomplishes two things. The increase in lift permits the plane to be flown at a lower airspeed, and the added drag lets the pilot come in for landings at a steeper angle than would otherwise be possible. This also enables the pilot to land the aircraft in a shorter distance.

Above Ferros's head was a silver metal handle, which he turned round and round to bring the Helio's flap's fully down. Checking to make sure the flaps on both sides of the wings were functioning properly, he then cranked the handle the opposite way, to bring the flaps completely up to their zero (normal) angle of deflection. He then turned in just enough flap angle to permit the shortest possible ground run.

Ferros started his take-off. Everything was normal until he began to climb above the runway. He then heard a pop sound, and suddenly the Helio-Courier began an uncommanded hard roll to the left. Ferros immediately put in full right aileron to counteract the turning force. It required both hands just to keep the ship from rolling over on its back, and he still found he was drifting to the left.

At first Ferros thought he had been hit by something. Pushing in on the radio transmit button on the control wheel, he declared an emergency and informed the tower he was coming around to land.

With the aileron locked all the way over to the right, Ferros made a skidding turn around to the airport. As he came abeam the control tower, one of the controllers, eyeing the disabled aircraft through a pair of binoculars, informed Ferros that it appeared to him that one of the Helio's flaps had retracted.

Ferros then realized that he had very likely suffered what is called asymmetrical flap deployment. In effect, with one flap now up and the other in the take-off position, the wing with the flap down was generating more lift than the "clean" wing, hence it was trying to push the aircraft over onto its back. Uncorrected, such a malfunction can easily prove fatal to an inexperienced or unsuspecting pilot.

Ferros decided to experiment. He gingerly began to turn the overhead crank to reduce the wing's flap deflection angle. As he moved the handle to raise the flaps, he found he needed less pressure on the right aileron to hold the aircraft level.

By the time he had turned the nose of the ship in the direction of the runway, Ferros felt he had the machine back under his control. He landed safely.

But it had been close. On the ground the Aviation Section mechanic examined the aircraft. Sure enough, the flap on one wing had broken free from its mechanical control and had sprung back to the neutral position.

The incident had shaken Ferros. He knew that had it happened at night, or if the aircraft had been heavily loaded with passengers and fuel, or if he hadn't had the amount of flying time he had in that aircraft, he wasn't at all sure the incident would have turned out the way it did.

CHAPTER 12

Captain Michael Chumley

Atlanta Auto

ON THE DAY OF THIS INCIDENT CHUMLEY WAS JUST COMING back from what had been a very routine photo mission. He had on board his Bell 206B JetRanger just a lone civilian photographer to do some photographic work for industry and trade. Chumley had decided there was no point in taking along his trooper/observer, and left him to wait by the helipad at the State Capitol building.

Chumley and his passenger/photographer completed the assignment—the taking of photos of various government buildings and facilities—without incident, and the trooper headed the JetRanger back to the capital to drop off his passenger and retrieve his observer. As he neared the capitol landing pad, he noticed his oil pressure warning light come on. His eyes quickly moved to the oil pressure gauge, which looked to him as if it was falling like "a long-sweep second hand." This, Chumley knew, was not a good thing. He immediately entered into an emergency autorotation and—as it was so close—headed for the landing pad from which he had taken off earlier, at the very start of the mission.

To the uninitiated—even when expected, as practiced in training—autorotations seem like a whole bunch of Disneyland "A" rides wrapped up into one short and particularly scary escapade. When they happen for real, the "aw shucks" factor can get very high.

When engine power is lost to a helicopter's main rotors, the machine doesn't just fall out of the sky—a popular general misconception. The force that still remains contained in the whirling blades, which generally weigh from two to several hundred pounds in turbine-powered machines, is formidable. There is sufficient energy remaining so that if rotor speed is maintained to a landing, it will permit a helicopter to touch down without damage.

The procedure sounds deceptively simple. If the helicopter is flying along at least several hundred feet above the ground's surface, and/or if the machine is traveling at a reasonably high airspeed—between fifty to sixty miles per hour—autorotations can be entered successfully. That is, so long as the pilot immediately recognizes there is a problem and performs several functions very quickly. Not to accomplish the latter will permit the main rotor blade's rotational speed to slow down to a point where—now no longer rigid due to centrifugal force—the flexible blades will begin to flap. When that occurs, and depending on the exact construction of the helicopter, one of the blades will likely slice into the ship's cabin, cutting the pilot and copilot in half.

Modern turbine helicopters are designed in several ways to warn a pilot there has occurred, or there is about to occur, a catastrophic failure of some critical component. Except for an on-board fire, there are generally only two malfunctions that can take place relative to the operation of a helicopter which will require the pilot to execute an immediate autorotation to the ground; loss or imminent loss of engine power, or transmission failure.

Most machines have several ways of informing the crew that one or the other problem is about to happen. If the trouble is with the engine, there is a loud and very distinctive "engine out" horn, signaling exactly that. However, pilots I have spoken to, who have had the experience of an in-flight engine loss, tell me the silence of the turbine's normal whine is the loudest thing they heard during the event.

There is also a "caution/warning" panel, filled with a dozen or so rectangular red, orange, or yellow written warning indicators. Which one lights up will determine how the pilot will react. If the applicable horn or light goes on, and

if what they signal indicates an autorotation is called for—
and is verified by a prompt look at the appropriate gauges—
then the pilot performs the following actions, very rapidly:

- First and foremost, the collective is lowered, or
  "dumped" in pilot jargon. This reduces the rotating
  blades' angle of attack—how much of the blades' surface comes into head-on contact with the wind. The
  now engineless helicopter immediately heads for the
  ground at 1500 to 2000 feet per minute—that is, if
  the "auto" is begun at 1000 feet, the pilot has around
  forty seconds before making ground contact—at a
  sufficient airspeed to permit the blades to maintain
  their high rotational speeds as well as retain the momentum (energy) they contain, momentum that will
  be released in order that a gentle and damage-free
  landing can be accomplished. Also, if the collective
  isn't lowered soon after engine power is lost, the
  blade speeds will degrade, they will lose rigidity and
  begin to flap, and then ...

- Next the pilot must set up the proper attitude of the
  helicopter's nose—remember, gravity is acting as the
  "engine" now—so an airspeed of (again, depending
  on the machine in question) about sixty to eighty
  miles per hour should be maintained.

- And finally, the pilot—while accomplishing the
  above—must also look for a safe place to land. The
  preferable location for touchdown is a flat, hard surface. But wherever the helicopter is going to land,
  the best advice pilots give is to "fly it all the way to
  the ground." That is, to continue to keep the aircraft
  under control while maintaining the correct airspeed,
  as well as the correct skids level attitude, until contact
  is made with the surface or whatever else happens to
  be under the helicopter at the moment of touchdown.

Unlike a fixed-wing aircraft, which for each foot of altitude lost moves forward around ten feet, a helicopter travels

ahead only three feet for each foot of altitude lost. Or stated another way, if a small Cessna airplane lost its engine at a thousand feet above the ground, it could travel nearly two miles before touching down. A helicopter, losing its engine at that altitude, would travel a little more than half a mile before landing.

Once near the ground, at a height of around seventy-five feet or so, the pilot must then gently pull back on the cyclic—the aircraft's directional control, and now, without an engine, also the only speed control device the pilot has—in order to slow the helicopter down. If all is going well, and there is a flat surface under the aircraft, and there is enough energy remaining in the rotating blades, and if the pilot times the pulling up of the collective—in order to increase the bite of air the blades take, trading their momentum/energy in return for reducing the machine's descent—he will slow the helicopter to nearly zero airspeed just as the aircraft touches down to the ground. And the pilot will have made a good landing. Otherwise . . .

So there was Chumley, seeing the bright glow of his engine oil pressure caution light on his caution/warning panel. He immediately confirmed the fact that he was about to lose his engine in a couple of seconds by glancing over to the oil pressure gauge, whose needle he saw was dropping faster than the value of the dollar. And he knew that the JetRanger's turbine, which spins up to over 50,000 rpm, just does not do well without its very special oil.

Chumley dumped the collective, set the nose of the JetRanger to just the right attitude, and headed for the pad. The machine made for the ground like a brick without wings. Just prior to impact, uh, touchdown, Chumley pulled up on the collective, brought the JetRanger to zero airspeed, and set her down like that's how it was always done; neither the helicopter nor anyone inside being the worse for wear.

Chumley immediately shut the engine down, not waiting for the normally required two-minute cool-down period. According to him, had he kept the machine running, with the amount of oil remaining in that Allison, the turbine would have shut itself down long before the two minutes were up.

Getting out of the helicopter, Chumley saw oil everywhere; the engine's five and a half quarts of turbine oil had apparently begun to gush out thirty seconds earlier, probably while they were around 1500 feet in the air, and what was left covered the outside of the helicopter and was beginning to make a nice-size pool of glistening liquid under and around the machine's skids. Chumley figured the stuff was dumped over a nearby interstate and now covered a bunch of cars. Turbine oil is not particularly good for paint, and he figures at least a couple of people must have wondered what caused the funny spots on their nice shiny automobiles, but nobody ever complained to him about it.

As he stood outside the helicopter, taking a deep breath and looking over the mess his aircraft was making over everything underneath, the civilian photographer sidled up to him. Turns out the guy never even realized anything was amiss. He figured those Georgia Patrol helicopter pilots were always in a hurry to land like that. But Chumley did say the guy pointed to the ground and asked him where all that oil was coming from!

CHAPTER 13

Sergeant Michael Dougherty

Manhunt

WITH TWENTY AND A HALF YEARS IN THE GEORGIA STATE PA-
trol, Sergeant Mike Dougherty certainly can't be thought of
as a rookie. And although he has been with the aviation
branch of the patrol only since 1981, he holds flight ratings
for both single-engine rotary-wing and single and multien-
gine fixed-wing aircraft, including the much coveted—and
difficult to acquire—Airline Transport Pilot (ATP) rating
for the latter.

Before he entered the police service, at a time when he
thought of joining the Georgia Bureau of Investigation, he
had to make a decision; take the offered position in the
Georgia Patrol, finish up his college degree, then transfer
over to the GBI; or stay in school and try for the investigator
job when he graduated. He chose to enter the patrol, and
found he was enjoying the work so much he forgot all about
the GBI. He hasn't looked back since.

The incident began when the Aviation Section became
involved in the manhunt for the killer of a GBI agent. The
killing of the law officer occurred in Thomson, Georgia. Aviation helicopters assisted in the murderer's initial capture,
which was a coordinated air/ground search. It was during the
first capture that Dougherty and his copilot, while actively
engaged in looking for the subject, observed him from the
air. The fugitive, known to be armed and already a killer,

149

would not stop for the airborne law officers. Dougherty's copilot fired at the man from the moving machine with his service handgun. It was a desperate move, as firing from such an unstable platform was most unlikely to result in a hit. Thus, not unexpectedly, the trooper's round did not find its mark. But the shot from above rattled the fleeing suspect. The aviation unit doggedly kept after the killer until he was ultimately captured.

Two months later the desperate man managed to escape from custody. He took to living in the woods, and for several months after his escape had successfully managed to elude capture.

Both times the killer was being sought, it was the air arm of the patrol that located him. And during both events the air and ground units put in many hundreds of man-hours in the hunt.

The second and final contact with the fugitive put an end to it all. The killer chose to shoot it out with the law officers on the ground, which ultimately proved to be a fatal mistake on his part.

But not many members of Dougherty's unit—or for that matter, the pilots and crew members of most of the other civilian airborne law-enforcement units from around the country—can say they ever flew a mission where they fired on a fugitive from their aircraft.

CHAPTER 14

Sergeant William Smith

Let's Do Lunch; or,
Does That Man Have a Gun?

SERGEANT BILL SMITH, WITH TWENTY-TWO YEARS ON THE Georgia State Patrol force and over eight thousand flying hours, remembers the beginning days of the Aviation Section. When the program started, there was much that was not adequately budgeted for. At the time, even maintenance funding was tight. Current pilots in the unit probably don't realize that the early fliers within Aviation often had to perform maintenance on their machines to the extent permitted by the Federal Aviation Regulations.

The man Smith credits with building the aviation unit from the maintenance side was their head mechanic, Gail LeMieux. Several pilots who were interviewed from the State Patrol mentioned LeMieux, and the high quality, dedicated work that he performed. They were all bewildered by the man's recent and untimely death in, of all things, a bicycle accident.

Smith stated that LeMieux was remarkable in his ability to detect problems on an aircraft simply by the machine's sounds and its feel. Smith reports that when he'd land at the Atlanta base, LeMieux would come from inside the hangar, circle the idling machine a few times, and without touching the helicopter, and before it shut down, would have a list of five or six things that had to be done to the aircraft.

One day, while up in Atlanta, Smith and other Aviation members were performing some routine maintenance on several aircraft. At lunchtime Bill Byrd (now a lieutenant), Gail LeMieux, and Bill Smith jumped into a marked patrol car and headed out to a popular local hot-dog stand. Once the food was purchased, and on the return trip to the hangar, the three troopers spotted a car up ahead weaving all over the road. Smith described the man's vehicle as going from shoulder to shoulder of the crowded highway they were on.

Realizing that something had to be done to protect innocent citizens, they pulled the car over. Having stopped the other vehicle, they watched as the driver unfolded himself from his car. As Smith related the story, "He was a big man."

Smith, as did the other troopers, looked over at the driver and as one felt they had a potentially serious problem on their hands. And because they had all been working on aircraft but a short time earlier, only one of the three had thought to bring a gun with them.

Byrd patted the man down and put him in the back of their patrol car. As he was doing so, one of the other troopers notified the Cobb County police by radio to come and get the guy.

When the local officer arrived, they transferred the prisoner—who was first patted down by the Cobb County officer—from the trooper car to the responding officer's police vehicle. The Cobb County officer didn't handcuff the man. He figured that if he had tried to do it at that moment, there would have been a major problem. And anyway, the man was being placed into a secure compartment, the rear of the police cruiser, which had a cage between the officer and the prisoner. There was also a plastic shield—it was supposed to have been bullet-proof—between the two men.

That done, the three troopers figured their work was complete and drove back to the State Patrol hangar.

Smith related that several hours later a telephone call was made to the hangar. It was from the chief of the Cobb County Police Department. It seems there had been an incident after the three troopers had left the scene. The Cobb County supervisor was trying to tie all the pieces together as best he could, and wanted the troopers to come down to police headquarters and give a statement as to what had transpired during the arrest of the drunk. Although Smith wasn't present when the next part of this story took place, he described what happened from the information he received from the Cobb County supervisor.

It seems that on the ride to the Cobb County lockup, the prisoner told the officer driving him that he had to go to the bathroom. He repeated this request several times, each time being told by the officer that the ride would only be a few minutes longer and he'd just have to hold on.

Finally the drunk in the back said, "Pull the car over and stop now." To which the police officer responded that he had already told the man three times that wasn't going to happen. As he was telling the prisoner he wasn't going to comply with his demand, he looked up into his rearview mirror and saw a revolver pointed in his general direction.

The officer slammed on the brakes, and as the car came to a stop (I guess the drunk did get his way after all!) the patrolman opened the door and bailed out. As he was doing so, the prisoner let off a shot, which had no difficulty in penetrating the supposedly bullet-proof plastic between the two men and which knocked the rearview mirror off. Fortunately, the round missed the officer.

The officer, using the walkie-talkie attached to his belt, called for assistance. Police cars, responding to the call of "shots fired," were coming in from everywhere. Meanwhile the officer, who had ducked under the patrol car, was now pinned down by the big man locked in the back of his cruiser, who would, every now and again, let a round go at the responding officers.

A good citizen, driving a pickup truck, somehow managed to get his vehicle into a position that permitted the trapped officer to escape unscathed and be driven away in the truck.

That didn't solve the problem of the belligerent, armed drunk. Ultimately the officers surrounding the police car convinced the man that his position was hopeless. They talked the man out of the car without any bloodshed.

After the dust settled, the question that had to be answered was how did the man get past two pat-downs, performed by two different law officers. It seems that the man had worn the pistol around his neck on a chain. He was so large that as the two officers had concentrated on his waist area, searching for a weapon, they didn't think to feel around the front of his chest.

The story unfolded further in that the arrested man had been released from prison only four days earlier. He had spent the time during his newfound freedom drinking and popping pills. Smith believes that under the right set of circumstances, such as would have occurred had a lone police officer made a car stop of this man's vehicle, the ending to the story could have been a far more tragic one.

Morning Encounter

Everyone in the Aviation Section had been summoned to Atlanta. Smith figured that whatever was going down, it was going to be big. He got up at four A.M., dragged himself out of bed, and drove himself to his airfield, Reidsville Municipal, by five A.M. A small 3800-foot-long strip located in southeast Georgia, the airport is quite isolated. There are no homes within a mile of the field, and absolutely no activity at that hour of the morning.

Drug trafficking during that period was mostly by air. Airplanes "were just falling out of the sky" in and around his part of the state at that time, Smith recalls. It was a major and expensive business, and the pilots of the illicit flights were often forced, by circumstances and greed, to undertake their missions during impossible weather conditions and without assistance from ground controllers, whom they actively sought to avoid.

Smith pulled his car around to his hangar, located opposite the aircraft ramp where newly arriving planes generally parked. Getting out of his vehicle, he heard the drone of an aircraft overhead. He noted the pilot had the plane's power pulled back, as if he were setting up for a landing. It was still dark out, though he could still make out an overcast above the field. He searched the sky for the ship but couldn't see the plane through the gray cover. Smith mentally shrugged and figured that perhaps the person inside was going to attempt to make an instrument approach to the field.

In the hangar he began to prepare his aircraft for the flight to Atlanta. All the while he had this nagging thought that something wasn't right about that lone airplane flying overhead. Maybe it was the early hour that was making him nervous, or perhaps it was the less than perfect weather. Whatever, it was eating at the trooper.

Five minutes later Smith heard the squeak of tires touching down on the macadam runway. He stopped preflighting his airplane and stepped to the hangar door. The aircraft, a twin-engine Piper Aztec, had indeed landed, and he watched as it slowed down.

The trooper also noted that the plane was showing no external lights.

Now, at a minimum, when an aircraft is flying after sunset or before sunrise, the ship is required by FAA regulations to show at least red, green, and white running lights. Most prudent pilots will also have a rotating beacon or strobe light turned on. Unless there was some sort of electrical failure aboard that aircraft, there could only be one reason why there were no lights showing.

Smith watched as the Piper taxied to the back side of the field's ramp, the airplane turning to face the runway. The plane then just sat, her twin engines ticking over at idle.

The trooper contacted the nearest Georgia State Patrol post, telling the trooper on duty about the aircraft. Smith said he was going to have a little talk with the pilot. He requested backup.

The dispatcher assured Smith both trooper cars working at that early hour would be right over.

Smith, still watching the idling aircraft, considered his possibilities. If he waited for the responding units to get to the airport, and he fully expected they'd be traveling with their blue lights flashing—making them visible for at least a couple of miles from where that twin sat—if there was anything to his suspicions, the plane would just taxi out to the runway and take off. As it stood now, Smith was surprised the individual inside the aircraft hadn't already spotted his State

Patrol car, whose front bumper was sticking well beyond the edge of the hangar.

On the other hand, if Smith chose to make a move without backup, he had no idea what odds he'd be facing. It was not uncommon for shipments of hundreds of thousands of dollars worth of drugs to be protected by heavily armed, and very desperate, people.

It didn't take the trooper long to come to a decision. It might be a minute or two before help got there, and that can be a long time when somebody's shooting at you, but he'd be damned if he'd just sit there and risk letting that aircraft get away. He hopped into his patrol car, threw on the blue lights, and headed for the twin.

No sooner had he started for the aircraft than the pilot fire-walled the twin's throttles and made for the runway. But Smith knew the airport and its taxi-ways. He had figured his approach so as to cut off the plane before it could make it to a place it could take off from.

Smith had made his decision. He was going to stop that bastard any way he could. He mashed down on his accelerator pedal and headed right for the now quickly moving airplane.

As Smith ran the trooper car right into and behind the airplane's right wing, he could hear the sound of tearing metal. The bumper of his car had torn off the torque link on the Piper's right main wheel. It was the torque link that caused the landing gear to track straight ahead. That gear now began to twist sideways, like a broken castering wheel on a shopping cart.

Smith backed off, preparing to make another run at the aircraft, this time intending to ram it smartly in the side. He hesitated when he saw that the Piper, instead of increasing her speed, was in fact slowing down. Had he looked under the wing, he would have seen the airplane dragging its right main gear wheel sideways.

The Piper came to a stop. For an instant Smith wondered what he would say if it turned out he'd run down some otherwise innocent person, and if in fact he had somehow misread what he'd seen.

During the short standoff, Smith informed his dispatcher

he had stopped the aircraft, and would the backup units please expedite their arrival.

The Piper's door opened and, fortunately for that aircraft's pilot, the man came out nice and slowly. Smith, alone on a deserted airfield, was in no tactical position to take chances. Had the man inside done anything even remotely unexpected, the trooper would have had no option but to have fired on him. Or, as Smith put it, "I woulda drilled him if he'd have sneezed."

The trooper, who was using his own vehicle both as cover from possible incoming gunfire as well as to conceal himself behind its blinding high-beams, ordered the Piper's pilot to come over to him. He quickly handcuffed the unresisting drug smuggler as the first of the responding police backup units arrived. To Smith's surprise, it wasn't a Georgia State Patrol vehicle that got there first, but a car from the local department. The Georgia State Patrol dispatcher, fearing for Smith's safety, notified the local authorities as well. A local officer happened to be nearer.

Upon arrival, the officer apologized. He would have been on the scene sooner but a big motor home stopped in front of him on the airport access road, blocking his path. The driver said he stopped because the flashing blue lights of the patrol car were coming up rapidly behind him. The officer had to get out of his cruiser and order the motor home out of the way.

Less than a minute after Smith heard the story, he realized the motor home was there to pick up the drugs. When the two Georgia State Patrol vehicles arrived, the trooper quickly explained to the other law officers the importance of finding the motor home.

Although it had been only a few minutes from the time the local officer saw that other vehicle to the time the three officers, in their separate cars, went searching for the motor home, it was never located. They did find a marine radio lying in a ditch where the big vehicle had turned around. And inside the aircraft they discovered an identical radio, which had a consecutive serial number stamped on it.

Soon after the initial flurry of activity, the park superintendent where the airfield was located came on the scene.

He informed the lawmen that that motor home had come in the night before. Two men had been inside, and one had asked the superintendent if it would be possible to leave the gate to the facility unlocked that night, as they were expecting another friend to arrive, and that he'd be coming in around three A.M. Naturally the superintendent, thinking nothing unusual about the request, obliged.

Inside the aircraft the troopers found 1100 pounds of marijuana. The story slowly began to unfold. The pilot was a furloughed Canadian airline pilot. He had been laid off due to the slow economy. To complicate his problems, he was also having marital difficulties. He had been offered fifty thousand dollars to pick a plane up in Savanna, Georgia, fly it to Jamaica, then return to Reidsville to unload the contraband. He was then to return the aircraft to Savanna.

For his part in the operation, the pilot was ultimately convicted and sentenced to five years in prison and a $25,000 fine. The end result clearly did not help to resolve any of the man's problems.

Wanna Sell Some Dope?

The Georgia State Patrol works closely with that state's Bureau of Investigation, particularly on matters involving the narcotics trade. During one particular investigation a GBI agent made contact with some gentlemen who had $100,000 to spend and who were looking to buy some high quality dope at a volume discount. For the money, the men wanted a thousand pounds of marijuana and several kilos of cocaine. Naturally the undercover GBI agent—after suitable negotiations—told his potential customers he would be delighted to oblige them. Such an operation is known as a reverse sting in law-enforcement parlance.

The GBI called on the aviation unit to haul the "dope" for them—actually bogus white powder with just enough real cocaine and marijuana, borrowed from the GBI evidence room—to make it a felony transaction. Smith, playing the role of a flying dope dealer, took one of the state's Cessna 401 twins, now loaded with the contraband, and departed for the meet location just as the sun set.

Smith pointed out that when doing business with dope dealers, he had found them to be notoriously unreliable. They were rarely on time, often got lost, and were just plain incompetent. Fortunately for the lawmen involved in this transaction, their undercover officer—being a State Trooper—was most professional, and had worked out the meet and drop-off arrangements in a most efficient manner.

The chosen airstrip was at an isolated location. The undercover officer had a VHF aircraft frequency radio with him. As Smith approached the field, the undercover would radio in "code" that they could execute plan Alpha—whatever that was—and was just sounding real good on the air, all for the benefit of the dope buyers standing around him

Smith, with a GBI agent riding along as "copilot," orbited about five miles from the end of the runway and heard the undercover officer transmit that it was safe for him to land. The trooper made an uneventful approach and landing, and rolled up to the dope buyers' car, an El Camino. A third GBI undercover agent, acting as crew chief, opened the rear door of the Cessna and began to throw bags of "grass" and "cocaine" from the aircraft.

Smith, watching from the pilot's seat, saw the group of dope buyers run around, bump into each other in the dark, fall down, and generally found they gave the appearance they were bit players in an old Mack Sennett silent film skit. While this was all taking place, Lieutenant Bill Byrd, along with four other law officers, was standing by in a helicopter about a mile from the ongoing antics.

Smith radioed Byrd that they'd dumped off all the drugs and Byrd could come on by any time now. Smith then added power to his idling engines, but held the brakes for a few moments. All eyes of the people on the ground were transfixed on the Cessna, and the din of the powerful engines kept them from hearing the rotor beat of the incoming Byrd in the JetRanger.

The people standing by the Cessna never knew the chopper was on the scene until it turned its bright searchlight on them. Pandemonium broke out, with people running every which way. In the confusion of the arrests, the undercover on the ground "escaped."

Realizing the predicament he was in, one of the bad guys jumped into the El Camino and attempted to flee. Byrd, after unloading his officers, made a beeline for the car.

The El Camino raced along the runway, with the Jet-Ranger keeping just off the driver's side of the car. Byrd, his helicopter putting along at a leisurely pace, looked down at the driver, who could only look back at him and give the car more gas. Unfortunately for the car's driver, he was rapidly running out of runway, and all the airfield's exits that could have been driven out of had now been blocked by large numbers of heavily armed police officers.

When the El Camino went past the end of the paved runway, it began to slow down in the rough ground beyond. The driver "bailed out" and ran into a nearby swamp, where he successfully eluded capture for all of about five minutes.

The end of the operation saw the confiscation of four cars, $90,000 in drug-buy money, and the arrest of a large number of individuals. Smith figures the dope dealers would have been a lot better off investing their ill-gotten funds in treasury bonds.

A Tough Way to Earn Some Money

During really busy periods of narcotics air smuggling, the State of Georgia, working closely with its own and other jurisdictions' law enforcement agencies, sets up a sophisticated interdiction protocol. The entire spectrum of technology used to thwart the drug traffickers is—and should be—a most confidential matter, but it's fair to say that among the resources utilized are high tech radar and communications equipment.

The equipment is useless without the skilled personnel to operate it, and the dedicated pilots who fly the missions. Smith, as well as several other pilots within the Georgia State Patrol, mentioned that when flying these missions at night, with the bad guys in the air not talking to anybody, nor running lights, nor operating their transponder—a radio signal-sending identification device—closing in on the targets often could get very interesting.

The enforcement aircraft would be vectored into the target from ground controllers. Calling out, "Five miles at three thirty; four miles at three forty" and so on, the radar operators would bring the Georgia State Patrol pilots right up the rear of the target aircraft. Problem was, at night, particularly under poor conditions of visibility, the trooper pilots might not have a visual on their target before the radar blips merged into one. At that point the troopers were on their own, and the "pucker factor" got real high.

Because the smugglers didn't use all the navigation and ground resources available, and because they often went into less than ideal airports under unfavorable conditions in order to unload their contraband unmolested, a fair number crashed.

While Smith was working in this program, a Forestry Service pilot found an aircraft that had cracked up and was little more than a burned-out wreck lying in the woods near a small strip. Investigation revealed that no report had ever been made of the accident.

Because the nearby community was so small, members of the local rescue squad remembered that a week earlier a man had called them for assistance from an airport telephone. He had told them a story about being beaten up—there were actually three versions of his tale which they recalled him telling—after being given a ride in a car by some drunks. He stated the drunks threw him in a ditch, and he had made his way, badly hurt, to the telephone.

The local medical facility couldn't handle the injuries the man had suffered and wanted him transported to a Savannah hospital. When asked whether or not he had any health insurance—he carried no identification on his person—he told them not to worry, and pulled out a large wad of money from his pocket.

Clearly there were a lot of things wrong with both the man's story and actions that night, but at the time there had been nothing to do but bring him to the hospital for treatment. But with the discovery and publicity of the airplane wreck, the ambulance attendant put two and two together and notified the authorities.

Investigators went to the Savannah hospital where the victim had been taken. To their surprise, the man was still there. It was clear that whatever had happened to him, he'd been broken up pretty badly by it. And when asked by the law officers about the circumstances of his injuries, he told an interesting tale.

It seemed that he and another man had flown to Belize, in South America, to pick up a load of marijuana. This was just one of many trips the pair had made together. Once back over U.S. soil, they would land at a small strip located just beyond the airport near where they had crashed, using the real airfield's navigation beacon to guide them in, then just flying a bit beyond to the more secluded landing spot. Another person would be on the ground with a powerful spotlight to guide them in.

The night he crashed, it had been very foggy. Too foggy to land at their usual place. In addition they were low on fuel, so he decided to put the aircraft down on the larger airport's runway instead. But to further complicate the pilot's situation, the man sitting next to him, a nonpilot, became panicky over their predicament. When the pilot attempted to land in the poor visibility, the man went berserk, throwing his arms around and trying to take control of the aircraft. The two began to fight, yet the pilot still somehow managed to bring the airplane in for a landing. Except that in the confusion of the moment, he'd neglected to lower the landing gear.

Later, when the accident investigation team saw the wreckage, the lead investigator stated it was clear that the airplane's propellers—the tips of which were badly bent—had made contact with a runway at some point of the flight. And when the investigators went to the airport runway, they could see the slice marks of the propeller's tips where they had impacted on the macadam.

The pilot, once he realized his mistake, and not wanting to belly in with a load of drugs in the aircraft, put power to the engines. The aircraft climbed up from the runway and he started to make a turn to come around for another landing attempt. But the right engine, badly damaged when its propeller hit the ground, now tore itself loose from its mount. With no other viable option, and not wanting to lose control of the aircraft, the pilot made a shallow approach into whatever was straight ahead, which just happened to be a bunch of pine trees.

The passenger, not hurt at all, jumped from the destroyed airplane, leaving the pilot for dead. The pilot, badly injured, crawled a half mile to the airport telephone, where he was picked up by the local rescue-squad personnel.

The man, understandably unhappy with his former partner, gave the authorities the man's name. It seemed that both he and the other individual had run away from a halfway house where they'd been confined after being convicted of smuggling narcotics. Once free, both men wasted no time and set up another illicit drug-trafficking operation.

The money man was never apprehended by authorities. Less than ten days after he walked away from the crash of the aircraft in Georgia he was back in Belize, in another aircraft with another pilot. Loaded with drugs the aircraft had been heading into Jacksonville, Florida when they encountered some bad weather. The pilot on that flight wasn't as skilled as in the first. The ensuing crash scattered airplane, dope and bodies all over the landscape, just two miles short of the runway.

The Shrimp Boat Is Coming

The Georgia Bureau of Investigation takes its anti-narcotics activities very seriously. Even when the information that surfaces from their intelligence gathering tells them that another law officer is involved in drug trafficking. It was one such case in McIntosh County, involving a corrupt deputy sheriff, that again brought the GBI and Georgia State Patrol aviation unit together as a team. One of the aviation unit members who was a participant was Bill Smith.

Because of the magnitude of the case, other state and Federal agencies became involved; the Drug Enforcement Administration, the Federal Bureau of Investigation, the Customs Service, even the Georgia State Department of Natural Resources participated in the investigation.

The GBI had an informant inside the criminal organization. It was to be a large transaction. A ten- to fifteen-ton shipment of marijuana, to be delivered via shrimp boat, was to make the trip from Columbia, South America, to Georgia.

The investigation had gone on for a long while. But eventually a two- to three-day window of opportunity was agreed upon by the bad guys involved in the smuggling venture, and they arranged for the boat to arrive to deliver the goods.

Both ground and air units were alerted and the prearranged plan put into action. Several aircraft would be used in the operation; DEA and Georgia State Patrol, with Smith as one of the pilots, had fixed-wing planes available, and the Department of Natural Resources assigned two of their helicopters to the activity.

Once the shrimp boat approached the mainland, its position was never in doubt. The more difficult part of the operation was in keeping all the players who were on the land side of the conspiracy under surveillance. To further complicate the law officers' lives, their radios had relatively limited range, and the operation, by necessity, was spread out over a wide area.

To help alleviate this situation, the fixed-wing aircraft were used to relay radio transmissions. The pilots would fly their aircraft in a fixed orbit at an altitude of between six and seven thousand feet. It was like having a relay antenna that was a mile high, and what would have been a communication limitation of only a relatively few miles was expanded outward so as to encompass a significant part of the state.

Each of the helicopters was assigned a different area of responsibility. One was to be used at the drop-off point, the other would deal with the shrimp boat.

The plan the people in the shrimp boat and their coconspirators on the ground had agreed upon was for the vessel to head up a river open to the sea. There were three islands on the river, and the drug dealers, as the boat came nearer the mainland, had set up lookouts on each one.

Not to be outdone by the criminals, agents from the various enforcement units involved also put personnel on these islands, although each of them were only a few acres in size. Although they were heavily wooded, it was a delicate process for the law officers to get people on the small bits of land without being spotted by the criminals.

The situation deteriorated when the weather went down. Smith recalls that as the operation progressed, the weather became unbelievably nasty, with a thick fog blanketing the area. Everything on the east coast shut down before that night was out. Virtually all fixed-wing aircraft flights had come to a halt. Except for the lone DEA aircraft. With one eye on the only open airport within range, the federal agent continued to bore holes in the sky, permitting communication to remain open among the law officers. Had the fog closed down that airport, there would have been literally no place for that aircraft to have landed safely.

At about 0230 hours the shrimp boat entered the river. As the tension mounted, one of the surveillance teams assigned to an island got on the radio and reported that they had been discovered by the bad guys and been forced to arrest them all. In with that particular group of smugglers was the GBI informant.

Smith, listening to the transmission, didn't think that the premature arrest was a major problem. After all, the boat was in the river, and so long as the traffickers were in custody, they couldn't do anything to stop the action or inform their friends.

But as Smith listened to the radio transmission, he noticed that the agents were trying to talk around some problem they were having. The operation supervisors asked the undercover agent how the mission was proceeding, and if there had been any change in plans on the part of the bad guys the other agents ought to know about.

The agents who had made the arrest hemmed and hawed, saying the undercover couldn't be spoken to, as he was handcuffed to the bad guys. Someone made the obvious suggestion that they remove his handcuffs and take him away from the other gang members. At this point the team involved revealed their dilemma. It seemed that between them nobody had remembered to bring a handcuff key!

They did establish that the shrimp boat was in the river, and that it was loaded with contraband. Despite the impossible weather, the helicopters launched. The one helicopter heading for the shrimp boat, a Hughes 500 turbine-powered machine, was forced to stay low over the water due to the terrible visibility, and ran into a fog bank. In an instant the pilot went from being able to see only a relatively few feet ahead to a condition of total forward blindness.

Night and fog. There is no worse combination a pilot has to face.

The pilot immediately switched his vision from outside the helicopter to his instrument panel. But the ship was doing a hundred miles an hour, and was less than a hundred feet above the water. The few seconds it took him to transition to his instruments were a couple of seconds too many. The machine hit the water.

The Hughes 500, its cockpit shaped like an egg so as to better protect its occupants, has a reputation as being one tough piece of machinery. That night it lived up to its billing in spades. On impact, the ship, although rolled up into a ball of scrap aluminum and having sunk twenty feet underwater, didn't even put a scratch on the two occupants. Both men aboard the aircraft popped their life vests while underwater and sprang up to the surface like two corks. Neither one of them would ever argue that the 500 series is one real well-built helicopter.

After that the weather just got worse. Nonetheless, although visibility was down to little more than fifty feet, the operation had to continue. Everyone on the remaining islands was picked up, as were other ring members staying in area motels. By the time the law officers got to the shrimp boat, which they found going round and round in a big circle, everyone who had been on that vessel had disappeared. On board they found the nearly fifteen tons of very expensive marijuana.

A number of cars were also confiscated, as was a substantial cache of money. And as for the destroyed Hughes 500, well, the Department of Natural Resources sent the GBI a bill for $250,000.

Like the man says, you wanna play, you gotta pay!

CHAPTER 15

No Names, Please!

SOME STORIES, WHILE WORTH REPEATING, AREN'T WORTH EM-barrassing those who were involved in them. The following tales were related with the understanding that those involved would remain anonymous. But they're true, and were told to the best of the teller's recollection.

Tales of Harry

Harry and the Chinese Funeral

Every agency, probably nearly every major law-enforcement unit, has a member who, while very competent in their job performance, just never seems to get the message. Rules are broken, policies and procedures pushed to the limit, until, inevitably, something has to give. And what most often "gives" is the person not in tune with what's going on around him. But sometimes, until they're gone, they can get themselves into some interesting situations.

One such example of the breed I've named Harry Naturally that's not the man's true name, which I've changed to protect the guilty.

Harry was a Vietnam vet. The Army taught him how to fly, and he was a fine pilot. But as they say, he had a lot of local character about him.

On the day in question, Harry was flying the director of the Georgia Bureau of Investigation. The pair had flown somewhere up in the northeast part of the state and were on their way back to home base, which was Fulton County Airport, situated on the west side of Atlanta.

As Harry was flying over the city, and within only a few miles of the airport, his flight path led him to cross over a large cemetery. Now, for some reason Harry had decided to complete this trip without benefit of an additional fuel stop. Maybe he had completed a flight of that length before, and had gotten away with it. Maybe the fuel gauge on the helicopter he was flying was a bit optimistic. Whatever the reason, it's a known fact that the very expensive and reliable Allison turbine engine that powers the Soloy Bell 47 just will not operate without fuel. And Harry had just used up the last of his.

As luck would have it, the moment the engine decided it would no longer run on air alone, they were directly over the aforementioned cemetery. Harry immediately entered into an autorotation (he didn't have much choice) and landed hard—the tail boom fell off—right in the middle of the cemetery. Fortunately, neither Harry nor his passenger were injured. But to further complicate matters, the helicopter had slid right up alongside a party of mourners attending a Chinese funeral, which was taking place less than a hundred feet from where the aircraft had come to a stop.

Witnesses later reported that pandemonium broke out. People began to run around in circles, yelling God knows what. The mourners didn't speak very much English, and Harry's Chinese was worse.

Rumor has it the situation set back Anglo-Oriental inter-ethnic relations for quite some time. And Harry's superiors wanted to know real bad what was so pressing about his getting back to the airport that he couldn't have taken the fifteen extra minutes and refueled his expensive, now scrap metal, helicopter.

Harry and the Conservationists

Georgia is a beautiful and rustic state. Not yet fully "discovered" by many of our nation's other citizens as an alluring place to work and live, over the years the state has wisely chosen to preserve many of its secluded and natural areas.

One such place, located off the state's southeastern coast, is named Cumberland Island. A wilderness area, it is only accessible by boat, with a ferry bringing the sightseers and tourists to and from the spot.

Because of the island's seclusion, it serves as a wildlife preserve. So long as the animals are left alone, those responsible permit most other activities to take place without comment or hindrance. This freedom from restraint, according to the trooper who related the story, also draws a fair number of people to Cumberland Island, who use it for whatever purpose pleases them. This includes, but is probably not limited to, walking about in the nude.

Harry, a person of somewhat puritanical values—that's to say, of the mind that it's okay for me to do what I want to do, but you better not be doing what I don't like or want you to do!—could not resist the joy of flying low over the beaches and harassing the people there. So, while on assignment in the area, one day he decided to swoop in low over the sand. He buzzed and whirled back and forth along the island's coast. Unfortunately for Harry, he became so distracted by the fun of his antics that he forgot the wildlife sanctuary status of the place. Well before he returned to his base, his supervisor's telephone was ringing off the hook, with people above him wanting to know what mission was so critical that a patrol helicopter had been assigned to fly out to Cumberland Island and terrorize the fauna.

As Harry ultimately found out, much to his chagrin, on Cumberland Island people can screw around with each other as much as they wished, it was the animals that you couldn't mess around with!

Harry and the Sandbar Landing

Harry and another trooper were performing one of the least liked missions a law officer has to perform. They were searching a river for the body of a four-year-old child who was known to have drowned there.

Harry's bad luck held true to form, and while he and the trooper were hovering over the Altamaha River, he noted that his Bell 47's cylinder head temperature-gauge needle had gone deep into the red.

Perhaps at that moment they were flying along a stretch of the river where the banks were particularly steep, perhaps it was the only place to go, but for whatever reason, Harry chose to land on a sandbar situated in the river directly below the helicopter.

As he set the Bell 47 down, the malfunction—the drive quill to the cooling fan had sheared—had caused so much heat to be generated that grease on the engine caught fire. Harry grabbed his extinguisher and quickly put out the flames.

Having suitably dealt with the emergency, he looked around. It then dawned on him that he and his helicopter were sitting six miles downriver, five miles from the nearest road. Harry immediately got on the aircraft's police radio and notified his supervisors of his dilemma.

Aviation personnel, wanting to remove the helicopter from its inaccessible location as soon as possible, knew that the most efficient way to retrieve the machine would be to airlift it out. They first tried the Army at Fort Stuart, about fifty miles from where the helicopter sat. The military person on duty there informed the aviation supervisor that in the spirit of public service they would be pleased to assist the Georgia State Patrol with the use of one of their helicopters. They offered to send a Huey, and charge the state only a thousand dollars an hour for the service, or, if that mission failed, a Chinook, for $2,200 an hour.

The response was, thanks but no thanks.

Then it occurred to someone that one of the units within the Georgia Air National Guard flew Sikorsky Sky Cranes. It took a few telephone calls, but the proper people were contacted and the Air National Guard agreed to do the job.

The first members of the Aviation Section that eventually got to Harry had to first fly in from Atlanta, then were met by a helicopter at a local airport, which flew them to the site of the incident. They reported that by the time they arrived, it was quite dark. Harry was dutifully on guard, sitting atop the machine's big Plexiglas bubble, flashlight in one hand and pistol in the other. Harry later reported that while he and the other trooper sat on top of the helicopter, there were all kinds of strange noises sounding around them, and glowing eyes stared at them from the surface of the water. And he knew there were some big ol' alligators living in the Altamaha River!

Large lights were set up by the helicopter, and other members of the Georgia State Patrol took over the task of guarding the machine. Eventually, two days later, the Sky Crane showed up and without any problem at all picked the Bell 47 up and brought it back to Reidsville Airport.

Various components on the aircraft were coming to the end of their time/service life limits and were due for overhaul or replacement. It was decided to transport the helicopter by truck back to Atlanta, where the work could be performed. The trailer they secured the helicopter to was a large unit, weighing in at nearly ten tons. It was a homemade job. In order to save money, the unit—never having had lavished upon it a generous budget—had put it together from bits and pieces of scrap. Unfortunately, the pickup truck someone sent to pull the trailer with was a small, half-ton model.

The road trip to the repair center started off okay. But somewhere on I-20 the driver encountered a steep downhill stretch. It was here, probably right around the time he stepped on his brakes, where the driver of the pickup discovered why it wasn't such a good idea to haul a really heavy load behind a much lighter vehicle. Especially when the heavy trailer being pulled wasn't equipped with any brakes.

First the trailer began to fishtail. Soon it was attempting to pass the pickup, which it ultimately succeeded in doing, dragging the pickup along for the short ride. Which was a ditch alongside I-20.

This resulted in a wrecked trailer, a wrecked helicopter, and the destruction of three other cars that happened to get in the way of the careening mass before the careening mass came to rest upside down in the ditch.

The last wheel on the wrecked cars had nearly stopped turning about the time all of the major local television and newspaper people showed up at the accident scene, taking videos and stills of the havoc that had been brought on by the smashup.

At least the helicopter was insured.

Harry and the Hog

The meat and potatoes task of the Georgia State Patrol Aviation Section is drug interdiction. Many flight and trooper hours are spent performing this dangerous job. Harry, as a member of the team, did his share of the work. But anything can become a bit tedious, and one day Harry found a way to liven up the work.

It was the end of the marijuana growing season, and Aviation had a number of their aircraft—nearly the entire unit was assigned—working around the southern part of the state, near the coast.

Harry and another pilot were flying a JetRanger to the unit's operational base when Harry spotted a group of wild hogs in a marsh clearing. The animals he saw were a mixed breed of abandoned/lost domestic swine and European boar. The boar had been brought over to this continent more than a century earlier for sport hunting, and significant numbers of the animals had escaped their fate and their areas of confinement, and most successfully adapted to the new world's forests. It is probably fair to say that the result of the mating of the two animals, the European wild boar and the American wild hog, was that neither animal inherited the good looks of the one species nor the kind disposition of the other.

These animals are very common in and around the southern United States, to the point of being considered vermin in some places. But mice they aren't. These are large, tough, mean-tempered, and potentially dangerous creatures.

Among the animals in the herd was a one-third-grown hog, which Harry decided would be fun to chase with the JetRanger. So, swooping down low, the pilot cut and weaved his way around the fleeing creatures, all the while managing to keep this one particular animal away from the rest of the group.

The hunt lasted for about twenty minutes, by which time

the hog just plain got tired and lay down in the mud to rest. Harry, seeing his quarry at bay, decided that the animal would be quite a trophy to bring back to show the rest of the unit. He landed his aircraft in the saltwater marsh, a few feet away from the beast.

The two troopers got out of the helicopter, the machine continuing to turn over at flight idle, and from inside the baggage compartment they took out a large, heavy canvas tool bag. Harry and his partner in crime walked over to the huffing and puffing hog. Unfortunately for the two troopers, the hog was unaware the pair had won this particular game, and when Harry grabbed hold of the critter, the hog exploded. He soon found that hog wasn't nearly as worn-out as they had thought he was!

It was a tough battle, and the hog nearly won, dragging the troopers all over the marsh. But dedication and persistence—even if devoid of common sense—paid off and the pig was theirs.

All the considerable time that the men had spent dealing with the reluctant swine, their helicopter had been sitting unattended. Its two hundred pounds of rotor blades had been dutifully turning around and around, the ship gently rocking on its skids, which rested on the marsh mud. The fact that the JetRanger had been left alone at flight idle was not a great idea, but in truth it would not have ordinarily been a problem. That is if, first, the skids had been resting on a hard surface, and second, the tide wasn't coming in.

The two troopers secured their protesting captive in the rear of the helicopter. As they entered the aircraft they noted that a good part of the machine's skids were now under the mud. Mud, they were to soon find out, of a particularly tenacious and gummy consistency.

Harry spooled the turbine up for normal flight's one hundred percent power and pulled up on the collective. What should have happened, lift-off, didn't. And from inside the machine they could see saltwater slowly creeping toward them. It was clear that they didn't have much time until their very expensive aircraft would become a permanent marsh fixture.

Harry pulled up on the collective, right up to the Bell

206B's torque limit. He played with the controls, moving them back and forth to free their three-thousand-pound hog catcher.

For a full ten minutes he fought with the machine, knowing that with the skids sticking the way they were, should one free itself before the other, he was very likely to have the helicopter roll over and beat itself to death in the mud.

With a mixture of luck and skill Harry managed to get the machine unglued, and successfully delivered their catch for the approval of the rest of the unit. History does not record the opinion of the person in charge of the group when he found out what had transpired, but suffice it to say Harry is no longer flying helicopters for the Georgia State Patrol!

BOOK FOUR

Arizona Department of Public Safety Aviation Division

CHAPTER 16

Lieutenant Richard Hanson

Water Rescues

To THE AVERAGE AMERICAN THE STATE OF ARIZONA IS MOST often thought of as a hot, dusty, desertlike place just emerging from the cowpoke era. In truth the state is quite different. The climate can be both very warm and very cold on the same day, depending on where a person happens to be at the moment. As for it being a place of much desert, that's true, as is the fact that there are more boats registered in Arizona than in any other state in the union. The reality of the situation is, the state is as sophisticated a place to work, live, and/or play as can be found anywhere in these United States.

Arizona's primary law enforcement arm, the Department of Public Safety, due to the state's large geographical size, has a substantial and very active aviation unit. The unit is currently headed by Lieutenant Richard Hanson, who commands over twenty sworn and civilian members of his department.

With nine aircraft in the present inventory—five helicopters and four fixed-wing—Hanson oversees a part of the larger public safety agency whose mission is three-tiered: Emergency Medical Service rescue, Search and Rescue, and of course, for purposes of general law enforcement.

The EMS part of the mission is conducted with Bell Model 206-L III helicopters, a machine that can be quickly and easily configured to a Medevac layout. The unit responds to many hundreds of medical emergencies of a varied nature each year. There are skiing, boating, mountaineering, and off-road vehicle accident victims to help. And, believe it or not, lots of problems related to flooding ...

Hanson stated that some of their most difficult rescues are water-related. It is hard to think of that southwestern state as a place where such problems are routine, but Hanson assured me such was the case. To support the large influx of people who have discovered the beauty of the state, many man-made dams and watershed districts have been created over the years. Normally these places pose no concern, but when heavy rains are added to the already present water, significant flooding of rivers and streams can occur.

In 1979 Hanson and his paramedic, Clarence Forbey, were flying out of Falcon Field, a Phoenix-based unit. There was a particularly difficult period of flooding due to heavy rains inundating a number of man-made lakes and dams of the Salt River project. With the lakes and dams reaching their capacity, water had to be released into the Salt River, which flows through the center of Phoenix. This in turn caused the various small creeks coming in from the foothills to swell.

Thus, a creek that was nominally only a few inches deep and which a four-wheel vehicle driver might have routinely crossed, can become a raging, vicious torrent of lethal water. According to Hanson, after a significant rain it has become routine to spend many hours retrieving people from the roofs of vehicles trapped in the middle of a fast-moving stream of water. And, literally thousands of people have been saved from drowning by the Aviation Division over the years. Nonetheless, even with the aviation section's diligent efforts, there have been numerous deaths attributed to this problem.

CHAPTER 17

Pilot Tom Armstrong

More Water Rescues

WHITE-WATER RAFTING AFICIONADOS ACTUALLY TAKE AD-vantage of swollen rivers. Each year many thousands of people safely engage in this exciting pastime and derive much pleasure from the beauty of the scenery and the rush of adrenaline that one gets from the adventure. But as with all sports, every now and again there is a problem. And more often than not, it's the Arizona Department of Public Safety aviation section that is called to aid those in need.

Just such a situation arose on an Easter Sunday a few years ago. The Gila County Sheriff's Office called Pilot Tom Armstrong and reported that a number of five-man rafts had become hung up at a small diversion dam on the Salt River. So, along with his paramedic, Clarence Forbey, Armstrong headed out to the scene.

As they neared the trapped rafts, Armstrong noticed Gerry Foster's news helicopter parked by a nearby aid station. Foster worked for station KPNX, an NBC affiliate in Phoenix. He was a respected member of the local aviation community and was often found at the scene of a disaster, frequently playing a role in the rescue of the victims. Armstrong called in to his dispatcher to notify the deputies at the aid station to tell Foster to come along. After all, five disabled rafts could mean a lot of people. Armstrong figured he might need all the help he could get on this one.

179

Foster quickly got into the air and followed Armstrong to the trapped rafters. After surveying the situation—there were several rafts involved, but not all of them held people—Armstrong saw that one contained a single girl and the other held three young women. Already one of the rafters had drowned, as had their guide. All the kids involved were students from the University of Arizona.

Both machines set down on the shore as the pilots tried to figure out what to do next. The Public Safety's Long-Ranger was a larger machine than Foster's MD-500, though both models were powered by the same engine. Foster's smaller helicopter therefore could carry more weight.

It was determined that the paramedic would jump into Foster's machine. Armstrong would then use the loud-speaker on the LongRanger to calm the young women and convince them to leave their rafts and climb aboard the other helicopter.

Armstrong saw that although the three women in the one raft were all wearing life preservers, the lone female in the second raft had her life vest tied to her waist by a rope. Because that raft was being badly beaten against the side of the dam by the rushing water, Foster and Forbey went after her first.

The frightened teenager made several tries to grab onto the skids of their helicopter as Foster again and again made an approach to her raft. It was becoming clear to Armstrong that the woman was becoming weaker with each failed attempt. With Foster's next pass, she fell from her raft and disappeared under the surface of the water. Armstrong could only see her vest bobbing on the river's surface as it moved rapidly downstream. He called out over the radio, telling Foster to go after the woman.

Forbey by this time had crawled out onto the news copter's skid. He lay prone on the skid tube, and when Foster brought the helicopter to a hover near where the floating life jacket bobbed in the water, Forbey managed to grab hold of the now unconscious woman's wrist.

The paramedic hung on with all his strength while Foster hovered back over in the direction of shore. Hanging onto the unconscious woman, Forbey realized that should he loose his grip, she would fall back into the water and certainly die. In his mind he wondered if it wasn't already too late.

As soon as he could, Foster worked his helicopter onto dry ground, Forbey still prone on the skid with the victim in hand. The paramedic released his hold on the young woman and immediately checked for breathing and pulse. There was neither. Forbey at once initiated CPR on the victim. Two quick breaths then compressions, followed by more life-giving air. He kept at it until he had brought her around. Without Forbey's quick action there is no doubt that the young woman would have died.

While the two helicopters were busy tending to the first victim, a group of experienced kayakers made their way to the stranded trio of women. By pushing the women's raft with their kayaks, they were able to guide the rubber boat to shore and safety.

Once all the stranded rafters were accounted for, two of the women were immediately Medevacked out by Armstrong in the LongRanger. They both recovered.

Once the excitement was over, Forbey went over to Armstrong and sheepishly asked if the pilot had been offended by his use of the news helicopter during the rescue.

Armstrong laughed and replied that he certainly had no problem with how the mission went down. Forbey smiled and responded that was good, because anyway, he figured that if they were going to have to risk losing a helicopter, he would have preferred it was Gerry Foster's rather than their own.

Cops and Robbers!

During the summer of 1990 Tom Armstrong and his partner, Paramedic Kevin Wood, were working out of Station 41 in Phoenix. Their office was a very small part of a large fire department facility that had originally been designed to house a training academy. Their helicopter had its own fenced-in pad out back, and the fire department had even built them a fuel island right next to it.

As is frequently the case with such facilities, the idea of

having a helicopter operate from the location had been an afterthought. The Aviation Division had needed an additional place to operate from, and the Phoenix fire chief, on hearing of their need, had been kind enough to offer one of his firehouses for the purpose. The construction of the landing pad and fueling location had even come out of the fire department budget. Still, it was a difficult approach, both heading in and out of the landing zone, with only a one-way direction suitable for both landing and take off.

The relationship between the fire department personnel and the Aviation Division pilots and paramedics couldn't have been better. The two units frequently worked side by side in the field, and within Station 41 the aviation people were treated just like fire department members. When a flying mission would cause Armstrong and his partner to return to the station late, one of the fire department guys would have dinner heating up for them.

The aviation people even slept in the same bay as the firemen. At the end of the dorm they had their own cubicles. When a mission came in for the flying unit, the fire department dispatcher would announce the call over the fire department loudspeaker. Armstrong contends that maintaining any semblance of sleep under those conditions is an art form. Lights in the dorm would come on just prior to the dispatcher making an announcement. He became adept at recognizing when the dispatcher was about to ask for the fire department or the aviation members to respond. When it was a fire department call, because of the use of ten-codes and urban addresses, there would be no pause before the dispatcher spoke. But with the Aviation Division, Armstrong found that invariably the lights would first come on and then it would take a moment before the dispatcher figured out exactly what to tell the fliers about what their immediate task was and where it was they would be going.

Around mid-morning one day, Armstrong was in Station 41 doing some routine paperwork. It was in the middle of August and the temperature outside was hovering around the 120 degree mark. With that heat, he figured the cleaning up of overdue clerical duties—or anything else that could be done indoors—was much to be preferred to being outside.

As Armstrong diligently worked at staying cool, his telephone rang. It was the Arizona Department of Public Safety communications center. The pilot and his paramedic were needed for a search. The previous day three men had been stopped by a sheriff's deputy out in the western part of Phoenix, near one of the many canal banks used in the area's irrigation system. The car stop had gone bad. Real bad. The deputy was jumped by the men and his own service handgun was grabbed. The deputy was killed—executed really—by one of the trio as the other two held the officer down. Now all three were being sought for homicide.

The car the men were traveling in had just been found abandoned off Route 10, to the east of the city, and a helicopter was needed to aid in the search for the killers. Armstrong and Wood took off from Station 41 and made their way to the ground units. Once there, they spent several hours flying over the rural region. It was farmland; flat cotton fields and adjacent desert. Armstrong kept the Long-Ranger at a low altitude while he and his partner eyeballed the brushy ground, swooping in and around abandoned buildings and unattended farm equipment.

After a number of hours the terrible heat of the day began to drain on the pilot. There was no air-conditioning in the helicopter. Making matters worse, he and his partner were wearing Nomex flight suits and gloves as well as heavy boots. In addition, regulations forced them to wear heavy military-style flight helmets, or "brain buckets" as they were often called.

The helmets generated so much heat around the head during warm-weather flying that Armstrong wondered whether people forced to wear such tortuous gear were actually losing brain cells in the name of safety. And if that were so, he calculated that on that particular search he must have dropped at least ten IQ points. In short, the pair were hot, miserable, and extremely thirsty.

Armstrong knew that eight miles down the road from their search area sat Casa Grande Hospital, with an air-conditioned cafeteria and lots of cold liquids to drink. He figured it was time for a Coke break. He pointed the nose of their helicopter in the right direction and headed for some cool air.

Just as he was about to make his landing approach to the hospital pad, his paramedic told him to hang on. Wood wanted to radio the hospital to let them know that they were there neither to pick up or drop off a patient. There was certainly no point in getting the people down below unnecessarily excited. It took a minute or two of orbiting around the hospital before the call was completed, after which Armstrong brought the LongRanger onto the helipad.

Armstrong shut the machine down and he and Wood walked into the emergency room. The doctors and nurses they met were curious as to what was going on, having seen the helicopter circling their facility prior to landing. The pilot explained about the incident with the deputy the previous evening and about their search for the killers. Armstrong was careful to assure everyone that there was no problem near the hospital, that the killers were nowhere in the vicinity, that he and Wood were there simply to grab a couple of cool drinks.

Armstrong and his partner continued on to the cafeteria, and each bought the largest container of ice-cold Coke they could find. When the pair settled into their hard, cool seats, a nearby wall telephone rang. One of the hospital staff picked it up and called out to the pair that it was for them. Wood sighed, got up and walked over to the phone.

Armstrong didn't pay much attention to his partner at that moment, being more concerned with starting on his drink. Barely drawing a sip from the straw, he saw Wood hang up the phone and head back to the table. By the look on his face, it didn't appear he was intending to sit down once he got there.

Wood said, "Come with me and draw your weapon."

Police officers quickly learn that when your partner utters those kinds of words, you don't get into a debate with the guy, you just pull your gun.

As they headed out of the cafeteria Armstrong asked Wood what the deal was. His partner responded that two of the deputy's murderers had given themselves up downstairs, had in fact turned themselves in at the hospital's gift shop on the ground floor, to a security guard who was standing there. The third man was still missing, and it was that individual they were now looking for.

By the time Armstrong and Wood worked their way down to the front door, the Case Grande Police Department had the first two perpetrators in custody. At that point other local officers were on the scene. Better equipped for the job of searching the large facility—they had portable radios for communication with each other, as well as more sophisticated weapons—Armstrong decided to do the only responsible thing left. He and Wood went back to the cafeteria to finish their barely touched Cokes!

Later the two Aviation Division members learned that it had been their orbiting of the hospital that had caused the killers to give up. Seeing the helicopter overhead—and probably envisioning it had the fictitious abilities of such make-believe helicopters as depicted in the movie *Blue Thunder*—had fooled the pair into thinking the game was up. Tired and thirsty, the two men decided to stop running from the inevitable. As for the third man, he was found a couple of days later in a Phoenix home, asleep in bed.

CHAPTER 18

Senior Flight Officer Michael McArthur
Pilot Tom Armstrong

Flood Patrol

PILOT MICHAEL MCARTHUR AND ARMSTRONG WERE OUT
and about on one more of their seemingly endless flood
patrol missions. As they flew back and forth in their Jet-
Ranger, looking for stranded people to pluck from atop vehicles and residences, McArthur spotted a couple standing
on a dry spot near a house. The home was otherwise surrounded by water.

Armstrong began to circle the place as McArthur stuck
his hand out the window, his thumb first up then down,
asking the people below if they wished to be picked up. The
man waved them on, so Armstrong brought the helicopter
about and continued toward Tucson International Airport,
to load up on fuel.

Refueled, McArthur and Armstrong once again continued
on their patrol, flying the reverse of their previous course.
When the helicopter came over the house with the couple
who had earlier waved them off, the crew could no longer
see anyone below. Since the water was now so high it was
up to the middle of the first-floor windows, it was obvious
that nobody could have gotten away from the place. Both
McArthur and Armstrong, concerned for the welfare of the
man and woman, decided to circle the house until they spot-

ted someone below. It took a few moments for McArthur to locate the pair, now standing atop a half wall in their patio. The top of the wall was just barely out of the water. Where they were now stranded was difficult to see from the air, and had he and Armstrong not been looking for the two people, they never would have found them by routine patrol. It was clearly time to perform a rescue.

Flying over to nearby dry land, McArthur jumped from the JetRanger and popped off the helicopter's back doors. He and Armstrong flew back to the house—it was an old farmhouse—and Armstrong planted one of his skids on the tin roof. McArthur got out, ran across the corrugated surface to its edge and looked down to where the people were waiting below.

The first thing the couple did—McArthur figured them to be in their sixties—was to hand McArthur a little dog. The officer tied the dog to himself, as the animal was unhappy with the situation and in its fright seemed to want to run around in circles. Next he attempted to assist the woman up onto the roof from below. Unfortunately for McArthur, she was a rather large lady and her bulk was catching on the lip of the roof covering.

The officer's first thought was to attempt to break a hole in the roof to permit her and her husband to climb on through, but he found that the tin was affixed to the house too securely to manage that. In desperation McArthur used one of his boots to pound the edge of the roof until it lay sufficiently flat against the side of the house to make the rescue possible. Seeing a horse cinch hanging from a nearby nail in the patio wall, he had the man hand it to him and used it to assist the woman up from below. She then literally used McArthur as a ladder, climbing over the officer the rest of the way to the roof.

He escorted her and the dog over to the JetRanger, which took the woman and the dog over to dry land. Now McArthur, alone on top of the trembling house, went back to help the husband climb up from the patio. Using the cinch the same way he had to bring the wife up, it only took a few moments for the husband to make it onto the roof.

As soon as Armstrong returned, McArthur wasted no

time in securing the man in the back of the ship. Climbing aboard the JetRanger, he noticed the house had begun to shift, and as they slowly moved away from the building he watched as the structure seemed to unhurriedly twist in the flowing water, then in slow motion collapse into itself.

McArthur wasn't sure whether it was the blowing of the JetRanger's downwash that was the straw that broke the camel's back or just that their timing had been perfect. Whatever the reason, another few seconds and both he and the home's owner would have been treading water.

CHAPTER 19

Lieutenant Richard Hanson

Rescue!

RICH HANSON ISN'T COMFORTABLE DEALING WITH TWO KINDS of emergencies: those involving young kids, and those having to do with burn victims. Children in need can be difficult for any police officer to cope with emotionally. And Hanson and his helicopter wouldn't be there if they weren't badly injured. With burn victims, young or old, the problem an officer has to grapple with is, the person you're trying to aid may be lucid at the moment, but if the burns are severe enough, the person the officer is talking to is not likely to survive the injury. It's tough trying to convince someone they're going to be all right while knowing they probably won't make it more than another forty-eight hours.

On one particular mission Hanson and his paramedic were called upon to respond to a crash scene. A camper-trailer towed by a pickup truck had had an accident. A family was traveling in the rig, three of whom were sleeping in the rear camper part of the setup. Traveling through rolling foothills, the vehicle jackknifed. The camper-trailer fell over on its side and a propane bottle inside ruptured then exploded. The back of the camper turned into an inferno. The two people who were lucky enough to be riding in the pickup were just shaken up by the incident. Inside the camper, the three individuals were all seriously burned.

Hanson still cannot shake the scene from his mind. A

woman, perhaps in her late twenties, was sitting amid the wreckage, attempting to tend to the needs of a young child. The woman's clothes had been singed off her body and most of her skin was just hanging on her flesh. Despite her terrible burns, she continued to try and comfort the child. Hanson speculates that at that moment she might not have been fully aware of her own injuries.

As he took in the horror of the surroundings, he knew as a paramedic that burn victims as badly injured as the young woman rarely live more than a few days. Hanson carefully placed her and the child in the JetRanger and flew them to a Phoenix hospital.

Even after discharging his patients at the medical facility, the incident disturbed him. He had trouble getting the image of the woman helping the child from his mind. So when he got off duty that morning, he drove over to the hospital to see how she was doing. He walked up to one of the doctors he knew, who explained that the woman had passed away shortly after Hanson had dropped her off.

Hurt kids and burn victims. Hanson will tell you they're both tough to deal with.

Search and Rescue

Arizona contains much remaining wilderness. Hikers and hunters take advantage of these largely pristine places. Most of their adventures end happily. A few don't, and that's when Hanson and the Department of Public Safety Aviation Division come into play.

Hanson and his JetRanger were called out on a search and rescue mission. A bear hunter had been reported lost in the area of Piney Mountain, which is located in the central part of the state. Near to the area to be searched, he and his paramedic picked up a Yavapai County Fish and Game officer who knew the locale.

For the better part of two hours the trio flew over the wilderness area, searching for some sign of the lost man. Hanson had some concern because there were no refueling points, such as an airport, situated nearby. Fortunately, the unit had a refueling trailer for just such eventualities, and

when Hanson saw that the search was going to take a substantial amount of time, he radioed to his Flagstaff base to
have ground units drive the fuel trailer down to them.

Figuring the soon-to-be-needed fuel was en route, Hanson
decided to extend his search pattern beyond the point of no
return. That is, either he was going to be fueled somewhere
near where he was, or in an hour or so the JetRanger they
were in was going to get awful quiet.

Just about the time Hanson was about to call it quits and
fly the machine over to where the fuel truck would eventually arrive, the three law officers spotted the lost man. He
was nearly atop Piney Mountain. Hanson slowly circled
around the man, who waved his arms at the helicopter.

It was impossible for Hanson to determine if the man
below was injured. And, anyway, Hanson figured doing a
medical diagnosis from several hundred feet at sixty miles
an hour wasn't such a good idea, so he looked for a place
to drop off his paramedic, to permit a thorough evaluation
of the lost hunter. He also decided, should the man need
immediate first aid, that the other law officer with them
would be of more value on the ground than flying along
with him going for fuel, so he'd be let out also. Seeing a
nearby pinnacle, Hanson flew the JetRanger over to it.
There was enough room on the outcropping to permit him
to place just the front of the helicopter's skids on the firm
surface and permit the two officers to get out of the machine. Hanson made sure they took a portable radio with
them so communication between them, the helicopter, and
the ground units could be maintained.

He then headed for the place where the fuel truck was to
meet him, a small dirt airstrip which was relatively nearby.
As he worked his way to the refueling point, just as he came
over the Verde River, he noticed the caution light for his
fuel boost pumps flicker on. The JetRanger has three fuel
pumps. There is the main one, driven by the turbine engine,
plus two electrically operated units. The electrical ones are
set fore and aft of each other, and are there as a backup
system.

Hanson glanced at his fuel gauge, which showed he had
around fifteen gallons remaining, enough for over half an

hour of flight. Still, he was suspect of any reading below twenty gallons on a fuel gauge. He calculated, however, that based on the amount of time the machine had been operating, he still had between twenty and thirty minutes of flight time remaining, more than enough to set the aircraft down at the refueling location.

Hanson nonetheless was aware that in the nose-low position he was now flying in—as would happen when the helicopter was low on fuel with only the pilot aboard—when the fuel pump caution light flickered, it meant the pump was sucking air. Prudence dictated he should set the machine down as soon as practical.

As he descended, Hanson attempted to radio to his dispatch center in Flagstaff that he wasn't going to make the refueling point. Initially he received no response, and when communication was finally established, he was still not able to inform the ground people where he was setting the machine down. Knowing that no one would know where he was going to land, he also tried to reach his medic and the other officer who had been let out of the helicopter only a few minutes earlier. That attempt proved unsuccessful too, but Hanson decided he was running out of time and continued to head for a flat part of the river bottom.

As he was getting close to his intended landing spot, he noticed a mesa, about a hundred yards away, that would be a far better place to land the helicopter, both for refueling and communication purposes. He pulled power and headed for the other location.

Just as he moved out of range of the river bottom, but not yet within distance of the mesa, he lost his engine. Low, slow, out of altitude and ideas, he did the only thing possible and swung the JetRanger around to try and make the riverbed.

Helicopters only glide so far. Hanson's made it into the trees just short of his destination. On impact he was thrown from the ship and jettisoned into the river. The JetRanger landed inverted in the water.

Hanson speculates that had he not been ejected from the helicopter, he probably wouldn't have survived the accident, since the machine settled with the cabin section underwater.

As it was, he realized he was injured fairly seriously, ten miles from where he was supposed to be headed, and with the two other officers several miles away atop Piney Mountain. And nobody knew where he was.

Hanson, a trained paramedic, wasn't sure how badly he was hurt. His back was in terrible pain, and he thought he might have suffered some internal injuries from the impact. Going into the water, he retrieved what medical supplies he could from the helicopter.

He started two IVs on himself and built a makeshift backboard in an attempt to immobilize his spine. Then he waited.

It took about three hours before one of the men on the mountain established contact with another Public Safety unit. Between them it became clear that Hanson and his helicopter had not returned. At first it was assumed that Hanson had simply put the JetRanger down somewhere between the mountain and the refueling location. A news helicopter pilot, out to cover the story, put some cans of Jet-A in his rear cabin and decided to follow the river, hoping to find Hanson.

It didn't take long for the other pilot to spot the wreckage. The man landed his machine on the sandbar, the very spot that had been Hanson's original, intended landing place. The other pilot jumped from his ship and ran over to the injured Hanson, informing him that an Aviation Division Medevac helicopter was only ten minutes behind. Then, in order to get the information out that there indeed had been an accident, the reporter/pilot got back into his machine and took off, to get sufficient altitude to make radio communication possible with the incoming helicopter.

Hanson was successfully Medevacked from the scene, thus acquiring a perspective of helicopter flight he hadn't ever anticipated seeing. He then spent four months in a body cast, and was out of work for some time before he was fully healed.

During his convalescence, Hanson had plenty of time to try and figure out what had gone wrong. He knew from previous experience with that helicopter that he'd had between ten to fifteen gallons of fuel left when the engine decided to quit. Was it his nose-low attitude? Perhaps some dirt in the bottom of the fuel bladder had gotten sucked up into the fuel line and that was what caused the problem?

With the helicopter lying upside down and in pieces in the river, there was no way anyone could determine exactly what went wrong with the machine. Much to his personal and professional annoyance, Hanson could never figure out why that engine flamed out on him.

And the lost hunter? He was just fine. And he had gotten his bear.

CHAPTER 20

Pilot Ellery Kramar

Inter-Agency Cooperation

IT CAN BE VERY DIFFICULT TO UNDERSTAND WHY TWO PUBLIC
safety agencies might squabble. Sometimes it's over budget,
sometimes over ego, more often when it happens the problem revolves around territory. Inevitably the only people
who suffer are the citizens caught in the middle of the
dispute.

Pilot Ellery Kramar recalls a time some years ago when
two different rescue units, each from a different county,
were in the middle of such a battle. As the silliness is now
past and both agencies are under different leadership, I've
decided to eliminate the names of the counties and the exact
location involved in this tale, seeing no reason to open old
wounds. But the story is true.

In this case a hiker had fallen during an outing. She lay
at the bottom of a small canyon, unable to walk out by
herself. Kramar and his paramedic, Pete Perkins, got the
call when they were already in the air coming back from
another run. They quickly flew out to the accident scene.
Kramar decided to refuel first, as the sun was going down
and he had no idea how long the rescue would take.

The area where the hiker was lying was surrounded by
huge boulders. It was going to be a tough rescue, and Kramar decided to notify the adjoining county's rescue team as
well as the team already headed to the site. The reason

Kramar wanted the second team in place was that they and his agency had practiced both rappeling and long-line extraction, and from what the pilot knew of the terrain below, those skills were going to be needed for there to be a successful rescue.

Once the LongRanger was refueled, Kramar and his paramedic flew to the top of the canyon, where they were met by a waiting rescue team. He picked them up, and as he flew them down into the canyon, he observed how much of a hike it would be to manually remove the patient from the treacherous area. At that point the pilot knew it was only logical to go the long-line extraction route. But what he hadn't figured on was ego and territory.

What Kramar wished to do was have those rescuers who were trained in rappeling to be lowered from a hundred-foot rope to the victim. Kramar would then fly to the top of the canyon, affix the stokes basket to the same hundred-foot line, and fly that to the victim. The hiker would be placed aboard the stokes, with one of the rescuers fastened to the line to act as both protector and emotional support. A short flight to the canyon's rim would permit either the transfer of the victim to a ground ambulance or the helicopter, whichever conveyance seemed to make the most sense, considering the nature and extent of the victim's injuries.

Kramar radioed to the search coordinator his observations and intentions.

Kramar was not aware that the rescue team on the ground, when hearing the plan to airlift the victim out, had told the woman that if she chose to go out that way, she would be dangling from a hundred-foot rope underneath the helicopter all the way to the hospital, thirty-five miles away. This understandably both terrified the victim and served to convince her she would be better off carried out of the area by hand.

When the two rescuers were lowered, they explained to the hiker that what she'd been told was not correct. But the first group of rescuers then claimed "jurisdiction" over the injured woman. With the situation becoming tense between the parties, ostensibly there for the protection and safety of the victim, it was decided on the part of the rappel team to forgo further debate. The woman would be taken out by the first rescue unit.

The rappel team radioed to Kramar to come and get them and, using the very same stokes basket that would have carried the hiker to the top of the canyon, both men were flown away from the scene, to the very place the victim would have been taken. It took all of five minutes for the ride.

Meanwhile the injured woman had to be carried for over six hours over dangerous terrain by rope rescue in order to reach the top of the canyon.

Kramar reports that now, happily, the rescue team that had then shunned the long-line recovery system are now enthusiastic supporters of the procedure. Which is fine. But it's still distressing to contemplate how self-important we humans are, so much so that we'd rather place the safety and well-being of another person in jeopardy simply because our egos demand we do things "our way."

CHAPTER 21

Pilot Windsor Wally "Duke" Moore
Senior Flight Officer Michael McArthur

10,000 Feet of Fog

WHEN THE AVIATION DIVISION WAS FIRST FORMED, A SYSTEM was put in place where each of the five crews would work a straight seventy-two-hour duty once every fifth week. They operated very much the way firemen do, being on standby most of the time but ready to fly when needed. Crews were assigned to a different community each time, and the theory was that such a routine would give aviation capability to rural parts of Arizona that would ordinarily not have access to such sophisticated and expensive equipment. Normally the crew would park their helicopter at a hospital landing pad or by a district Department of Public Safety office if one were nearby.

During one such stint Pilot Windsor Wally "Duke" Moore—his mother had been enamored with the Duke and Duchess of Windsor when he was born, hence the name and nickname—and Michael McArthur were assigned to the Kingman area, in the northwest part of the state. About a day and a half into their seventy-two-hour tour, they received a call. There was a reported homicide in the town of Peach Springs, a community of 1200 people. The town was to their northeast and is located on the Hualapai (pronounced "Wal-a-pie") Indian reservation. Only a few miles away lay the Grand Canyon and the Colorado River.

By late afternoon the two deputies from the Mohave County Sheriff's Office who were to investigate the matter arrived at the helicopter. On takeoff the weather was cold, with high scattered clouds above them. It wasn't great flying weather, but then again, it wasn't terrible either.

Landing on the main street of Peach Springs, near a Hualapai Indian police cruiser, McArthur and Moore shut down and secured their machine.

A pickup truck, which had a camper attached to the rear bed and in which the body lay, was only a short distance away. The two deputies, after conferring with the local police, went over to the vehicle to conduct their investigation. Once photos were taken of the scene and other basic investigative steps completed, McArthur was invited to hop in the back of the truck to view the deceased. He did so, then called over to Moore to take a look.

Now Moore will be the first to admit he doesn't relish gawking at dead human bodies if he can avoid it. But it's hard for a cop to demur when invited to do so, and he went over to his partner and peered inside the small camper compartment. The dead man—an apparent suicide, as it later turned out—had placed the muzzle of a 30-06 rifle against his chin. He had pulled the trigger with one of his toes.

The scene Moore looked upon, one most experienced law officers see a number of times in their career, was that of a person who, from the chin up, had no face. The force of the high-powered rifle's discharge had removed just about every bit of bone and flesh from beyond the point where the muzzle had sat. A single eyeball, incongruously sitting in the middle of the void that had only a few hours before been a human face, stared back at Moore.

The sight unsettled Moore. For Moore and most other cops, you only see such a scene for a few seconds, but you can never forget what it looks like.

The hours dragged on. It was after midnight by the time the two deputies had interviewed all the witnesses and finished writing their notes. By then a heavy fog rolled in, coming off the nearby Colorado River—caused by the temperature difference between the water and air. A light wind had blown the gray blanket over the town. Much to Moore's discomfort, visibility was nil.

Moore and McArthur had seen the phenomenon before, which was very common for the area. Such a dense fog would normally lie only fifty or sixty feet on top of the ground. Above the gray cover they would nearly always find a cloudless sky with unlimited visibility. It would be a simple matter to punch a hole through the fog to the clear air and return to their base of operations in Kingman.

Moore told McArthur that if they were going to be heading back to Kingman that night, they were going to do it right then or forget it until the morning. McArthur walked over to the deputies and herded them back to the Jet-Ranger.

Moore tuned in the Peach Springs VOR—a radio beacon used for navigation—and set his heading indicator. He was an instrument-rated helicopter pilot, which meant that he had received training in how to fly these machines with reference solely to the machine's attitude and navigation gauges. But the JetRanger they were in was designed for day/night visual flight. It had only basic attitude gauges for flight control by reference to instruments alone.

Moore had another problem. The air was so saturated with moisture, both the outside and inside of the cabin's windows had beaded up with water. McArthur had to use a towel to wipe up the water on the outside as well as to keep it clear on the inside.

Moore told McArthur to keep an eye on some nearby electrical wires as he pulled up the collective lever. Moore broke ground and went to near max power, settling on a relatively slow forward speed of forty knots. His main desire was to gain altitude to clear the fog. Once that was done, he planned to lower the helicopter's nose to pick up airspeed and make good time back to base.

Moore fully expected to clear the fog within the first few seconds of flight. That didn't happen. Four minutes passed, then five. All the while the helicopter remained encased in a dense gray shroud. He was in a serious dilemma. With the lack of outside visibility, he had no idea what solid objects were around him. Thus, there was no way he could return to land. Moore did the only thing he could under the circumstances. He turned to the proper heading he had already set up on his VOR, kept the nose of the JetRanger pointed in the direction of the station, and kept the power up.

The deputies in the rear had no idea of the dangerous predicament they were in. One of them exclaimed, "Hey, this is neat. How many of these helicopters do you guys have?"

McArthur responded softly, "I hope we have two tomorrow." Moore recalls that McArthur never said another word. His partner just continued to wipe off the windscreen as needed and remained silent. Moore figured that McArthur knew better than anyone there that the only person who was going to pull them from their precarious situation was going to be the guy at the helicopter's controls.

Moore remembers the feeling of fear that pervaded the front cabin. The minutes ticked away as Moore continued to fly the machine with reference to only a few basic attitude instruments. Finally, somewhere between 9500 and 10,000 feet, the JetRanger cleared the clouds. The two men up front could see that the ground was covered with the dense fog for miles around them. Now Moore pondered just how far it was spread out before them and where they'd be able to eventually land.

Moore turned the helicopter in the direction of Kingman, began to calculate fuel flow, and asked McArthur to look up radio frequencies of possible landing sites en route. When they were about two-thirds of the way to Kingman, the clouds began to break up. Over the town of Valentine they could make out ground lighting. Moore decided the most prudent course of action would be to head for them. Lowering the collective almost to the point of executing an autorotation, he permitted the helicopter to rapidly loose altitude so they were once more near the ground and visual flight references.

In a few minutes Moore found the highway that led into Kingman and followed it all the way in. The entire time the deputies in the rear had no clue as to the danger they had faced.

Back at the motel, Moore jumped into a shower and stayed under the hot water for a very long time trying to rid himself of an adrenaline high.

It was just one more time that Moore had beat the odds, but he admits that this particular incident haunted him for years afterward. This one had been a little too close.

CHAPTER 22

Pilot Ellery Kramar
Senior Flight Officer Michael McArthur

Plane Crash!

SITTING AROUND THE SAINT JOSEPH'S HOSPITAL LOUNGE IN Phoenix, Pilot Ellery Kramar had no desire to do any more flying that day. The weather outside was lousy. It wasn't so much the wind and rain that Kramar wasn't comfortable with, but the low ceilings made for terrible forward visibility. No, he was content to wait comfortably inside while his paramedic, Mike McArthur, received his required inservice medical training, which had been scheduled for that day. Naturally, as the two were a team, Kramar and their Bell 206L-III LongRanger had gone along for the ride. Just in case.

Kramar's hopes for a quiet day were upset when a call came in from headquarters about a possible aircraft down. Commercial airliners flying in to Phoenix were picking up an Emergency Locator Transmitter signal. This type of radio-sending device is aboard all United States registered aircraft, and is designed to emit a radio signal should an aircraft crash. The signal can be picked up by a conventional aviation radio as well as a multinational satellite system, which are capable of pinpointing the precise location of the sending ELT transmitter. In this case it was known that the ELT signal was coming from about fifty miles to the northeast of the city. That information, plus the fact that a twin-engine aircraft had departed Phoenix for Albuquerque, New Mexico, earlier in the day and had been lost from the local air traffic controller's radar screen, told Kramar his relaxation time had just come to an abrupt end.

Kramar searched out McArthur. He quickly explained the aircraft they would be searching for was a chartered prisoner transport flight. There was a pilot and one guard aboard, plus an unspecified number of prisoners. That day the plane had made its first stop in the L.A. area, picked up some prisoners, then headed to Phoenix, did the same, and was making its way to Albuquerque when it went down. Its final destination for the day was to have been Florida.

Kramar and McArthur at first tried to head directly for the crash site. The ceiling over Phoenix was between 800 and 1000 feet, which was okay, but as they headed north, the terrain rose, forcing them to fly closer to the dense clouds. It effectively put them and their Bell LongRanger between a rock and a hard place.

By the time they got to Scottsdale the gray overcast was down to barely 200 feet above the ground. Beyond them lay snow and rain showers, with the clouds all the way to the deck. Kramar headed back to try another route.

He then made his way to the north of Scottsdale, and despite the poor visibility, was successful in getting through a pass there. That done, and the elevation once more dropping down now that they had passed beyond that particular ridge line, Kramar pushed on to the Verde River. To their east was all mountains, a bad place to be in that weather, and right where Kramar and McArthur were heading.

Although Kramar hadn't been given an exact location as to where the ELT signal was coming from, with his long experience flying in the area he had a pretty good idea where the aircraft might be. That and the fact that the plane was flying along a Victor Airway, an invisible road in the sky delineated by a radio signal emitted from a ground transmitter referred to as a VHF Omni-Range, or VOR for short. Anyway, Kramar figured that even if the ceiling remained low to the ground, he could follow a real highway until he got near the crash site.

As he approached the place where he felt the plane might be found, he began picking up an intermittent ELT signal. He knew that had he been able to fly higher, he would have heard the emergency transmission sooner. And the stronger the ELT signal in his headset, the more Kramar felt compelled to find its source.

As they neared the Bartlett Reservoir, Kramar found the weather was making him fight for every mile gained. The cloud masses were moving close to the ground and in such a way that when he'd find himself in a valley whose next ridge was obscured by cloud, he'd have to wait a few minutes for the cloud to move off so he could make it over the ridge and down into the next valley. There he would repeat the process, all the while getting closer to that compelling ELT signal.

Eventually Kramar's persistence bore fruit and he found himself by a local highway. He kept the helicopter over it and headed north in the direction of the town of Payson. By this time he was attempting to use his on-board DF-88, a direction finding device for locating VHF radio transmission, the same frequency on which the ELT is designed to send its signal. It told him the transmitter they were tracking was east of the highway.

By the time they got to a position south/southwest of Mount Ord, they were flying in formation with another helicopter, a Hughes 500, flown by Pilot Gerry Foster, who was also a reporter.

It was Foster who first spotted the wreck. He radioed its location over to Kramar and McArthur. They looked over to where Foster indicated and saw the twin-engine Cessna pancaked in on the floor of the valley It appeared that the machine had hit in the bottom of a wash and continued to move in an uphill direction. Both wings had broken at their roots and lay with their tips touching the earth. The engines had been ripped from their respective mounts. One drooped to the ground, the other lay on top of the pilot's seat, with the pilot lying crushed underneath. The cockpit was sheared open like a big sardine can. It seemed to Kramar that the aircraft must have made contact with the earth while it was in a flat stall. There seemed to have been relatively little ground run after impact.

Kramar landed and he and McArthur grabbed their gear and prepared to aid whoever survived.

There had been seven people aboard the aircraft, five prisoners plus the two crewmen. The prisoners' seats were laid out in a reclined position, in a way consistent with the Cessna hitting the earth flat and very hard.

McArthur got to the wreck first. To his surprise he found that three of the passengers—all prisoners—had survived the impact. The remaining two were dead.

One of them, a man wearing a Harley-Davidson T-shirt, called out weakly, "Help me." Another man was standing outside the aircraft. Though, like all the other prisoners, he was still in his restraints, which remained fastened to the inside of the plane, he had somehow been tossed to the outside of the aircraft. And to McArthur's bewilderment, he appeared uninjured.

A third prisoner had been thrown to the rear of the Cessna. He had impacted with such force that his head had penetrated the metal bulkhead. The man was in very bad shape.

The pilot and copilot were dead. McArthur noticed that the copilot was wearing a holster, and that the holster was empty. "Harley-Davidson" was sitting directly behind the copilot's position. McArthur looked over to him and asked, "Okay, where's the pistol?"

Harley Davidson responded with a lethargic, "I dunno."

McArthur found that his compassion for the injured man was quickly draining away. In language Harley-Davidson was sure to understand, McArthur told him, that unless that pistol was produced forthwith, as far as MacArthur was concerned Mr. Davidson could remain shackled in his seat until he froze to death.

Mr. Davidson considered McArthur's words for a moment, then replied, "It's in there," and indicated a piece of wreckage a few feet from where he sat. McArthur reached in and recovered the "lost" revolver. He unloaded the weapon and handed it over, without ammunition, to the cameraman who had come along with Foster in the Hughes 500.

It took a few minutes for McArthur to locate the keys to the prisoners' restraining devices. Even then he found that the unlocking system was not a straightforward affair. The strangely shaped key—round and hollow—had to be pushed in, turned, pushed in again, turned in the opposite direction, then pushed in still farther and again turned before it would unlock the shackles.

As McArthur and Kramar were going about their business, an air-evac helicopter from Good Samaritan Hospital landed nearby. The crew jumped out and began busily removing Harley-Davidson as well as the man who had been thrown unharmed from the wreckage. They were placed in their helicopter and flew off. As they left, it occurred to McArthur that he and Kramar were now left with the most badly injured of the trio. And their helicopter was sitting a fair distance away from the crash scene.

Kramar and McArthur loaded the third victim onto a stretcher and carried him back to their ship over the rocky terrain. The trip was a difficult one, not made any easier by the fact that it was both raining and snowing on them as they struggled over the rugged ground.

Once secure in the LongRanger, Kramar hit the starter button, only to find there wasn't enough energy left in the battery for a good start. He tried once more, with the same result. Finally, in pure desperation, McArthur jumped out and ran the main rotor blade around the machine to take a load off the starter motor. Once he got the blade moving, he quickly moved to the rear of the machine and turned the tail rotor blade to keep the main rotor going—the blades are connected by a series of rods and gears.

The trick—one not found in any Bell manual, nor was it a procedure that would likely ever be recommended by that company—worked. Kramar hit the button and the engine whined to life.

Kramar and McArthur flew the victim back to Phoenix Memorial. But their effort was for naught, as the man died the next day due to internal injuries.

Later Kramar and McArthur learned that the Cessna had been caught in icing conditions, and the pilot had requested permission from the ground controllers to fly at a lower altitude. Icing is one of the most insidious enemies a pilot has to face. It's not the weight of the frozen water on the aircraft's surface that causes the problem, but the disruption of the airflow over the machine's wing. The irregular shapes formed by accumulating ice negate the ability of the wing to generate lift. Unless the ice melts off, and regardless of the power of the machine's engines, an airplane can literally stop flying and start falling.

And so it would seem that a few pounds of frozen water brought down the twin.

CHAPTER 23

Pilot Dave Ruhlman

Aircraft Down

DAVE RUHLMAN HAS FLOWN ASSORTED HELICOPTERS FOR WELL
over half his life. First in the military, then for over twenty
years with the Arizona Department of Public Safety, he's
put in over 8000 flying hours in the complex machines.

As senior pilot with the Arizona Department of Public
Safety's Aviation Division he has performed many varied
missions. One type that he particularly prides himself in
doing well is the search and rescue work of the agency.

Ruhlman believes that to do that kind of a job right requires more than just hopping into an aircraft, cranking it
up, and taking to the air. He likes to get into the mind of
the person whom he's looking for. Where would that individual go? How would that person react to being lost? Does
that person have a survivor mentality?

One incident in particular that sticks in Ruhlman's mind
was the case of a lost airman and his three passengers. It
was winter in Arizona. A state of many contrasts, in January,
Phoenix, which is situated at sea level, might have bright
blue skies with eighty-degree weather, while a raging bliz-
zard could be bedeviling the residents of Flagstaff, which sits
at an altitude of 7000 feet only a scant hundred miles away.

An off-duty fire fighter had chosen one of those kind of
days to take his teenage daughter, her boyfriend, and another teenage friend, on a weekend plane trip to ski country

situated an hour and a half flight time northeast of Phoenix. He was a VFR pilot, able to legally fly only under visual flight rules. And he was leaving good weather and heading for bad.

Departing Deer Valley Airport on a Friday, there had been no indication anything was amiss until the parents of his teenage passengers became concerned when their children failed to return as planned on Sunday evening. The parents called the fireman's former wife—the couple was divorced—who herself began to worry. Authorities were notified and a search commenced.

The first inquiry the search people made was to the destination airport. No, the man's aircraft had never landed there. Other airports were queried and the same answer received. Finally the Civil Air Patrol, local military units, and the Arizona Department of Public Safety's Aviation Division became involved.

Although Ruhlman's agency was involved in the effort, his helicopter, a Bell 206L LongRanger, was in for scheduled maintenance. He was assigned to the Flagstaff office, and when his aircraft was down for repair or maintenance, he didn't fly. Without an aircraft, Ruhlman could only sit on the sidelines and watch. He was sent home to burn up some of his comp time. The pilot, terribly frustrated at his lack of involvement, heard and read about the search through media accounts.

Meanwhile, Ruhlman fretted. The search was turning into a long and unusual one. He knew that his agency's Tucson- and Phoenix-based helicopters had flown many hours seeking the lost plane, as had the aircraft from the other units concerned with the mission. But heavy winter storms were making it difficult for everyone, and the white powder was covering up what might have been recognizable traces of where the lost airplane had set down.

Each day that went by without a sign of the missing people had the news media turning up the heat. And all the while Ruhlman became more and more frustrated. He had a theory about how to look for lost people. He takes pride in his methodical approach to what he considers an investigator's job. Ruhlman starts by evaluating what was known about the place the individuals were supposed to be headed and how these people would likely have tried to get there. He asked questions about the personalities of those involved. Were they cautious or risk takers? How have they reacted under similar kinds of stress in the past?

Ruhlman likes to talk to the lost person's friends. What was the individual like? How was he dressed? Was he an outdoors type or a couch potato? As far as Ruhlman was concerned, it was a matter of analyzing the available data and then going out and putting it all together.

The three families of the missing people were trying everything possible to aid in the effort. They spent large sums of their own money on private helicopters. The desperate families, contacted by assorted psychics, asked for and received permission to have these people flown around in Arizona Department of Public Safety helicopters, looking for their lost relatives.

Even ego and territory intruded into the effort. A relative of one of the missing teenagers was an airplane pilot. He volunteered himself as well as his own private aircraft to fly search missions with the Civil Air Patrol. Ruhlman was astonished when CAP not only wouldn't permit the man to assist in the effort, but told him that if he flew below 10,000 feet anywhere within the search area, they'd have the FAA revoke his pilot's license.

Finally, after three weeks of fruitless searching, with the combined efforts of many different agencies, Ruhlman was told he'd be getting his helicopter back on line the upcoming Saturday. Coming to work on the Friday before, he spent the entire day doing his homework. He called every National Guard pilot who had flown missions on the search. Making a list, he compiled where they had flown, where they had looked, what they were looking for, rumors, leads, anything that might fit into the puzzle.

On Saturday morning, with his helicopter now out of maintenance, Ruhlman was ready with a prioritized list of places to look for the missing aircraft.

First he flew to the center of the search area, the town of Young, a small mountain community. Stationed there was a sheriff's deputy who, by Arizona statute, was in charge of the effort.

He landed at first daylight. To his surprise, a number of family members of the lost people were there to meet him. Ruhlman recalls there was a feeling in the air bordering on despair. It was a windy day and CAP wouldn't go up due to the turbulence. Ruhlman found he was to be the sole aircraft flying that morning. The families' mood, although unspoken, told him that he and his helicopter were the only help these people had to depend on at that moment.

Ruhlman is a quietly religious man. He remembers that he had prayed the night before. He asked God that he be permitted to find the lost aircraft and its passengers. The pact he made with God was a simple one. If he could find the lost plane, he'd not seek any personal publicity for locating them.

After a briefing at the command center—there was no new information available—Ruhlman took off. He already was aware that the weather on the day the flight began had been poor, to the extent that the tops of the mountains along the route had been obscured in cloud. The radar tapes showed the aircraft leaving Deer Valley Airport and moving in a northeast direction, then, 110 miles away, the airplane disappeared somewhere within twenty miles of Young.

Ruhlman figured there were two reasons the missing aircraft had been lost to radar coverage. One possibility was that the plane had mechanical difficulties and descended, or, the pilot was ducking below the weather to stay clear of cloud. And the cloud he was avoiding was masking the mountains all around him. It was a guess, but Ruhlman figured the pilot was trying to "scud run." That is, he was flying low and around the clouds in an attempt to make it through the mountain pass and to his destination airport.

One lead had bothered Ruhlman from the moment he heard it. Several of the National Guard Huey pilots who had been in on the search had reported that in one particular mountainous region, not far from where radar last had the lost plane, they had smelled the odor of burning human flesh. They had only noticed the scent for a few days after the plane had been reported missing. These men had all flown in Vietnam, and Ruhlman didn't doubt for a moment that they knew what they were talking about.

Another lead Ruhlman had faith in was that of a person who had been cutting wood with a chain saw, in an area in line with the last known radar track of the aircraft, on the day the lost plane had left Deer Valley Airport. The man told Ruhlman that he heard a plane flying overhead. The weather was so bad that day that the man said he couldn't see the aircraft, but he figured the plane must have been quite low for him to have heard it over the racket of his chain saw.

There were other leads, some very interesting, but Ruhlman decided that the first two were the ones he'd check out first.

While still at the command post, the mother of one of the missing young women came up to Ruhlman and told him this day was her daughter's birthday. She told Ruhlman that she knew he was going to find her daughter. The words struck the pilot in a way he finds hard to describe. On one hand he desperately wanted to bring relief to the grieving and distraught families. Nonetheless, although Ruhlman had his hopes, he was also a realist. Three weeks had passed since the plane went down. In the interim there had been several snows. High winds had knocked down the tops of many pine trees, obscuring the telltale sign of damaged treetops as an indicator of their having been in contact with a crashing aircraft.

Still, there was something in the mother's words that told Ruhlman the lost plane was going to be located that day.

For five hours Ruhlman, his paramedic, and the deputy searched the area. It was a difficult task. Broken treetops were common, and under the blankets of fresh snow odd shapes bulged, making it impossible to know what was concealed under the white powder.

Because of the remoteness of the area, Ruhlman had to fly a long distance each time he needed to refuel. The task was becoming tedious, but Ruhlman persisted. After entering each of the high probability areas, he would fly a grid search. That is, first he'd pilot the helicopter in one direction for a fixed period of time, then swing around and come back in the opposite direction, for the same amount of time. That way each covered area would be looked over twice.

His paramedic sat in the left seat, next to Ruhlman, each man going over the area checked by the other. Finally, after the fifth hour, the paramedic spotted the downed aircraft from his side of the helicopter. Neither Ruhlman nor the deputy who was sitting in the rear behind him could at first see the aircraft from their vantage points. He flew the Long-Ranger over the site. The aircraft had crashed and burned. Over the weeks, the wreckage had become buried progressively deeper in snow. It was no wonder the aircraft had been so difficult to locate.

The terrain was inhospitable, eliminating the possibility of landing. Orbiting the site, Ruhlman called in their coordinates for ground crews to come in. It was clear to him, even from the air, that no one had survived the crash.

As soon as he had transmitted their find, news helicopters from Phoenix were on the way to the site. Inside the cockpit during the ride back to Young there was little conversation. Ruhlman wanted to tell the family himself. Perhaps if he chose the right words, it would make it easier on them.

Once that was done, the mission over, Ruhlman and his paramedic flew back to their base in Flagstaff.

When the reporters arrived in the search area, there was no one to interview but the deputy. Ruhlman remembers hearing the deputy tell the press how he had spotted the downed plane and his thoughts and views on the event. Ruhlman recalls that the man became a celebrity overnight.

Ruhlman had no problem with the other man getting all the press. He had kept his pact with God. He found the wreck, and afterward he hadn't sought any gain or publicity for his act.

B-52 Down!

As a senior pilot for the Department of Public Safety, Ruhlman finds that sometimes the use of examples is the best way to get a lesson across. Pilots come into the unit for many reasons, Ruhlman knows, but more often than not the

driving force is the opportunity to aid others. And sometimes that desire can put a new pilot in serious peril.

When Ruhlman first entered the department, he already
had extensive flying experience. A veteran combat pilot from
Vietnam, he had done and seen things that rarely have to
be dealt with by most pilots. The military position was often,
"We'll do it, or we'll die trying." Such a gung-ho attitude
worked well in combat units, but could get a person into
real trouble back in the States.

On one particular evening, it was just after dark, he recalls
the weather outside as being terrible. A severe winter storm
front was coming in and snow was just beginning to fall
outside their Flagstaff hangar. The wind was starting to
pick up.

Someone picked up the ringing telephone. It was Scott
Air Force Base, where the facility that military arm uses for
all its aerial search and rescue work for the entire country
is situated. With the sophisticated radio equipment there,
they can pinpoint the location of an aircraft's on-board
Emergency Locator Transmitter anywhere in the continental
United States.

Ruhlman was informed that they had a B-52 go down in
their area. The pilot's adrenaline began to pump, but as he
talked to the person on the other end of the telephone, he
looked out the hangar window and watched as the swirling,
blowing snow was caught by the outside lights. He knew
it wasn't a night in which a light helicopter ought to be
out flying.

He was told that the crash site was about one hundred
miles to the northeast of Flagstaff, on a large Navajo reservation. The Air Force advised Ruhlman that the B-52 had
been on a low-level training exercise when it ran into trouble. They believed a number of the crew got out, perhaps
as many as ten. But they were scattered all over the landscape. The ground people with whom the Air Force had
been talking had told them the terrain was so rugged only
helicopters could reasonably be expected to make any expe-
ditious rescues.

The winter storm was coming from the northwest. Ruhlman considered his options, and the fact that very likely

there were injured Air Force personnel out in the middle of nowhere who would probably die if not gotten to soon. Hanging up with Scott, he and his paramedic talked over the situation. The men convinced themselves that just maybe they could beat the storm front to the crash site.

The men lifted off from Flagstaff. Soon after departing, there was no ground lighting for them to use as reference, and the night was heavily overcast with ominous winter clouds. They decided to put on their night-vision goggles, which helped. Ruhlman was aware that although their airport was at an elevation of 7000 feet above sea level, the terrain continued to rise in the direction they flew. Only ten miles ahead of them was a 12,600-foot mountain.

The farther the two men got, the progressively worse the weather became. By the time the helicopter was three-quarters of the way to the crash site, Ruhlman found himself fighting a raging snowstorm. Snow and ice started to accumulate on the windscreen, and Ruhlman could only speculate as to how badly his main rotor was icing up. All it took was just a little disruption of the blades smooth airfoil before the helicopter would no longer be capable of flight.

He said to himself, "Man, I shouldn't be doing this."

The whole scene wasn't feeling right to the experienced pilot. Yet there was that nagging thought in the back of his mind. There were people out there who needed their helicopter.

Without any outside lighting visible, Ruhlman was flying solely by reference to his instruments for some time, taking an occasional peek outside when a rural home's lights came into view. But now he had to admit he couldn't be sure what was out there ahead of them. He couldn't even tell how far beyond the front of his helicopter he would be able to see obstructions before coming on them. The terrain he was over was basically flat, but he also knew that as he approached the crash site, the ground slowly rose about two thousand feet. And Ruhlman could barely make out what lay below them.

He turned to his paramedic and informed him that as it stood now, there was no way he would be able to avoid—

or even prevent—their impacting into the side of some unseen mountain.

Ruhlman made the only possible decision a rational human being could make. He decided to land the helicopter right where they were. He still remembers feeling like he was in a life raft and was abandoning the survivors of the *Titanic*.

Ruhlman lowered the JetRanger's collective and let the machine slowly settle to the ground. As he waited for the engine's needed two minute cooling-off period to be over so he could shut down the aircraft, all he could do was watch the white flakes of snow hit his windscreen. He wondered what it felt like to be lying out in the middle of the desert, waiting for a rescue helicopter that would never get there.

Just before turning off the engine, Ruhlman radioed the Navajo police as to their location. He and his partner sat in the cabin of the JetRanger for nearly an hour before the four-wheel-drive sent by the police picked them up. For the next three hours they bounced and wallowed along brutal roads.

Finally making it to the vicinity of the crash site, Ruhlman saw that two survivors had already been found. Although they were both suffering from broken bones, he was glad to see that they would live. The servicemen confirmed that there had been ten crew members aboard the B-52. The only person among the crew who they were sure didn't make it was a colonel, who was along to conduct a check ride for the two pilots. He'd been sitting on the console between the front two crewmen and hadn't been wearing a parachute. Also, one of the crewmen's ejection seats ejects downward. Because the altitude was so low when they were ordered to abandon the aircraft, there wasn't much hope left for him either.

Ruhlman and his partner, along with the reservation police officer, started to drive along the route the downed B-52 had taken. Ruhlman wasn't sure which was the smoother ride, searching for the downed airmen over the desert or the earlier three-hour journey over a "road" to get to the crash site. For hours they slowly moved ahead. Ruhlman spotted first one then another of the survivors. The officers also came upon the body of one deceased member of the crew. It looked to Ruhlman that the dead man's chute had failed to fully deploy before he had hit the ground.

Now Ruhlman and his paramedic had to try and figure out how they were going to get the injured personnel to a medical facility. It would take at least two hours by four-wheel-drive to get to a paved highway, and only then could they head to a hospital. As they discussed the problem, the men heard the sound of a large turbine aircraft overhead. Ruhlman looked up and quickly recognized the ghostly gray form above him as that of a military C-130. As they watched, the big aircraft began dropping aerial parachute flares over the path of the crash site, brightly lighting up the terrain. About ten minutes later Ruhlman heard the distinctive beating sound of a large helicopter. It was a Jolly Green Giant, which had flown in from Albuquerque, a 300-mile flight. Ruhlman knew that aircraft had the equipment on board to see through cloud and snow, with its sophisticated search and rescue electronic gear. The big machine quickly found the remaining survivors of the B-52 crash and the whole crew was flown out by them for needed medical attention.

Ruhlman and his paramedic had no option but to spend the remainder of the night at the crash site. The next day they were flown back to their helicopter by another Department of Public Safety JetRanger. As they made their way over the treacherous roads, Ruhlman reflected that from where they had put down the day before, only ten miles farther on the fog had gone clear to the ground. And just beyond that point he now saw that heavy power lines crossed the roadway he had been following. Had he continued the trip, he and his paramedic would have certainly hit those wires. Their chance of surviving such an accident would have been slim to none.

What comes to mind from Ruhlman's story is a little saying often recited to new pilots by more experienced aviators:

There are old pilots and there are bold pilots. But there are no old, bold pilots.

Lost Pilot

One winter day Ruhlman and his paramedic were heading to an automobile accident about fifty miles outside Flagstaff. Weather was poor, with low clouds and poor visibility, with snow alternating into sleet then back again to snow.

The pilot and his paramedic picked up the victim, who was in critical condition, and headed back in the direction of a nearby hospital. Visibility was so poor that Ruhlman had to fly low over an interstate to ensure he wouldn't "bump into" anything on the way.

Nearing the hospital, which was located only about five miles from his base airport, Ruhlman heard a transmission over the Unicom (general aviation) frequency. "Can anybody hear me? Can anybody hear me? I'm lost and in the clouds and don't know where I am." The tone of the pilot's voice had an edge of hysteria that clearly told Ruhlman whoever made it was in serious trouble. It was the kind of call, Ruhlman remembers, that made the hair on the back of his head stand up.

Ruhlman transmitted to the lost pilot that he was an Arizona Department of Public Safety helicopter, and asked him to identify himself. The man in the other aircraft replied that he was a single-engine Cessna, and he believed himself to be somewhere north of Prescott, heading for Flagstaff.

Ruhlman could tell by the strength of the transmission that the man wasn't too far away. The Cessna pilot reported he was in and out of clouds and that he couldn't see anything. He also told Ruhlman that he was at about 9500 feet. Ruhlman was also aware that just to the north of Flagstaff was a mountain 12,600 feet high.

Ruhlman knew he had to do something to help the lost pilot. He told his paramedic that the patient would have to be unloaded with the helicopter still running, and that he would be departing as soon as the paramedic and their auto accident victim had cleared the machine.

While still making his way to the hospital, Ruhlman directed the lost pilot to fly to a heading of 180 degrees, or due south. He figured that having the other pilot do that would accomplish two things. First, it would force the man to turn away from the mountain he was probably heading right for, and second, because the ground elevation got lower in the new direction, there would be less chance he'd hit something.

Ruhlman finally put his JetRanger on the hospital helipad and impatiently waited as the unloading process took place. As he sat on the ground he lost contact with the other pilot. His low altitude created an interference problem due to local obstructions. His patient finally unloaded, Ruhlman once more took off and headed for where he believed the man was now heading. As he gained altitude he once more made contact with the other pilot, who reported that he could see a ski area below him. That ski area, Ruhlman knew, was on the side of the mountain he had wanted the other pilot to avoid.

Ruhlman quickly transmitted, "Turn south! Turn south!"

Once the pilot executed the turn as Ruhlman commanded, the helicopter pilot asked the other man if he could see anything of the sun. The lost flier replied no, he couldn't exactly see it, but he could tell where it was because the clouds were brighter in one particular place. Ruhlman told him to fly toward the light.

Five minutes later the Cessna pilot broke out on top of the overcast, and shortly thereafter found a hole in the cloud cover and made it safely underneath. Nearby he saw the city of Flagstaff, from where he easily found the airport and successfully landed.

Much to Ruhlman's surprise, the man, once secure on the ground, called the media to report the event. There was a big to-do in the papers and on television about Ruhlman's talking the pilot to the ground and saving the man's life.

About a year later the same man, again coming into Flagstaff, undershot his approach sufficiently to rip one of his airplane's wheels off on the edge of the macadam at the beginning of the runway. He skidded to a stop, winding up in the weeds and doing a fair amount of damage to his aircraft.

On hearing of the accident, Ruhlman decided that what that guy really needed was to find another hobby.

One Accident Too Many

We all make mistakes in life. Most of us are wise enough to learn from then, and if the first one isn't fatal, avoid committing the same error twice. And then there are those of us who choose to just carry on.

It was 1979. At the time, Ruhlman—who had decided he needed a change of pace—was on leave of absence from the Arizona Department of Public Safety and was flying for the Federal Park Service. He had gone into the law-enforcement job after getting out of the service, where he had served one and a half tours flying Hueys in Vietnam.

It was like trading in one kind of combat flying for another, and Ruhlman just wanted to get away for a while.

The Park Service job kept him around the area of the Grand Canyon, performing mostly search and rescue missions.

One night while on duty he received a call that airliners in the area were picking up on ELT signal.

Ruhlman figured it had to be fairly large aircraft lying out there. Nothing small should have been flying in the snow, freezing rain, and heavy turbulence that made up the evening's weather.

With dawn and a break in the weather, Ruhlman headed out in his JetRanger to try and find the downed airplane. The ceiling was just high enough for him to scud-run to the canyon's rim and then down into the wide chasm below. Moving across the canyon, he made his way to the north rim—where, according to Scott Air Force Base, the ELT would be located—and continued flying under the 100- to 200-foot gray overcast.

Although flying low to the ground, Ruhlman found that he began to pick up the ELT signal about a mile or two from where it was supposed to be coming from. Coming over a rise, he could see, sitting in the middle of a snow-covered meadow, the downed aircraft—a small, single-engine Cessna—along with its male pilot, who was waving his arms, as well as his female passenger standing next to him. Both people appeared fine.

The story that unfolded was that the pilot, coming in from Utah, had been heading for the Grand Canyon when he had run out of fuel. This happened at night, during the terrible weather.

He and his passenger had been incredibly lucky. Ruhlman figured that what saved the two was that the pilot had pancaked his aircraft into the flat meadow, which had been illuminated by its phosphorescent blanket of snow.

Two years passed. Ruhlman by then was back flying for the Arizona Department of Public Safety. One day he responded to a report of a plane crash by the Grand Canyon, above five miles from where that small Cessna had earlier made the emergency landing with the man and woman.

Once at the scene, it was clear to Ruhlman that no one could have survived the impact. Indeed, the remains of the victims were not even recognizable. The pilot, in the dark, during terrible weather, had apparently flown himself and his passenger into a box canyon. With no visible way out, he had smashed into the side of a cliff.

There was no more for Ruhlman to do at the scene, and as other units had taken over the task of removing the bodies, he left for another mission. Several days later Ruhlman found out that the two people aboard that aircraft had been the man and woman—now the man's wife—from the incident two years earlier.

Another bold pilot, Ruhlman thought.

Lost Governor

In the early eighties Bruce Babbitt was governor of Arizona. An avid environmentalist, he enjoyed the outdoors and was an enthusiastic hiker and fisherman.

During one such trip, at the far north end of the Grand Canyon, he and his Department of Public Safety security people had taken themselves down to the Colorado River, which flows at the canyon's bottom. Some rafters had come by and, recognizing Babbitt, came over to the shore to invite the governor along for a ride downstream.

The Public Safety security personnel who were with the governor weren't all that happy with the thought of turning their charge over to the rafting people, but he was the boss and that's the way it was going to be. One of the security people went with him while the other three hiked back to their vehicle, intending to meet up with the governor at a trail located near where his raft ride would end.

The plan was for the three surplus security people to get to their car, drive east ten miles to a main highway, then go twenty miles on that highway, make another turn back in the direction of the canyon and drive ten miles to where they could again enter the canyon and meet the governor by the predetermined trail. At any rate, that was the idea.

The security people managed to get to their car and headed off to look for the governor's destination trail. Unfortunately, while the security men were very competent and professional people, the fact was, they were out of Phoenix. The Grand Canyon and its surrounding wilderness area were as foreign to them as another country would have been. To complicate their lives, the maps they were using were Arizona highway maps which didn't show trails or dirt roads.

Good soldiers, off they went, unsure were they were headed. This was not a good feeling to have if you were responsible for the safety and well-being of the state's governor.

So, crisscrossing the unfamiliar area of northwest Arizona, the security people eventually, just before dark, made it to the rendezvous point. And they waited. And as time went on they became increasingly nervous. But they waited some more. Until finally the group decided either they were at the wrong place and Governor Babbitt was sitting on the Grand Canyon's cliff somewhere, impatiently waiting for them, or that the Governor was lost, or even worse, that he might be lying injured somewhere.

A call was put into the nearest Department of Public Safety helicopter unit. In summary the unit was told, "You gotta get up here and help us find the governor!"

A JetRanger responded and flew up and down a number of the hiking trails which were thought to possibly be the ones the governor might be walking out of. No luck. By this time it was dark, and there wasn't even a moon to aid the pilot. In addition, with the night came chilly air, and the Plexiglas of the JetRanger had begun to fog over. The pilot landed the machine and told the security personnel they needed both a helicopter with a heater—which his machine didn't have—and a pilot with more experience flying in and around the Grand Canyon.

Ruhlman remembers receiving the telephone call at home. Would he do the search with the helicopter coming in from Phoenix—a Bell 206-L LongRanger that had a heater? Ruhlman said sure.

By then it had been confirmed that the security people were at the proper location. So now it was a matter of finding the missing governor. With the uncertainty of the situation, the imagination of the collective group of worried security people began to create an unlimited number of tragic scenes: the governor had been flung out of a raft and was clinging to a rock in the middle of the Colorado River; he broke his leg hiking out and was lying in agony on the side of the trail; he was kidnapped; and on and on.

Ruhlman was asked if he would fly his LongRanger, on this moonless darker than dark night, down into and to the bottom of the canyon. He said sure.

He handed his paramedic a pair of handheld night-vision goggles. In the rear of the helicopter sat the county sheriff, Ruhlman's sergeant, as well as his lieutenant. The lieutenant had been ordered, by the director of the Department of Public Safety, "Find the Governor!"

Ruhlman wasn't sure which was making him the more nervous, flying into a big pitch-black trench or having three bosses sitting behind him in his helicopter.

Ruhlman pulled up on his collective and took off. Coming over the canyon's rim, he found that without moonlight to at least throw some illumination on the earth below he was strictly flying by reference to his instruments. His paramedic could see the wall of the cliff to their left and called out turns to the pilot. As the LongRanger descended into the canyon at between 200 and 300 feet per minute, Ruhlman found he could begin to make out the faint outline of the river under them. He headed for it.

Once near the water, Ruhlman found that he could follow it using his powerful front-mounted searchlight. Ruhlman was comfortable with what he was doing. He knew that so long as he stayed over the river, he wasn't likely to bump into anything. Meanwhile, the passengers sitting in the rear hadn't a clue as to what was going on. As they could only look out the side windows of the helicopter into pitch-blackness, the trio were terrified. Such is the life of management.

Up ahead Ruhlman spotted a campfire and some rafting boats. He found a suitable sandbar and set the LongRanger down. Sure enough, there was the governor. It seemed that the raft trip had taken longer than anticipated. And once darkness fell, there was no safe way the man could have walked out of what is still a pristine wilderness area.

Governor Babbitt apologized profusely. He was genuinely embarrassed by all the fuss that had been made over his losing touch with the security people, and was truly concerned over the danger that had been engendered by flying the helicopter down into the canyon.

Ruhlman, along with his passengers, left the governor with the rafters. He had decided to remain there until morning, at which time he was going to hike out of the canyon.

The end result was that the governor, after reflecting on the cost of the helicopter in the unnecessary rescue effort, chose to pay his own Department of Public Safety for the use of the LongRanger!

CHAPTER 24

Pilot James Knapp
Paramedic Lee Sentner
Coconino County Deputy District
Attorney Camille Bibles

Kidnap/Homicide

FLAGSTAFF IN JUNE. COMPARED TO THE HEAT OF YUMA, IT was like being in heaven instead of the other place. The Wilsons of Yuma counted themselves fortunate when Richard Wilson, the owner of a construction company, had been able to find sufficient contracts to temporarily move his wife, Nancy, their four children, and their two horses up to Flagstaff for the summer of 1988.

Everyone in the family was excited about the move. It would be a change of scenery, a change of climate, and moreover would give everyone a chance to meet new people. It would be a wonderful adventure for all of them, especially the children.

The Wilsons' nine-year-old daughter, Jennifer, had shown particular enthusiasm over the prospect. An athletic, social child, she had written about all the great things she planned to do with the family while they stayed in Flagstaff. A popular child in school, she had no doubt she would make some new friends during the summer.

The drive from Yuma to their "new" place, loaded down

with all the clothes and stuff such a move requires, as well as the additional burden of having to trailer two horses behind them as they drove up, took the family a bit longer than had been anticipated. Arriving in Flagstaff late on Sunday, June 5, by the time they unloaded most of what had to be taken from the cars, it was well after dark. They chose not to put the horses in the stable where they were to be boarded, even though the place was only a mile or so down the road, but instead placed them in an open field, tied up to a fence for the night. They reasoned that the stable was closed at that late hour, and anyway they decided it would bc simpler and safer to take care of the animals first thing in the morning.

And with the whole summer to look forward to, there was certainly no need to rush.

Jim Knapp likes to take his time when preflighting a helicopter. He knows that it's not for lack of a good reason that pilots refer to these machines as "a bunch of dissimilar parts flying in close formation." With twenty years as a pilot with the Department of Public Safety plus another four piloting National Guard helicopters, he has found in his 8500 hours of flying that it always pays to be cautious.

While Knapp poked in and around his Bell LongRanger, his paramedic, Lee Sentner, did his own preflight, making sure there was the proper type and amount of medical gear aboard their ship.

As they both methodically went about their respective chores, it promised to be a routine morning for the pair.

Early Monday morning saw Richard Wilson leave his family for a business meeting in Wisconsin. Not that the rest of the Wilson clan didn't have plenty to do. The first full day in Flagstaff would be spent taking care of all the preliminary housekeeping details that come with setting up in a new apartment. There would be food shopping to do, along with picking up cleaning supplies for the place, and of course they had to deal with the little matter of the two horses that had been left tied up outside.

Jennifer was very excited by the prospect of the day's

adventures. She couldn't even be persuaded to eat breakfast with the rest of the children, although they all had to wait for a family friend to arrive to help with the horses and things. Instead, while everyone else was eating, she chose to deal with a far more important task, that of doing her hair. It was a new style she was wearing—a recent birthday present—and it had to be made up just so.

Once the friend got to the Wilsons, the family started to load themselves into their car to pick up the horses. Jennifer asked her mother if it would be okay to ride her brother's bicycle to where they were tied up. There was no reason for Nancy to refuse the request. She said sure.

The family and friend, once at the horses, went about putting the two animals into their trailer. Everyone pitched in, for once that had been accomplished they would continue on to the boarding stable down the road.

Jennifer balked at the idea of completing the ride in the back of her family's car. An assertive and self-assured young lady, she wished instead to continue on to the place riding her brother's bicycle. Nancy considered the request. After all, they were out in the country. It would be a short bike ride on a rural dirt road. At any rate, the child would hardly be out of sight. She gave her permission to Jennifer, who immediately started peddling off before the horses had been completely secured in their trailer.

It took only a few minutes more for the job to be done, after which Nancy called for her other three children to get into the car for the short ride to the stable. Slowly driving off, they were halfway to the stable when Nancy saw Jennifer peddling up ahead of them. Pulling alongside her daughter, she encouraged her to keep going, that they'd see her up ahead. Nancy then pulled away for the stable.

It would be the last time Nancy Wilson saw her daughter alive.

As Nancy drove away from Jennifer and on toward the stable, she noticed a blue pickup truck on the road ahead, coming toward them. For the moment she thought nothing of it.

Once at their destination, the group began the process of

removing the horses. It took several minutes to ready the stalls and get the animals settled in. Before the job was finished, Nancy's eleven-year-old daughter went up to her and voiced concern over Jennifer not yet having arrived.

Nancy realized her other daughter should have gotten to them by now. Everyone hopped in the car to backtrack their route. As they drove along, the same blue pickup they'd seen earlier now raced past them, moving in the opposite direction. Again, at the moment Nancy thought little of it.

A short distance farther on, they found Jennifer's bicycle lying alongside the road. Thinking that perhaps Jennifer had wondered off looking for flowers or perhaps had gone exploring, they began to search the immediate area. They looked in vain.

With a feeling of dread only a frightened parent can know, Nancy called 911.

Knapp remembers it being a quiet Monday morning until the Flagstaff Police Department called requesting assistance in the search for a missing nine-year-old girl. Sentner, as paramedic, had the job of getting the mission information. As Knapp prepared their LongRanger for the flight, Sentner was given a description of the girl and her clothing, right down to her white-topped tennis shoes.

Knapp and his paramedics flew out to the place where Jennifer was last seen. Landing in a vacant grassy field to the side of Old Country Club Road, Knapp kept the helicopter running while his partner stepped out for a briefing by local police and Sheriff's Department personnel. Sentner was given what additional information the other officers had gathered. That included the matter of a stolen blue Blazer pickup truck recently taken from the sheriff's auto pound, and which seemed to match the description of a suspicious car Mrs. Wilson had seen just before finding the abandoned bicycle. He was also informed that, just to be on the safe side, all routes leading in and out of the area had been sealed with police roadblocks.

As his paramedics spoke with the other officers, Knapp looked out his windscreen. Sheep Hill, one of many such small knolls in the area, was only a short distance away.

He'd be flying over that hill many times over the next few hours.

There are monsters in this world. Creatures that walk among us, appearing to be human beings, but whose inner persona have evolved into an entity far different from the rest of the fraternity of people. The word "brute" doesn't capture it. Nor do the words "creature" or "animal" or "beast." They are monsters.

Psychologists sometimes tell us we create these monsters, that they are formed in dysfunctional families, and our society, with its reverence for violence, reaps what it sows. Perhaps.

Others say they are just one part of who we are. Some of us have more of the thing that makes monsters inside us than others. That may be so.

But it remains quite correct to say that when you come in contact with one of them, all the questions about how they became what they are become moot. And on that particular Monday morning, little nine-year-old Jennifer had met up with a monster.

His name was Richard Lynn Bible. On that early summer's day when Mr. Bible first came in contact with Jennifer, he was twenty-seven years old. At the time, he was living in the woods, more like a wild thing than a person. He was in fact hiding from the Sheriff's Department for a string of thefts and burglaries. And he was only recently out of prison. Mr. Bible had a history of violence and of committing criminal acts. Six years earlier he had been sentenced to prison for an offense involving his sixteen-year-old cousin.

He had taken the teenage girl to the base of Sheep Hill, tied her up, and threatened to kill her. To enforce his will, he took a knife and tortured her by making cuts between her eyes and on her neck. He also sexually assaulted her. The young woman survived Mr. Bible's attentions by managing to talk her way out of the situation.

The truck Mr. Bible was driving on the day he met Jennifer was one he had stolen from the Sheriff's Department auto impound area a day earlier. It was a blue Chevrolet Blazer.

* * *

Knapp and Sentner began their search for Jennifer using what information was available. Sentner felt that it was quite possible the little girl had fallen from her bicycle. He reasoned that she might have had an accident, hit her head, and now, dazed and confused, was wandering along one of the many dirt logging roads in the area. Sentner could imagine the child, perhaps not far away, walking about aimlessly, in need of medical attention.

It was the kind of hopeful thinking that a person trained to aid other people might try to convince themselves was true. At any rate, Knapp and Sentner started their search for the little girl by flying over the local roads.

The pair kept at their quest for nearly two hours. They'd slowly fly up one trail, come to its end, then seek out another and work that one until there were no more roads to look at.

Low on fuel, they headed back to their Flagstaff base to load up on Jet-A. Then they returned to begin a methodical grid search of the area.

Sergeant Pat Tarr of the Coconino Sheriff's Department was taking part in the hunt for the missing Jennifer when, about five miles from the initial search area, he recognized Bible driving along in the stolen blue Blazer, the same color vehicle earlier reported as having been near where Jennifer was last seen. Knowing that there were arrest warrants out for Bible—for eighteen counts of burglary—and aware that the gentleman was only recently out of prison for a violent sex crime, the sergeant attempted to pull the Chevy over. Bible chose to run.

At speeds up to 115 miles per hour, Tarr kept after Bible and his stolen Blazer. Radioing for assistance, soon half a dozen police cars had fallen in trail behind the sergeant. Knapp and Sentner were also monitoring the police frequency. The pair was still involved in the job they had been doing for the last several hours, performing a grid search of the area. They also happened to be only a mile or so from where the chase was going on.

On hearing of the in-progress pursuit taking place on old Route 66, Knapp broke off from his assignment, pointed the nose of his helicopter in the direction of the chase, and pulled up on his collective. At full maximum continuous power, it took only a few minutes for his helicopter to come over the ongoing chase.

Below him Knapp saw a blue Blazer running along at a high rate of speed, followed close by a half-dozen police cars, their emergency lights flashing. Knapp discovered that his LongRanger was the only helicopter in the air at the moment committed to aiding the ground units. He put his aircraft a couple of hundred feet over the Blazer and watched it bounce up and down the road as its driver drove it as fast as the vehicle could be made to go. Knapp glued himself in position. The Blazer was now his.

Perhaps the Blazer's driver became aware of the helicopter, perhaps he had planned on doing the maneuver that followed all along, but Knapp saw the vehicle make a quick turn onto a Forest Service dirt road shortly after the helicopter joined in the pursuit. Knapp stayed right above him.

The move caught the police cars following the other vehicle by surprise and gave an eighth of a mile lead to the Blazer. As Knapp watched, the blue pickup started up a hill, and then he observed a man jump from the moving auto and run into the woods. Knapp radioed that information to the ground units. Because of the helicopter, the tactic didn't do the escaping man very much good. In fact, the ground units now ignored the still-running car and focused in on their quarry. Had Knapp and Sentner not been in place, that tactic might have proven far more effective.

Knapp began to fly in an arc around the man's position. The dense woods precluded him from seeing the individual, but he still had a good idea of where he might be hiding. And so long as the helicopter was flying overhead, Bible wouldn't be going anywhere. Knapp intended to stay put at least until more ground units got there.

Among the units that responded to the scene was a K-9 team. The handler and his dog had been assigned to help find Jennifer, but now were brought in for the search for Bible. The dog was released by the officer working him, and jumped into the now stopped pickup truck, sniffed around a bit, then ran off into the woods. As the animal moved about in circles, sniffing the ground, a young officer who had followed the dog found himself standing on a rock ledge. He looked down under a rock outcropping. Partially covered with leaves and branches, he saw the face of Richard Bible.

The monster was captured.

But when asked about his involvement with the missing Jennifer, Bible responded with a curt, "Prove it."

Camille Bibles knows all about monsters. She is a deputy county attorney with the Coconino County District Attorney's Office, and her job, once they're caught, is to try and keep them away from the rest of society for as long as possible. And sometime it's not an easy job, "proving it."

Bibles is no relation to Richard Bible. Due to the possibility of confusing the two names, from this point I shall refer to her as Camille.

Upon his arrest, Bible immediately cloaked himself with all the protection afforded him by the United States Constitution. He denied all knowledge of Jennifer and otherwise chose to remain silent.

But sometimes, when law enforcement is doing its job, questions can be answered in ways other than the human voice. A serologist, examining the clothes taken from Bible on his arrest, found a tiny speck of blood on the back of the man's shirt. The drop was in a shape that was consistent with the kind of splatter seen when someone batters in the head of another human being.

The amount found was no larger than a comma on this page. But there was enough to show that it wasn't blood from Bible. It was a rare type, a type that could be from one of Nancy Wilson's children. Except that Jennifer was still missing. And without Jennifer there could be no positive match.

Camille remembers that eighteen days after Jennifer had been reported missing, some hikers came upon a child's white high-topped tennis shoe in the woods. Flyers had been placed everywhere with descriptions of Jennifer's clothing at the time of her disappearance, and that style of shoe was part of the description. The people immediately made for a telephone to contact the police. The place they hiked off of was Sheep Hill.

Officers returned to the site and after some searching soon found the crime scene. Camille describes it as being one of the messiest homicide scenes she had ever had experience with. Jennifer's clothes had been tossed in all different directions. Her clothesless body, hands tied behind her back, was found under a tree, with a tree limb lying on top in what appeared to be a hurried effort at concealing the dead little girl. Jennifer had been killed by blunt trauma to her head.

From where Jennifer was murdered, Camille stated that a person standing there could look down and see everything of the beginning search activity. This fact convinced Camille that Bible, afraid of being found out by the helicopter—which Camille thinks Bible saw when Jim Knapp and his LongRanger landed on the road below the hill—had panicked. It probably spoiled some of his sport as well, as he had to hurriedly camouflage the spot where he'd done his deed, then attempt to run and hide from the authorities.

Camille, one of the prosecutors during Bible's six and a half week trial, argued in open court that it was the sight of the helicopter, and the flying machine's constant crisscrossing of the terrain, that caused Bible to bolt so quickly from his makeshift lair.

Camille had been originally brought into the case because, besides being an attorney, she possesses a science background. And this was to be the first case in Arizona where DNA analysis would be utilized. And all from the tiny speck of blood taken from the back of Bible's shirt.

When DNA is broken down for scientific examination, it shows up as bands of varying widths and darkness on sheet film. Such a test would graphically demonstrate that a child would get one band from their father and one from their mother. Camille believes that the evidence the jury must have found most persuasive was the DNA test done on Richard Wilson which showed among the strips a unique band, as was the case with the test done on Nancy Wilson. When matched up with the DNA sample taken both from the blood in Jennifer's body and the spot on Bible's shirt, the bands matched those of Jennifer's parents. It demonstrated a clear link between the Wilsons to their child and the tiny spot of blood.

As it turned out, Bible didn't have to say anything. It was Jennifer's blood that ultimately condemned him.

Bible was convicted of first-degree murder, kidnapping, and child molestation, and sentenced to die by lethal injection. With that sentence comes an automatic appeal to the Arizona State Supreme Court. It is likely that should the sentence be upheld, the case will go to the United States Supreme Court. After all, Bible has his rights.

It's been five years since Jennifer was killed. She would have been in high school now. It's been five long years for the Wilson family, knowing that the person who took their daughter's life is still alive, working the legal system and enjoying his existence.

This country has a fine legal system, and a humane one. It's only that at least in this case, at the moment, to those involved in the Jennifer Wilson murder, it doesn't seem to be all that just.

BOOK FIVE

Los Angeles Police Department Air Support Division

CHAPTER 25

The Unit

WHEN VIEWED WITHIN THE CONTEXT OF THE POLICE AVIATION scene, the Los Angeles Police Department Air Support Division must be considered one of its major players. The numbers alone that are generated annually by the LAPD air arm are staggering. Just in 1992 the Air Division accounted for the following police and public safety related activities:

Responses to Crimes in Progress	33,628
First at Scene of Incident	13,152
Vehicle Pursuits	607
Foot Pursuits	940
Fires Called In	127
Felonies Initiated Air Crew Initiated	2,034
Felony Arrests Air Crew Assisted	6,134

For a city of 3.2 million people —with several hundred thousand additional if undocumented aliens are counted—its 7600 officers do yeoman work, and this is nowhere more evident than in the proactive tasks assigned to the Air Division.

Begun in 1956 with a single helicopter, the officers assigned to the seventeen helicopters in the unit's current inventory fly a staggering number of flight hours each year. The unit flies twenty-four hours a day, seven days a week. There is virtually never a time when an Air Division helicopter isn't up somewhere over the city of Los Angeles. Its pilots average between 650 and 800 hours per year per flying member.

The Air Division wrings the most utility it can out of each

of the craft purchased. A number of their JetRangers hold the record for having the most flying hours ever recorded on this model aircraft. Where most aviation units retire their helicopters after between 5000 and 7000 flight hours, the LAPD air arm has a program that totally rebuilds their ships when they reach 14,400 hours. Three of the unit's flying machines have gone through this process twice and have accumulated over 30,000 flight hours each!

This aggressive professional flying outfit has more than enough stories to its credit with which to write a book about. Here are but a few of them.

CHAPTER 26

Sergeant/Pilot Brent Carey

An Almost Perfect Homicide

SERGEANT BRENT CAREY GETS TO DO A LOT OF SURVEIL-
lance work in his Air Division helicopter. He doesn't mind.
He's been shot at three times while flying department aircraft over the last ten years, so he figures that maybe just
watching people is a bit safer than getting involved in trying
to lock them up on the spot.

Carey recalls one recent case he was called in on. A few
years ago a woman reported to the LAPD that her husband
was missing. The matter wasn't viewed as anything extraordinary by the police. When uncomfortable with their lives,
some adults will occasionally take the path of least resistance
and run away. With no reason to believe otherwise, the department's investigators figured that was what had happened
in this particular domestic situation.

There was just one aspect of the case that made the in-
vestigating detective uneasy. Very soon after he became involved in the matter, he discovered that the woman was
having an affair with another man. It looked to the detective
that there was no real time interval between the disappearance of her husband and her becoming involved with this
new flame, to the point where her lover had moved in
with her.

But with nothing more than a queasy feeling in the stomach to go on, the case was filed as a standard missing persons report.

Two years later the detective received a call from a "friend" of the couple, one of their drinking buddies. The detective figured that the man must have had an argument with the woman's male friend. He just didn't seem like the kind of guy who would all of a sudden decide his conscience was bothering him about something he had known for a while.

Whatever the man's real reason, he claimed the couple killed the woman's husband.

He knew this, he said, because on the anniversary of the homicide the couple celebrated by making a pilgrimage to the dead man's grave site. Once there, they would both piss on his grave. The last time they had gone, he, a close friend, had been invited to go and partake in the little ritual.

To the regret of the detective, the area described by the couple's acquaintance was very vague. It was also extremely large in size and located somewhere in Tajunga Canyon.

According to the informant, on the day in question the three had gone up to the canyon area armed with several six-packs of beer. They drank the beer, which permitted the trio the luxury of engaging in their whim several times during the evening.

The detective believed the man's story and set about to find the body.

The first step after managing to limit the scope of the territory to be searched was for the Air Division to be assigned the task of using Forward Looking Infrared to check out the environs. The device was capable of sensing differences in temperature and showing the images on a televisionlike screen in the cockpit of the helicopter. It had been hoped that the decaying body would emit enough heat to distinguish it from the surrounding terrain.

The attempt was unsuccessful, probably because if a body is in the ground for two years, heat differences between it and the earth are too small to be picked up with FLIR.

The investigators next tried to locate the grave by searching for it on foot, but even with some idea of where to look, the size of the canyon area was too vast. The ground search proved fruitless. Finally it was decided they'd have to wait for the next anniversary of the homicide and arrange to follow the car with the three people inside. Since the site was located in a place that could be reached only via narrow and twisting mountain roads, a surveillance by car was out of the question. If the detectives were going to be successful in this investigation, they would need the services of the Air Division.

Carey was the pilot chosen for the mission. He and his observer stood by their JetRanger, waiting by the radio for the green light from the units on the ground. The investigators had set up the surveillance at a country and western bar located in the San Fernando Valley. It didn't take long before the couple and their friend met. At about six P.M. the detectives watched the three get in their car and start on their journey.

Carey received the call that the operation was a go and took off in his JetRanger. Following the directions of the two ground units already tailing the suspects, he was able to quickly position his helicopter four thousand feet above the vehicle as it headed toward the canyon. The two police cars then lay back and let the Air Division team do their thing.

The suspects' car didn't have to travel very far. It took them little more than fifteen minutes to get to the Tajunga Canyon area. Carey and his observer watched from overhead and reported to the ground units what they were seeing. The car pulled off the shoulder of the road and the three people got out and walked into the woods.

It had earlier been explained to Carey that special weapons team members had already hid in the general area where it was believed the trio would go. When the suspects arrived, the ground units in the woods did have some visual contact with them, but because of the trees, weren't able to see exactly what they were doing. Carey and his observer didn't have that problem from several thousand feet in the air. About seventy-five yards from the parked car, the trio came out into an open grassy area. Beer was broken out and the three began to drink.

While being watched from the orbiting JetRanger by Carey's observer—who used high-powered binoculars—after some time the people got up and walked over to the edge of the clearing. It was at that spot where the little ritual took place.

No police action was taken at that point, and in fact the three individuals remained at the site for quite some time. Since it was known where the couple lived, it made sense to permit them to have their fun, let them leave, and then dig up the ground to see what was buried there. It would have been awfully embarrassing to have swooped down on the three only to find there was no corpse.

The detectives needn't have been concerned. Once the little group left, Carey and his observer gave precise directions as to where the three had relieved themselves. The investigators on the ground had the unpleasant task of digging the area up. But their efforts were rewarded when they uncovered human remains under the ground's surface.

Warrants were obtained and the couple was soon brought to justice.

There is probably a lesson to be learned somewhere in this story. Perhaps it would be that first, it's not a good idea to commit a homicide and then tell somebody about it. Second, if you do murder somebody, hope they don't put the Air Division people on to you.

CHAPTER 27

Police Officer/Pilot
Charles "Chuck" Perriguey

Car Chase

THERE ARE A LOT OF CAR CHASES IN LOS ANGELES. MAYBE it's the road system, perhaps it's the West Coast's car culture. For whatever reason, the LAPD Air Support Division seems to spend a good deal of its time going after people who appear to believe it's a good idea to try and outrun police officers. You'd think they'd learn that once a helicopter is overhead the game is over.

Sometimes the chase turns out to be more humorous than exciting. Sometimes it's just some kid with more hormones coursing through his blood than he has brain cells in his head. But sometimes it can get really serious. That's when people wind up dead.

The advantage a helicopter enjoys over police ground units in a pursuit situation is profound. Besides the tactical advantages and the reduction in police liability, there is the obvious asset that most of the patrol aircraft used by the Air Division can fly at speeds of over 120 miles per hour. They needn't make sharp turns around narrow streets and they don't have to worry about civilian ground vehicles interfering with their route of travel.

Twenty-year-plus veteran police officer and Air Division

Pilot Chuck Perriguey was up for the second of his two and a quarter hour patrol flights one evening when a call came over the air from the Communications Division. They reported that California Highway Patrol units were on the Harbor Freeway, attempting to stop a fleeing vehicle.

Perriguey glanced to the south and three miles away could make out the dome lights of the pursuing vehicles. He swung the nose of his JetRanger around and headed for the action. The speed of the stolen Buick Riviera involved was fluctuating from between eighty and a hundred miles an hour. Not fast by pursuit-speed standards, but enough to get people hurt.

Perriguey needed to communicate with all the ground units involved. As LAPD cruisers had also taken up the chase—and as they use a different frequency from the CHP units—the pilot switched over to the statewide CLEMARS system, an acronym that stands for California Law Enforcement Mutual Aid Radio System.

Radioing both the CHP and his own communication's section that he was now over the suspect vehicle, Perriguey turned his thirty-million-candlepower Nightsun searchlight on the car. Maintaining communication with the ground units, he ensured that they were kept aware of the exact location of the fleeing auto as well as where it might turn off. This was important because now that they were entering Los Angeles proper, his own department would be responsible for blocking off the exit ramps the stolen car might take.

Flying over the Buick, Perriguey made sure his helicopter's powerful light stayed on the car. It was also important that he light up some distance of the road ahead. The purpose of that tactic was first to ensure that the driver of the vehicle being pursued was aware that he was under aerial surveillance and that further flight was pointless. Secondly, it was intended to warn any incoming traffic that might get in the way of the fleeing car, and so help them avoid being injured.

The driver in the Buick didn't intend to let anybody or anything get in the way of his escape. As the driver of the car came up behind traffic that was blocking all four lanes of the freeway, Perriguey watched as the stolen car swerved into the left lane of the roadway. Sparks flew from the side of the car as it rubbed up against the railing of the highway's concrete center divider. Perriguey figured that maneuver would be it for the vehicle, but he was wrong. The Buick passed by the traffic in his way and kept on going. The pursuing police vehicles were left behind. They weren't about to endanger the lives of innocent civilians by pulling a similar stunt.

Perriguey, who of course had remained right behind the suspect's car, now realized his helicopter had become the only game in town.

About a mile up the road the stolen car encountered more freeway traffic. This time the driver opted to attempt to squeeze by on the right side of the roadway and drive onto the shoulder of the highway. The aggressive maneuver didn't quite work. The Buick went out of control and rolled down the steep side embankment to the street below.

The vehicle rolled a number of times, eventually coming to rest on its roof. Perriguey watched the surreal scene from a few hundred feet overhead. He knew that broadcasting his observations of the chase and crash had attracted a good deal of attention from ground units—over a dozen LAPD cars had reported they were en route—and he was expecting backup to arrive within a few seconds. From the looks of the banged-up car, Perriguey figured its driver was going to be in need of some serious medical attention.

But what he did not expect to happen was what he now saw. The driver of the stolen car climbed through an open window and took off running from the scene. And except for the Air Division helicopter's occupants, there wasn't a police officer within a hundred yards of the bolting suspect.

It took the officers from the pursuing police vehicles from atop the freeway better than half a minute to jump from their cars and run down to the stolen Buick. By that time the suspect had fled down the residential street and turned into the driveway of a private home. The neighborhood the man was in was a veritable maze of byways and alleys for somebody trying to hide from the police.

It would have been a perfect place to escape, except for the fact that a helicopter was there.

During the time it took for the ground units to get to the scene, the lone Air Division JetRanger hovered overhead. Perriguey watched as the man jumped one fence after another as he attempted to blend into the night. But the brilliant Nightsun searchlight illuminated the suspect and half a football field area of ground around him. With the Air Division overhead, he found out the hard way that there was literally no place to hide.

As the man futilely attempted to get away, Perriguey calmly reported to the ground units the suspect's every location. Officers formed a cordon around the area, and following Perriguey's directions, slowly worked their way to its center. Within a few minutes of his running from the crash, LAPD and CHP officers made the arrest.

CHAPTER 28

Police Officer/Pilot Don Reuser

Narcotics Work

PILOT DON REUSER HAS SEEN A LOT OF TIME IN THE AIR IN HIS over nineteen years with the Air Division; he has a total of twenty-three years in the department. If one were to include his military Huey time, his flight logs would show that he acted as a helicopter's pilot-in-command for about 14,000 hours. That's a fair amount of experience by any yardstick.

Another member of the Air Division told me of Reuser's extensive military background and the medals he was awarded during his year in Vietnam. In response to my questions on the subject, Reuser reluctantly offered that he had two Distinguished Flying Crosses, forty-nine air medals—four with B devices—and a Bronze Star. It was clear he had been accorded others, but wouldn't elaborate further.

When asked the circumstances on the action surrounding his being awarded the Bronze Star, Reuser simply stated he responded to a group of servicemen who had been pinned down by enemy fire. I pointed out to Reuser that the Bronze Star was not handed out to people just for coming to work on time, that there had to be more to it than that.

By his telling, he simply dropped down in his Huey, picked them up and took them to the nearest aid station. He did casually mention that his helicopter had taken eight hits during the action. But otherwise he made the story sound as if he'd faced as much danger as going to the local grocery to buy a quart of milk.

As with the other LAPD pilots and observers he flies with within the Air Division, Reuser is first and foremost a police officer. Like the other members of the unit, the main difference in how they and ground units operate is the manner by which they get to the scene of the crime.

It can also be said that, depending on the task, Air Division members may get to wear several different hats. One example is those times they're called on to conduct an aerial surveillance of a drug operation. Not only might they play the role of pilot, but also that of detective and arresting officer!

A few years ago, for example, Reuser and his partner/observer James Mahon—now recently retired after over twenty-five years on the job—were part of an operation aimed at closing down a drug-smuggling ring. The LAPD had an informant in the case. (What successful operation doesn't!) The investigators knew where the drug dealers would start from, that a plane would be landing somewhere in the desert to drop off the goods, and that the dealers would be bringing fuel to the aircraft.

In short, what the police didn't know was from where the aircraft would be coming in, or exactly where it would land.

From a police perspective, for the whole business to come to a successful conclusion would require a lengthy ground and air surveillance of the parties involved.

For this case Reuser traded in his JetRanger for a Cessna 210. The Cessna is a powerful single-engine aircraft, her high-wing configuration most useful in that their location permitted the aircraft's occupants an unobstructed view of what was going on below them. Fully fueled, it would also permit an aerial operation that lasted for over six hours.

While Reuser and the other members of the Air Division waited by their aircraft, the ground units surveilled the smugglers known location in Los Angeles. It took several weeks, but finally the group members made their move. The Air Division officers were told the drug dealers had left their main residence and headed out in the direction of Las Vegas. The people were seen traveling in three vehicles: a passenger van, a station wagon, and a pickup truck with a camper shell on top. Inside the camper shell the investigators reported there were two empty fifty-five gallon metal drums.

The ground units reported that the small caravan's first stop was at an airport. There, the empty drums were filled with aviation fuel. It looked like a go for the rendezvous.

At around four P.M. Reuser got the signal to take to the air. Once airborne, it only took a few minutes for the Cessna 210—guided by a department helicopter already on station— to come over the three vehicles. Once Reuser was in place, the JetRanger broke away from the surveillance. It was now up to Reuser and Mahon to stay with the suspects.

The three vehicles headed out on the freeway toward the desert. The Cessna hung like an invisible police cruiser a mile above the smugglers. The ground units lay well back from the suspects, being told every move the three vehicles made, every exit they passed.

When they got to the town of Baker, the little caravan exited the freeway, took a side road, and then made for the desert. Reuser and Mahon had no problem staying with the vehicles, which was fortunate as the ground units were unable to assist at that point because of the flat terrain and the likelihood of being seen.

The Cessna followed the three vehicles to a dry lake bed, a not uncommon place for dope smugglers to land contraband-laden aircraft. The spot they had chosen was close to Edward's Air Force Base, whose military pilots use the dry lake beds of the region for far more legitimate purposes.

Reuser relayed the information to the waiting ground units. He figured that the dope dealers would stay where they were, and use either a radio or some light device to communicate with the aircraft they were clearly expecting to arrive.

As Reuser and Mahon circled overhead they could see that a number of the people below had gotten out of one of the vehicles and had piled into the remaining two. They then headed back in the direction of Baker in the two cars.

By this time the sun was getting low on the horizon. Reuser speculated that perhaps the smugglers intended on meeting the aircraft the next day. Whatever the reason for their return into town, their movement called for a rapid change in plans. The ground surveillance teams would have to close up on the suspects and attempt to pick up whatever intelligence they could and perhaps figure out what the group's next plans were.

Reuser stayed above the two smugglers' vehicles. After some time orbiting the town, he was told by the ground teams that once the group had gotten back into Baker some of the party had made for an auto parts store. It appeared the vehicle they'd left sitting out in the desert had blown a radiator hose. The people had also booked a motel room.

The ground units contacted Reuser. They felt confident they had a good handle on the smugglers' activities. Both the police and smugglers would be in Baker for a while. They suggested that he land the aircraft at a small local airfield until they notified him that his aircraft would be needed. Reuser concurred with the recommendation.

The airport Reuser flew to was to the west of Baker. The place was small, with a single 3000-foot runway, no runway lights for night landings, and a single rotating beacon to tell incoming pilots where it sat. By the time Reuser landed, the sun had set.

In the desert, once the evening comes, if there isn't a full moon, it can get very dark. And there was no moon that night.

The little airport had no taxi-way for Reuser to follow. The pilot had to travel back along the runway until he came to a small paved section that had parking space for four small aircraft. The only light Reuser had was his own taxi and landing lights and the fireflylike blips of the airport's white and green rotating beacon.

There was only a single aircraft tied down at a small ramp. Reuser took the space next to it and shut down his Cessna.

Reuser and Mahon's aircraft had no police markings. The machine sprouted a couple more antennas than most planes, but with all the other antennas sticking out of a modern airplane, they weren't out of place. They were working an investigation, and in anticipation of a situation such as the one they now found themselves in, the two officers were dressed in civilian clothes. After all, there was no point in stirring up the locals by having them walk around in LAPD uniforms if they should have to make an unexpected landing at some out of the way airport.

Still in radio contact with the ground units, they were asked if they wanted something to eat. Their resounding yes had them soon partaking of the customary gourmet cop dinner of hamburgers and fries, washed down by a fine vintage of Diet Coke.

While at the airport, the investigators reiterated to both men what was already known. The bad guys had purchased a radiator hose and booked a motel room. They were still moving around, but it seemed to the investigators that they were getting ready to wrap it up for the night. When they finally put the dope dealers to bed, they'd be back for Reuser and Mahon and bring them into town to a local motel.

With that, the investigators headed back to the rest of the surveillance ground team, leaving the two Air Division officers with not much to do and no place to do it. Just standing around their Cessna quickly became boring for the pair. In desperation, Reuser broke out their Starlight scope. The device is used to amplify ambient light tens of thousands of times and permits the user to literally see in the dark.

Reuser and Mahon took turns watching the jackrabbits run around the airport. They also listened to the surveillance radio on the movement of the smugglers as reported by the ground units, and generally amused themselves as best they could under the circumstances.

Without the Starlight scope both men were enveloped in the opaque blackness of night. Except for the small rotating beacon and the lights of the occasional car as it passed along the highway abutting the airport, it was like being in a coal bin.

The two officers were fortunate that the evening was a warm one. It was April; had it been closer to the winter months, they might have faced uncomfortably cold temperatures wearing only their shirtsleeves.

By now they had been standing about for nearly two hours. It was close to eight P.M. Bored with hanging around their airplane, the officers decided to take a walk.

Noise travels a long way in the desert. The officers could hear the sound of an aircraft's engines in the distance. Reuser figured the ship to be a twin. This didn't particularly concern either of the men. After all, they were at an airport. The only thing was, while the night was clear and the noise of the airplane reasonably close, they both figured they should be able to see some aircraft lights showing by now. Still, while the droning of the plane's engines got louder, nothing was visible in the night sky.

The officers started to slowly work their way back to their Cessna. Soon they stood under the aircraft's high wing, still looking for the twin—now quite close but still invisible.

As the officers watched, they caught sight of the aircraft— with none of its lights on—as it made a low pass over the runway. Reuser saw that he had been right, it was a twin-engine aircraft. The plane climbed, and he watched as it prepared to land at their little airport. Now he could make out that the ship was one of the larger model Cessnas. And it still had no lights showing.

Reuser contacted the ground units with a question: What kind of an aircraft where they expecting? The investigators replied that they only knew it was a twin-engine Cessna.

The twin Cessna set up for landing. Reuser, his full attention now on the aircraft, was stunned when he heard one of its two engines shut down. He couldn't imagine why the pilot would do such a dangerous thing just before landing. The twin, only one of its engines turning over but now with its landing lights on, set down on the dark runway. The aircraft came to a stop at the end, turned and headed for the small parking area.

By this time both Reuser and Mahon were inside their aircraft trying to sort out this new wrinkle. Making contact with their ground surveillance people, Reuser read off the tail number and other identifying information to Mahon, who in turn transmitted the intelligence to the units in town. The officers in Baker, after reviewing what was now known about the aircraft, decided the plane was probably the one they wanted.

Both of the Air Division officers had to lower themselves below the bottom of their Cessna's windows to avoid being seen by the occupants of the closely taxiing twin. Reuser kept his door cracked to enable him to hear what was going on outside.

The ship finally came to a stop on the ramp. The side door opened and three people stepped out, two men and a woman. To Reuser's surprise the trio, now out on the tarmac, laughed and joked among themselves. It became clear why they landed on a single engine when one of the men—clearly the pilot—said to the others, "Could you believe it, we ran out of gas."

Then one of the group suggested to the other, "Well, they're a couple of airplanes here. Let's just steal some gas."

The trio closed their aircraft up and walked past the Air Division's Cessna. Fifty yard away, at the base of the pole that supported the rotating beacon, rested a public telephone. By the banter of the three it was clear that the stealing of fuel would come after they made some calls.

As soon as the group passed their Cessna, Reuser and Mahon quietly exited their ship and worked their way as close as possible to the beacon. In between the green and white flashes of the rotating light, the two officers inched their way forward. They knew it might prove valuable to hear what was going to be said on the telephone.

The conversation the officers did manage to hear cleared up any doubts regarding the nature of the trio's activities. On the telephone one of the people stated they had run low on gas, had made several low passes near the dry river bed—presumably the one where the Los Angeles group had first gone to—but as no lights were showing from ground vehicles, they weren't sure they were in the right spot. The speaker told the other person on the line to have fuel brought out to the airport. He also mentioned a telephone number, which Reuser managed to hear a part of. That partial number, Reuser would find out later, was to the residence the ground units had been watching in L.A. for the last several weeks.

Before the man hung up it was clear that he was told the people in town would be notified and send a car out to get them.

As the three headed back toward their aircraft, Reuser and Mahon scurried back to their Cessna. Mahon stayed with the Air Division aircraft while Reuser worked his way to a place opposite the twin on the other side of the runway. He badly wanted to find out what was inside the body of that ship.

Once the trio got back inside the aircraft, Reuser decided it was more prudent to get back to his own plane. As he got inside, he closed his door, but because it would have made a loud, distinctive noise to have closed it fully, he was forced to hold it partially shut. With the same hand, he held onto a two-cell flashlight, kept aboard the aircraft "just in case." Mahon was lying down in the back seat, softly speaking on the radio to the ground units, who were now heading to the airport.

At this point Reuser had his five-shot .38 Smith & Wesson revolver in his hand. The only reason officers carry such a light firearm is because the weapon is so concealable. There is nothing else to recommend about the little gun, which is of limited effectiveness. Except in the movies, but there the people who get shot with such small handguns have to follow a script and lay down and die. Reuser was under no such illusion. If the bad guys had any kind of serious weaponry aboard that aircraft, he and Mahon would be in real trouble.

From inside his plane Reuser could hear the door open on the twin. As the people stepped from their aircraft, he could hear them discuss among themselves the idea that since the walk to town was only a couple of miles, they might as well head in that direction. When they were near the Air Division aircraft, one of the men exclaimed, "Hey, the door's open on this one." Reuser and Mahon could then hear the three heading their way.

With that, Reuser decided that his options had just dropped down to one. When they were right up to the aircraft, he kicked open his door, shone the light in their eyes and, pointing his snubby in their faces, announced, "Police!"

The chase was on. Not seeing any weapons in their hands, neither he nor Mahon wanted to shoot at them—again, notwithstanding movie lore.

As Reuser raced in the direction of the three suspects, he saw the lights of his backup police units coming onto the scene. The suspects had by this time run across the road next to the airport and were out into the desert proper. The ground units, seeing where they ran, cut out for them in their large American sedans. Reuser watched as the big Buicks and Chevys made like dune buggy racers.

Mahon had the sense to grab hold of the Starlight scope, and with the perfect 20/20 night vision it afforded, directed the officers to the three would-be escapees. With his assistance, it didn't take long to capture them.

With the alleged smugglers now in tow, Reuser and the rest returned to their twin-engine aircraft. Before they even came close to the door, Reuser could smell a powerful pungent odor which he knew to be that of marijuana. One peek inside the ship explained the reason. The cargo consisted of big bales of grass.

The three people under arrest vehemently denied any knowledge of the aircraft or the marijuana inside. They claimed they had just been taking a walk along the road when all these crazy people started to run after them.

Hearing their protestations of innocence, Reuser smiled. For when he and the other officers had looked inside the craft, they had found numerous Polaroid photos of the group they had in custody, and of others loading the illegal cargo aboard the airplane.

It turned out that they made a round trip to and from a Mexican location to pick up the contraband. Later investigation showed that the two men were the pilots and the woman was both the brains and money supplier for the operation.

With all the fuss that had gone on in the desert, citizens, unaware of who was whom, called the local police. San Bernardino County officers responded, and after some initial confusion—the "how come you didn't tell us you were coming" kind—assisted the Los Angeles officers in rounding up the rest of those involved in the smuggling operation, who had remained in town.

The judicial actions that resulted from the arrests seemed to Reuser to go on forever. Each defendant demanded a separate trial, and they all took place in a court in Barstow, about halfway between Los Angeles and Las Vegas.

One of the defendants—one of the two pilots Reuser and Mahon helped capture—was thirty-five years old, nearly completely bald, with just some fringe hair around the outside of his scalp. He was a thin, nervous, Don Knots type; so nervous that it made Reuser jumpy to be around him. The man quickly earned the nickname of Balding Bob.

Balding Bob made it clear he did not wish to go to jail. After he was convicted on the smuggling charge, it didn't take much prodding for him to became an informant for the state's attorney.

Reuser, there primarily for his aviation expertise, along with state and federal investigators, sat down to talk with Balding Bob. The man claimed to have flown hundreds of dope runs in and out of Mexico and now was willing to work for the government to stay out of prison.

And in fact Balding Bob did serve as an informant for the government on several cases. Unfortunately, his desire to stay out of jail did not preclude his lust for money. He also decided to stay in the drug-running business at the same time he worked for law enforcement.

One day while Reuser had some business up at one of the Los Angeles area airport control towers, an unusual call came in. It was from the American consul in Mexico. He was calling about an aircraft with an American registration which they believed came back to the Los Angeles area. The plane had crashed in the Mexican jungle and there had been fatalities. The consul was concerned about notifying the next of kin.

Reuser started making some telephone calls. The registration number had come back to a post office box number in West Los Angeles. Customs quickly confirmed that box was a known front for drug smugglers. They also verified that the registration number was to an aircraft which they had suspected was involved in smuggling.

A few more calls to Customs and Reuser found that when the aircraft had gone across the border to Mexico, the pilot had filed a flight plan. It came as little surprise to him that the pilot was Balding Bob. He and several others aboard the plane had perished, putting an end to Balding Bob's dual careers as a police informant and drug smuggler.

Aircraft in Trouble

Modern general aviation aircraft fly many millions of hours each year without mishap. These machines are remarkably reliable and afford a safe, fun, and exhilarating means of transport for many people. Airplanes are kept aloft by their wings. When the wings are pushed through the air via propeller or jet engine, they generate lift, which in turn enables the machines to fly.

Popular myth has it that when an airplane "loses" its engine, that is, the engine quits, the aircraft plummets from the sky. Nothing could be farther from the truth. A light airplane flies as well with or without its engine operating. The only practical difference is that with no functioning engine to push air backward and move the aircraft forward to cause air to flow over its wings (and create lift), gravity takes the place of the motor. So although the plane is still perfectly controllable—like a glider or sailplane—in a relatively short period of time it will come down to earth.

Depending on where the pilot finds him or herself when the engine decides to stop will determine to a large degree where the plane ultimately lands. If the problem occurs over an urban area, it could easily ruin a pilot's day.

On a late August evening Reuser was on duty, piloting his JetRanger over the San Fernando Valley section of Los Angeles. Because of the area's crowded airspace, Reuser was monitoring the Approach Control frequency of a nearby airport. He overheard a troubling exchange. A single-engine Cessna pilot reported to the ground controllers that his aircraft was experiencing engine trouble. The oil pressure was low and the engine had begun to sputter.

As Reuser listened it occurred to him that the middle of Los Angeles was not a good place for a pilot to lose an engine. Approach Control must have had the same idea. They radioed Reuser and asked if he could assist the pilot in distress. He responded that he would certainly try.

Reuser radioed the Cessna pilot, hoping that the man could baby the engine a little longer until close enough to an airport to make a safe landing. Unable to spot the small plane in the clear night sky, he asked the man to turn on his landing light. Immediately he spotted the aircraft a few miles off the helicopter's nose and headed in its direction.

The pilot reported to Reuser that his altimeter showed him to be at 4000 feet above sea level. Reuser figured the terrain below was around 1500 feet ASL. That would leave the pilot about 2500 feet between him and the ground should the engine decide to quit completely. The experienced Air Division pilot quickly calculated that without the engine running, the aircraft would be able to glide about five miles before touching down. He was also aware that the nearest airport was over ten miles away.

Reuser radioed the pilot that the Air Division JetRanger was going to head over his way and escort him to the closest airport. The officer figured the least they could do is follow the man and try to ensure his safety.

After speaking with the Cessna's pilot for a few minutes, Reuser figured they had one good thing going for them. The man appeared to be a mature individual. He voiced concern over his plight but his voice was calm and not panicky. It would require calm, rational decision making to deal with this situation.

While they flew along, a second Air Division helicopter came up to the two aircraft. The other JetRanger was working his sector on routine patrol and the pilot figured he too might be of some assistance.

Less than five minutes after Reuser had made contact with the Cessna pilot, the man radioed the JetRanger that his oil pressure had dropped to zero. And his engine had quit.

Reuser was intimately familiar with what lay on the ground below. It wasn't promising. To the south, which was the direction the small plane had come in from, were hills. To the east, west, and north there was nothing but rough terrain; small streets with wires running across them and private homes.

Reuser figured that for the Cessna pilot to make a successful emergency landing would require an uninterrupted stretch of clear flat ground that ran for a minimum of half a mile. The only thing remotely resembling that kind of terrain was the four-lane Ventura Freeway below them. And it was full of cars traveling at seventy miles an hour.

Reuser made a decision. He radioed the pilot in distress and told him that he should fly his plane in the direction of the freeway. Reuser would clear a landing place for him.

With little time to lose, Reuser, along with the second Air Division helicopter, dropped down to less than a hundred feet over the freeway. The second helicopter radioed for marked ground police units to drive onto the roadway and block it off at both ends. The radio cars responded they were on the way, but from their estimated times of arrival it was obvious they'd get there too late to be of much help.

Reuser realized the alternatives available had now been narrowed down to a freeway landing. He radioed to the other Air Division JetRanger, "It's up to us." Turning on his multimillion candlepower searchlight, Reuser set his helicopter up to face oncoming traffic. He shone the light in the direction of the cars heading his way and at the same time turned on his JetRanger's external siren. Reuser swung the nose of the helicopter back and forth. It took a few moments for the drivers to comprehend, but ultimately a line of cars stopped across all the four lanes of the freeway facing in the direction the Cessna would attempt its landing. The second Air Division helicopter had set itself up in a position to shine its searchlight on the part of the freeway where the Cessna would set down.

The Cessna pilot radioed Reuser that he saw the traffic break the officer had just created. The small aircraft swooped down over Reuser's helicopter. Under normal circumstances, with an operating engine and plenty of time to plan the descent, the pilot of a small Cessna could land the plane in under a thousand feet. But this was by no stretch of the imagination going to be a normal landing. An aircraft without operating engine has only two things going for it: airspeed and altitude. A pilot can trade one for the other, but in any case, once the "money" in the bank is spent, there's no putting it back. The Cessna pilot came in fast.

Reuser watched with growing concern as the plane began to overtake the traffic that had gotten past his impromptu blockade. Worse, a number of the cars ahead of the Cessna had begun to slow down, some even pulling off to the side of the road, curious as to what the two helicopters where doing hovering so low over the roadway.

Reuser turned his JetRanger around and, along with the second Air Division helicopter, flew alongside the landing Cessna. What Reuser and the other helicopter pilot didn't see, and what the Cessna pilot couldn't have done anything about it if he had, was a line of electrical wires stretching across the freeway.

Where a moment earlier he had seen the Cessna, Reuser was startled by a sudden, violent, blinding flash of light. The Air Division pilot didn't know what had happened, but his heart sank as he figured the pilot had come so close to making a safe landing only to have his aircraft explode at the last second.

It took a moment for Reuser's eyes to regain their night vision. To his surprise and relief he saw that the Cessna was still going. The plane had sliced through the power lines, and Reuser would later see that the only damage done to the aircraft was a black mark where the wing had cut through the cable.

To Reuser's gratification, he watched as the Cessna pilot made a smooth landing on the freeway. As the aircraft rolled along with road's surface, its wings just cleared the roofs of some of the cars that had parked alongside the roadway.

The plane finally came to a stop in the middle of the road. By this time Los Angeles Police Department ground units were on the scene and officers assisted the pilot—shaken but unhurt—in pushing his aircraft off to the side of the freeway.

And Reuser and the other Air Division JetRanger returned to normal patrol. Just another routine night over L.A.

Drugs in from the Sea

San Clemente Island sits nearly seventy miles off the coast of California, almost due south of Los Angeles. This island is a naval military reservation with an air base at one end used by Navy pilots to practice carrier landings. On the other end is a bombing range and an area for ship gunfire training. From the vantage point of the Pacific's surface, the island's land mass appears shaped like a wedge. Tall, sheer cliffs sit at one end and gradually descend down to the sea where a harbor is located. The island has little vegetation on it except for cactus. Those who visit come away feeling the place more closely resembles a desert setting rather than a warm weather paradise.

Air Division pilots sometimes find themselves in odd locations. San Clemente Island might not be the strangest one, but for Reuser during one particular narcotics case, it had its moments.

Information was received that a seagoing tug was to leave Long Beach and rendezvous with a foreign freighter off the Los Angeles coast. Intelligence had it that a substantial quantity of drugs would be transferred to the smaller vessel and brought to the mainland.

A Customs Service aircraft followed the tug to where it anchored off the southern tip of San Clemente Island. The vessel sat among a number of other legitimate craft, out in the area for fishing or as part of a pleasure trip. Once it was determined where the tug was, an LAPD ground unit was put in place on the island to keep an eye on it.

Reuser and Mahon's job was to take the Air Division's single-engine airplane, their Cessna 210, and fly out to San Clemente and follow the tug.

Reuser went through the formality of getting a Prior Permission Request from the Navy base so that he could land his small aircraft there. Dressed in civilian clothing, both men took off from Van Nuys Airport around four P.M. The trip to the island was a routine half hour flight. Coming over the airport, Reuser saw that the runway was configured literally like the deck of an aircraft carrier. There were even restraining cables that lay across sections of its surface to catch the tailhooks of Navy aircraft practicing for carrier landings.

Reuser checked out the runway and figured he could safely land on the first part of its surface, there being no cables running across that segment. He entered the pattern, and as he touched down and began to slow the Cessna up, determined the cables that lay ahead would cause no harm to his airplane.

He was almost correct. Pulling back on his elevator control to take as much weight off the nose wheel as possible, he permitted the Cessna to run over a cable. There was a bigger thump than he had anticipated, his panel full of radios and navigation gear immediately went into "off" mode. Whatever had happened had shorted out a bunch of the instruments. Reuser heard a sizzle sound come from the panel, which was followed by an accompanying wisp of smoke.

This he knew was not good.

A quick check of the gauges showed that the jar of the landing rollout had shorted out the panel lighting. Since there was an excellent possibility that the mission was going to be flown at night, he decided the most prudent thing was to fly back to Van Nuys, get the electrical glitch repaired, and return immediately afterward.

Which is what Reuser and his partner for the mission, Mahon, did. A few hours later, on their return to the island, they landed on the taxi-way parallel to the runway and avoided the cables this time.

It turned out to be a better plan.

Once parked Reuser and Mahon were picked up by members of the Shore Patrol—Navy police—and driven over to the Shore Patrol billets. They also met the LAPD narcotics investigators who were housed there and who had been keeping tabs on the tug for the last four days.

By the time the two men were briefed on their role in the mission, it was dark out. As Reuser headed toward the office where he and Mahon would get room assignments, he noticed a small animal scurry down the hallway. At first he figured it was a cat or dog. Since it was inside the building, it was logical to assume the animal was some kind of a pet.

The door to the office he and Mahon were in was open. The animal entered, and as the small creature walked about the room, Reuser did a double take. At first he thought he was looking at a small dog. It took a moment for him to realize that the dog was really a fox.

He turned to the man behind the counter and asked if the fox was a pet. The man replied that no, it was just one of the island's many foxes. Since the two-foot-long animals had no natural enemies on the island, and since hunting wasn't allowed, they had became quasidomestic.

Reuser checked the little creature out. He noted that half its length was made up of a bushy tail. The creature looked healthy, almost like a small collie, and seemed to be inquisitive about the two newcomers to its island.

The animal sniffed around the two officers. He then trotted over to their bags and first took the scent of Reuser's bag, satisfied himself, and then went over to Mahon's. He took a whiff of that bag, looked over to Mahon, then turned back to the bag, lifted a leg and proceeded to pee all over it.

Mahon, upset by the fox's ill manners, yelled and chased the animal out of the building. Reuser figured from that moment on that particular fox had a predator to worry about on San Clemente Island.

Worse, from Mahon's point of view, after that incident the nickname the "Fox" was appended to his name by Air Division members.

At the end of an uneventful three days on the island, the tug moved off from its anchorage. Reuser and Mahon took off to follow the vessel, only to find there was a low cloud cover obscuring their view. Quickly radioing their predicament, Customs sent over one of their twin-engine Grumman aircraft which had infrared viewing capabilities.

The Grumman tracked the tug several miles out to sea, where it was observed meeting with the mother ship. There, bales of marijuana were tossed overboard and picked up by the smaller vessel. Once fully loaded, the tug headed back toward the coast.

The area of low cloud and fog ended before the tug got too much closer to the coast. Reuser and Mahon were already overhead when the tug broke out from the clouds and fog bank, and they took over the surveillance from the Grumman when the vessel was within twenty miles of the mainland. They were assisted by Coast Guard radar, which had maintained a lock on the tug for its entire voyage.

The drug-laden vessel made its way into Los Angeles harbor, oblivious to the Air Division aircraft overhead, the Coast Guard radar surveillance, and the many LAPD officers in vessels. As the boat moved closer to a docking place,

Reuser and Mahon radioed more frequent reports of its whereabouts. The vessel had to move in and around various channels once it got past the breakwaters in order to get to its final destination. Reuser stayed close.

He finally saw the tug going into a dock. He radioed the units on the ground and in the water, which immediately descended on the docked vessel, taking the eight-person crew without a struggle.

On board, the officers found several tons of marijuana. The freighter was soon boarded by Coast Guards units, who took the vessel and its crew into custody.

Once the ground units informed Reuser that everything was under control, he felt comfortable returning to the Air Division base at Van Nuys Airport. After all, there was still paperwork for him and Mahon to finish up.

Drive-by Shooting

Why would a person drive past a total stranger and fire a gun at them? Sport perhaps? Ego gratification? The territorial imperative? Maybe a combination of all three.

Whatever the motivation, such behavior has become all too common in some parts of this country. And these random violent acts can be extremely difficult for law enforcement to deal with. Without rational motive, following a schedule the timetable of which might be a person's next need for an emotional high, the police can not anticipate such crimes, only react to them.

Reuser and Observer Mel Stevenson had to deal with just such a problem while working an evening tour one warm summer night. A call came over the air around 10:15 P.M. about a possible drive-by shooting. Witnesses had described the vehicle as a white foreign car. Reuser decided to head over in that direction while Stevenson kept an eye out for any vehicles fitting the description.

Before they even got to the scene, another drive-by shooting was reported over their police radio. This one took place within a mile of and east of the last shooting. Communications broadcast that information received from reporting witnesses indicated that the light-colored or cream car had two occupants.

The shooters were part of a group called the Hazard Gang, named for the park they hung out in. That night two of the gang members decided to go cruising outside their normal "turf" and simply drive around and pick out targets of opportunity.

The first victims had been standing in a group of half a dozen people. The blast from the gang member's shotgun hit two of them, fortunately causing no serious injuries. The second person attacked was a man riding on a bicycle. He wasn't to be so lucky. The car with the two Hazards members inside pulled up alongside him and the shooter opened up at close range. The bicyclist was wounded very badly.

Before each of the attacks, the shooter would yell out the name of his gang, just to make sure the victims knew where they came from.

Both men involved in the shootings had lengthy arrest records.

But at the moment both officers knew nothing of the perpetrators. They could only conjecture that based on the last broadcast direction of travel, the shooters' vehicle was heading for a local housing project, Pico Eleso Village. Instead of working his way slowly along the streets from the point of the last shooting onward, Reuser decided to take a chance and fly directly to where he believed the two men might be heading.

The Air Division officers were over the projects for only a few moments when they saw a light-colored foreign auto enter the east end of the housing area at a high rate of speed. Later they would learn the auto had been stolen by the two men riding inside.

Stevenson immediately put out a transmission that they were following a suspect vehicle. He broadcast to ground units the car's location and gave a running report on where it was headed. Reuser moved their JetRanger in close above the vehicle.

The car pulled into a parking lot and the passenger and driver jumped out. Reuser knew that no black-and-whites had yet arrived on the scene. The pilot turned on the helicopter's searchlight, knowing he could no longer be subtle.

Under normal circumstances the helicopter pilot would have focused his attention on the car's driver. But Reuser figured that since the crime was that of a drive-by shooting, it was the only logical that the passenger was the one who actually did the firing. It would be the passenger that he would stick with.

As the man bolted from the car, Reuser noted that he held nothing in his hands that even remotely resembled a shotgun. The suspect ran through the project, every so often trying to hide in the bushes planted along the building line. He even took off his long-sleeve shirt in an effort to camouflage himself. Now in a T-shirt, he attempted to blend in with local area residents similarly attired.

It didn't work. All the suspect's machinations managed to do was permit Reuser and Stevenson to keep an eye on him and at the same time note the position of the driver who was lurking off to the side of one of the project buildings. The man made the mistake of believing the helicopter could only deal with one person at a time. From three hundred feet in the air both Reuser and Stevenson had no difficulty keeping several blocks under good visual surveillance.

When ground units did arrive in the project, it took only a moment for them to be guided by Stevenson to the passenger suspect and take him into custody. Reuser then saw the driver, who Reuser speculated probably thought the officers would be satisfied with arresting just one of them, head back to the car. The pilot kept the man under view, all the while continuing the JetRanger's orbit around the passenger and his arresting officers so as not to alert the other man that he was being watched.

Reuser saw that the driver, after entering the vehicle, emerged with a jacket in his hand with something wrapped inside. To the officer's mind, whatever it was that lay in the cloth was shaped suspiciously like a shotgun.

Reuser decided he'd better not keep his thoughts a secret. He radioed nearby and arriving police cars. Meanwhile the man ran to one of the project's housing complexes. The pilot shined the thirty-million-candlepower Nightsun on the suspect, who then flattened himself out against the building's wall as if that would hide him from the light. Reuser reasoned the man had seen too many bad prison escape movies and was attempting to emulate them.

The man finally decided his ploy wasn't going to work and ran up to the front of the apartment complex. Just as he disappeared by the door of the building, uniformed officers arrived at the location, too late to see him enter. They therefore couldn't tell whether he had the shotgun with him.

Assuming that the man did in fact have the gun with him, Reuser continued to orbit the location for twenty minutes while additional ground units were brought up. Officers cleared three of the four apartments in the small complex, which surrounded the one the suspect was thought to be in, to ensure the safety of innocent civilians. A command post was set up and specialized weapons teams were alerted to the possible barricade situation.

The telephone number to the apartment the man ran into was obtained from neighbors. The number was called and a woman answered. She told the officers that no one had run into her apartment and the only ones inside with her were her family.

She was asked to please come outside so the police could talk with her. When the woman was out of the apartment, the officers asked if anyone else was in her home. She insisted that only her three children, ages nine to fifteen years of age, were still inside.

Would she mind if they came out also?

Once the three youngsters were on the sidewalk, the woman quickly explained that yes, the suspect had broken into her house. He had held the four of them as hostages with the shotgun, and when it was clear she and her children would be leaving the apartment, told her they would all be killed if she told the police he was inside.

The police first tried to telephone the suspect and establish communication with the man. He wouldn't pick up the phone. It was a decision the suspect would likely later regret.

Seeing little option in attempting to further try and open up dialogue with the holed-up suspect, a battering ram—sometimes referred to as the key to the city—was brought to bear against the apartment door. Behind the ram was a K-9 officer with his partner, a large police dog.

With a few hits of the ram, the door gave way. A moment later the dog was let loose, and by the yells of the suspect, it was clear to the officers outside that communication had at last been achieved. A bloody male soon emerged from inside the apartment. Officers reported to Reuser that no shotgun had been found in any of the rooms.

As the suspect was being led away, Reuser continued to orbit the building. He noticed an object lying on an overhang below one of the apartment's windows. During the barricade situation he had to fly over the scene in a high orbit. It gave the ground units the light and perspective a helicopter offers, but at the same time generated the minimum amount of noise and distraction. Now that the critical part of the operation was over, Reuser decided he'd come down a couple of hundred feet.

Sure enough the object he had seen was the shotgun. He reported his discovery to the officers standing around the front of the building. Somebody procured a ladder and a uniformed officer climbed up and reached over the top of the overhang to take hold of the weapon. To preserve whatever fingerprints were on the piece, he placed one hand carefully on the end of the shotgun's butt, and with his other hand grasped the weapon's muzzle. As he lifted up on the shotgun, the slide of the action moved home, chambered a round, and the gun discharged.

The officer cried out in pain and surprise. Clutching the hand that had been by the muzzle, he fell backward off the ladder a full ten feet to the ground. The drive-by shooters had claimed one last victim that night. The hand with which the officer had held the shotgun's muzzle had three fingers blown off.

CHAPTER 29

Police Officer/Pilot Dennis Abbott

A Short Surveillance Flight

WITH FEW EXCEPTIONS, THE LOS ANGELES POLICE DEPART-
ment's Air Division uses its helicopters more like routine
day-to-day police patrol and investigative vehicles than any
other airborne law-enforcement unit. From routine drunk
driver arrests to complex murder investigations, the department's echelon of top level management has tried to wring
out every bit of utility that can be had from these aircraft.

Sometimes the machines are asked to do more than what
they were ever intended to do. And sometimes duty requires
the pilots to perform at a level beyond what those in the
field have thought police officers could rise to.

Dennis Abbott, with twenty-five years in the department,
twenty of which were served in the Air Division, figured he
was in for an easy day. As with all division pilots, Abbott,
even with his 12,000-odd flight hours, had to pass a quarterly
check ride with the unit's chief pilot to continue to fly
LAPD helicopters.

The testing process takes the better part of a tour. So
between the "ride" and some overdue paperwork, Abbott
looked forward to kicking back for a change and relaxing.
And he had come real close to being right about it being a
quiet day. Except that fifteen minutes prior to the end of
his tour, Sergeant Richard Lucia told him they had just received a job. The lab squad was in the middle of a surveil-

lance. They needed Air Division to help them follow a vehicle heading out of town. The bad guys were supposed to be going to a place near Oakland, several hours ride out of the city. And it was Air Division policy that anytime a helicopter left the city proper, there was to be two pilots aboard. Before this mission was over, both Lucia and Abbott would be ready to recommend that number be raised to three or maybe even four.

Since Abbott was the extra pilot hanging around that day, he—plus Observer Skip Zavas—would be going with the sergeant on the ride. Abbott changed into civilian clothes (standard procedure when going on an out-of-town surveillance), grabbed his overnight kit—just in case—and accompanied Lucia and Zavas to the unmarked JetRanger.

It was supposed to be a routine mission; follow a motor home carrying narcotic trafficker suspects and its load of a substantial quantity of chemicals for the making of the illegal drug PCP. Abbott was assured by the sergeant the exact destination of the vehicle was unknown it was to be somewhere to the east of Los Angeles, perhaps a two-hour ride away.

When airborne, Abbott, Lucia, and Zavas were quickly directed by ground units to the location of the suspect's vehicle. It was already rolling along the highway, so the three men followed a mile above and behind the thirty-foot-long motor home as a half-dozen ground surveillance vehicles kept just behind and out of sight.

Nearly three hours later, now close to the town of Blythe, the Air Division officers decided they'd better refuel. They landed at a local airport and filled up the helicopter's fuel tank. Discussing the situation among themselves, the men figured the vehicle would have to be stopping soon somewhere close by. They jumped back in and once more took up their position over the mobile home.

That stop would turn out to be only one of many they'd be making on this mission. As the vehicle kept on heading east, every three hours the helicopter would fly out well ahead of the ground units, who would then take up the surveillance. The ship would be landed, refueled, and the seat positions rotated. Dinner, lunch, and breakfast would mostly come from airport candy-vending machines. This routine went on for two days! Nobody involved in the investigation had any idea that the final destination of the drug traffickers was to be in Dallas, Texas. Or that the JetRanger and its Air Division crew would be continuously on duty for an incredible forty-four hours!

Twenty-four hours into the ordeal, the motor home developed mechanical problems in New Mexico. The helicopter crew took advantage of the respite and landed so that one of the ground units could give them a ride into the local town where they had the luxury of a real breakfast.

In the city of El Paso the motor home had another incident. This time they hit a passenger car making a turn in front of them. Abbott circled his JetRanger overhead as the local police dealt with the routine matter. To the surprise of everyone in the JetRanger, the motor home's occupants managed to get into an argument with the responding police. It required the quiet intervention of the LAPD officers with the local police to extricate the drug traffickers from the scene.

Now that the Los Angeles units were in Texas, contact was made with Texas law-enforcement authorities. A fixed-wing aircraft from that state's Department of Public Safety was assigned to assist the Air Division helicopter in their mission. At Midland, the Texas aircraft took over the surveillance and the JetRanger flew straight on to Dallas.

Weather intervened once the Texas DPS aircraft was in Dallas. Thunderstorms and heavy rains forced the plane to land. The mobile home, for the first time without police surveillance in two days, disappeared within the big city. The LAPD units involved in the mission were crestfallen. After all the work they had put into the case they refused to believe the vehicle could be lost at its destination city.

Dallas police officers were contacted and alerted to the problem. The Dallas officers searched known drug locations for the suspect vehicle. It didn't take them long to come up with the right mobile home.

With a great deal of relief the LAPD units once more took up the watch on the vehicle. Now that the mobile home was again under surveillance, the Air Division officer located a motel for themselves and got some well-earned and badly needed sleep.

The end result of the case was the ultimate arrest of the suspects in Dallas and the seizure of $19.3 million worth of PCP.

As for the aerial surveillance conducted by Abbott, Lucia, and Zavas, it was the longest, in both time and distance, ever performed by LAPD Air Division helicopter. And, although it would be difficult to absolutely prove, it was very likely the longest surveillance—in hours and distance—by helicopter ever performed by any police force, anywhere, ever.

CHAPTER 30

Police Officer/Pilot Lewis Peake

Crash

PILOT LEWIS PEAKE REALLY LIKES TO FLY. ON HIS OFF-DUTY hours he even has a job piloting helicopters for various commercial enterprises. It was during just such an occasion a few years back when one of the very machines he loves so much almost did him in.

The West Coast is known for its high-tech industries. Among the large concerns that call California home are numerous defense contractors. Peake was working for a small aviation firm that held a contract with one of the major companies in the business. The job was to chase boaters from the firing lane on the Pacific Ocean in the area of cruise missile as well as from computerized torpedo test sites.

Peake and other pilots would warn civilian boaters prior to the test submarine's underwater launching of its missile. Peake figures it would have been bad press for the Navy should a yacht have a cruise missile launched through its stern.

On the particular day in question, the helicopters were assigned to keep the sport boats away from the danger area during a missile test. There were two JetRangers—Peake flying one—and another helicopter, an older Bell 47 on floats, which was coming up from San Diego after working the torpedo test job. The three men landed their aircraft on the Navy base on San Clemente Island.

The Bell 47 utilizes a conventional internal combustion engine. The JetRanger series are turbine (jet) powered machines. Once inside the company's office the Bell 47 pilot asked Peake, who was senior pilot for the company, if it would be all right for him to switch aircraft with the other JetRanger pilot in order to log some turbine time. Peake replied he saw no problem with the idea. The pilot left Peake to tell the JetRanger pilot of the revised plans.

A few minutes later the Bell 47 pilot returned and informed Peake the other pilot had no idea how to fly the Bell 47 helicopter. Would Peake, with a thousand hours of LAPD Bell 47 time, mind changing helicopters with him?

No problem.

Peake left the office and preflighted the older machine. It was the second preflight of the day for the helicopter, the other pilot having done an inspection that morning.

Peake started up the machine and he and his passenger, a Navy representative involved in the cruise missile program, lifted off. For reasons he still is not sure of, he came to a hover, then let the machine settle back to the ground. With the helicopter still running, he stepped out and secured a number of rags used to clean the aircraft's windscreens. He removed his wallet from the pouch of the helicopter and stuck it deep inside his flight suit's pocket, stuffing a number of rags on top of it. He then fastened the pocket he put the wallet in. Peake then removed his firearm from one of the helicopter's inside storage compartments and put it back on.

There were other personal items he removed from various nooks and crannies inside the machine, and placed those things in his flight suit as well. He has no idea why he did what he did, and in fact it made little sense as it was far more comfortable to fly without having bulges sticking out of his various suit pockets.

He then jumped back into the helicopter and departed. The first few hours were uneventful. Peake warned some boaters from the area, and upon finding a Russian trawler nearby, harassed it for a while.

There was also a whale that Peake spotted and flew

around, as well as some dolphins and a few sharks. Peake figured it wasn't such a bad job for an off-duty cop to have.

His radio came on with a request he contact the telemetry vessel. It seemed they had lost communications with the ship, and without them the test would have to be scrubbed. That would be costly in terms of both time and money.

It didn't take long for Peake to find the vessel. Orbiting the boat, it soon became clear to the ship's crew that they had a communications problem. Peake watched as the crew below scrambled about trying to figure out what the difficulty was. It only took a couple of minutes for them to discover they had blown a fuse.

The fuse was quickly replaced. They came back on-line and everything was once more set to go. Now the base called and reported a sailboat had wandered into the danger area. Peake turned to go and handle that situation.

Without warning the control stick in Peake's right hand began to vibrate badly. It was so severe he removed his hand from the collective on his left side and grabbed the problem control with both hands. For a moment it started settling down, then Peake heard a loud bang, feeling the noise vibrate through his back.

The stick shook again, the bubble of the helicopter nosed over, and from a hundred feet in the air the Bell 47 made for the water. Peake's last view of his airspeed indicator just prior to their impacting the ocean showed they were traveling at 85 miles an hour.

Peake remembers the next few moments very clearly. What took a few seconds lasted far longer in his conscious mind. He watched the bubble impact the water. The water then slowly came up the side of the Plexiglas. Spiderweb cracks formed in the plastic, giving way to the inexorable pressure until finally the water came through the windscreen and entered the helicopter's cabin.

Just prior to the water coming in, Peake heard a voice. Where the voice came from, whose voice it was, he won't even speculate. The words he heard were quite clear. They said, "You aren't going to die in the crash."

The next thing that happened before he blacked out was that his future wife's name came into his mind.

Peake then remembers seeing a bright light. It was a color of green he'd never seen before. There was no sensation of being cold or wet. There was no pain. It was just peaceful and quiet. Then he felt a pain in his chest and the light began to fade. All at once he felt the cold water on him and realized the pain in his chest was the fact that he wasn't breathing.

He figured he'd better get out of the helicopter. Reaching for the seat belt release, he found it jammed. He sat in his seat, holding onto the controls of the helicopter, and considered his problem. He tried to breathe through his nose, then through his mouth. Nothing came in. At that point he came to his senses. Realizing the helicopter was sinking underwater, he knew he had to get out of it. He worked his hand back to where the seat belt was fastened to the aircraft's structure. Working his hand along the belt, he came to the buckle. His fingers felt the mechanism and he discovered it had been struck by the cyclic in the impact and was damaged. It took him three tries to force it open.

Kicking free of the machine, Peake bobbed to the surface. The Navy passenger, an old World War II submariner, was already treading water. He later told Peake he was used to getting out of things underwater.

The telemetry vessel attempted to pull Peake from the water. He refused, telling the crew they'd have to first secure the helicopter before he'd come aboard. The cruise missile launch was imminent and the mission couldn't be continued while he was in the water. All Peake could think of was to get the helicopter secured to the vessel so the cause of the crash could be determined. Otherwise it was all too likely to be listed as "pilot error," and effectively put an end to his flying career.

The crew tried to hook Peake's life jacket with a hook. He grabbed hold of the end and secured it to the Bell 47. Seeing he was adamant, the crew then threw him a line, which Peake also fastened to the helicopter. He then permitted them to help him aboard the vessel.

The investigation showed that the bolt for the internal mechanism for the control stick had disintegrated. This caused the control to move full forward.

After a short rest, Peake went back to work at the Air Division. He told his fellow pilots what had happened and the problem that had been uncovered in the internal control mechanism. One of the pilots who heard the story went out to his department Bell 47 and, besides doing the normal preflight, made it a point to check the area that had caused Peake's accident and in the process almost killed him.

The pilot discovered that the very same piece that had failed on Peake's machine was cracked in his.

Armed Robbery

Officer Lewis Peake, with his two and a half decades of service with the LAPD, has been involved in a lot of perilous situations. But on the morning watch of January 10, 1982, he and his observer, Police Officer Skip Zavas, came onto a scene that closely resembled a running military-type firefight.

The shift had started slowly enough. Peake and Zavas were the sole Air Division unit working at around one A.M. and were concentrating their efforts over one of the busier Los Angeles areas. A radio call came over from a neighboring district. A citizen reported a possible 211 in progress, Los Angeles police talk for a robbery. The person gave as the location Rusty's Hacienda, a Mexican restaurant in the Hollenbeck area.

It is not uncommon for an initial call coming into communications to be false. Experienced police officers don't get their blood pressure up every time the radio crackles with "robbery in progress," "shots fired," or "man with a gun." Sometimes it's pranksters who make such calls, just wanting to see the flashing police lights. Sometimes it's honest citizens who mistake what they're seeing for something other than what they're reporting.

But every once in a while what the radio says is happening is right on the money.

Zavas, upon hearing the location, turned to Peake and informed him that he thought he knew exactly where Rusty's was. A sergeant then came on the air. He had been

279

driving by the place, actually coming from some routine administrative assignment at a nearby hospital, when one of the restaurant's workers had flagged him down, telling him of the robbery going on. The sergeant put the information over the radio. When a cop puts a robbery call over the air, everyone knows it's serious business.

Because of the sophisticated communications equipment installed in the Air Division's helicopters—air units normally monitor more than one police division at a time—Peake and Zavas heard the officer's call as it was being broadcast. But since the sergeant was not normally assigned to the division from where he was transmitting, his car's radio was not being heard by the patrol units—whose cars were on a different division frequency—around him. The other units were getting the information rebroadcast by the dispatchers.

Peake, who had half ignored the first call, now perked up. He nodded his acknowledgment of Zavas's directions and pointed the nose of his JetRanger toward Rusty's.

Five miles from their helicopter a scene out of the Wild West was taking place. Six heavily armed people were robbing Rusty's, a busy place on a weekend night. Five men and a woman were holding nearly two hundred patrons at bay, going from table to table, relieving the victims of their money and jewelry. The robbery team had first gotten everybody's attention in the place by firing shots into the ceiling.

All the male robbers were related, four brothers and a cousin who had been involved in a series of vicious armed robberies throughout the Los Angeles area.

Less than three minutes after hearing the call, the JetRanger was over the restaurant. Looking down on the street scene below, neither Peake nor Zavas saw anything out of place. No police cars were on the scene, nobody was excited and running around; below them the visible activity was routine. Peake got on the air and started to talk to the sergeant, who still had the citizen who flagged him down.

The sergeant was adamant about the nature and seriousness of the event. He added that not only were there half a dozen armed robbers in the place, but they were all scattered around the inside of the restaurant. He also told the Air Division officers and communications he was fearful the setting was ripe for it to be turned into a hostage situation.

Peake turned on his multimillion-candlepower searchlight and scanned the area. A police cruiser just rolling onto the scene came on the air and reported seeing some people come running out a side door. The ground unit then reported seeing a black car move from the side of the building and another man jump inside through the vehicle's open window. The officer had no idea if these people were victims, perpetrators, or what.

At first Peake and Zavas didn't see the auto. Then, coming out of the driveway, they picked up the moving police car. The Air Division officers weren't certain whether they should stay by the restaurant or head for the unknown entity that was the car. Peake called to the ground units, and once assured there were enough officers at the scene to surround the restaurant, headed toward the black-and-white police cruiser following the suspect vehicle.

It took only a moment for the helicopter to catch up with the pursuing police cruiser. Cresting a hill, Peake looked out ahead of the black-and-white and was shocked to see flashes of gunfire coming from every window of the black car.

Peake called to the pursuing police car to back off, that the robbers were shooting at them. What he was to find out later from a number of cruisers involved in the chase and running gun battle was that the bad guys were more often than not shooting at Peake and Zavas's helicopter!

The helicopter got ahead of the police cruiser and took up the position as the lead pursuit vehicle. All the while the men inside the car were firing handguns and shotguns at the low-flying JetRanger.

Up ahead Peake could see other police cruisers converging on the area. From his unique perspective it was clear to him that as a police car would come into view, the men i the car would fire their weapons at the black-and white' officer. Peake broadcast again and again the warning to the ground units that they were being fired upon. He directed the police cruisers to lay back, as his helicopter sat exposed in the air, hardly two hundred feet from the five madmen in the pursued vehicle.

One police cruiser, on a different frequency from the rest, was heading toward the melee from the opposite direction. Seeing the firefight, the cruiser's driver quickly pulled his car into an open driveway. As the suspect vehicle passed by, a fusillade of shots rang out, many rounds hitting the now stopped police car. It was a miracle that neither of the two officers inside were hit.

Peake not only was running the helicopter with its brilliant searchlight blazing, but had the siren on as well. The purpose of the light (a great target) and noise was not so much for any impact it might have on the bad guys, but because Peake had to worry about any innocent civilians who might come onto the scene.

The helicopter followed behind the suspect vehicle as it made a quick right-hand turn through a red light. A citizen's car drove right up to the back of the suspects' vehicle and fell in trail behind. To Peake's horror, he saw that the situation was now complicated by this noninvolved citizen's auto that had come between the pursuing police vehicles and the fleeing robbers. And the bad guys were still firing wildly at the cops!

Peake wondered whether the people in the middle car figured they were in a movie or were just oblivious to what was going on around them. Zavas yelled over the radio for the police car to get those people out of there. Peake watched as the black-and-white cruiser pulled out into the oncoming lane of traffic, raced up past the civilian car and cut it off, once more putting themselves in the direct line of fire. As Peake continued his pursuit he noted that the citizen's car hadn't even slowed down.

The suspect car tried to make another turn, lost control and hit the curb and a pole. Zavas broadcast to the responding units about the now-stopped criminals' vehicle and its location. Zavas's attention was focused on the responding police cruisers. Peake called over to his partner and told him to check out what was going on below. Peake pointed out to him that the robbers had set up a hasty ambush. The men had taken up positions behind their car with their shotguns and handguns pointed in the direction of the oncoming black-and-whites. And from where they were situated, the police cars wouldn't see them until they were within point-blank range.

Zavas immediately got on the radio and warned the incoming units about the trap. Peake dove the JetRanger down between the buildings to directly over the top of the suspects' ambush. While hovering only scant feet above the armed men, he threw his siren on full blast and over his PA system called out for them to surrender.

The warnings almost came too late. Two of the black-and-whites locked up their brakes but still skidded past the corner of the street where the robbers were barricaded. A firefight ensued, with the officers using their own cars as cover as the outlaws blazed away at them and the helicopter.

Three of the suspects ran, two into a nearby junkyard and the third down the street. Peake saw the two were heading toward a high fence they'd never be able to climb. The third man had what appeared to be the money bag in his hand. Peake stayed with him. Throwing on the JetRanger's bright searchlight, Peake remained with his man.

The suspect ran down an alley. He stopped when the light hit him, and began to fire his .45 pistol at the helicopter. Zavas called out for assistance as Peake watched the man dump his empty magazine and insert a fresh one. Still firing on the helicopter, he emptied that magazine, reloaded, and fired some more.

The suspect then ran from the alley and entered an empty lot. Turning once more on the JetRanger, he again opened fire as Zavas continued to call for backup. The man then ran out into the middle of the street, where uniformed officers at the scene exchanged gunfire with the suspect. Once more the robber ran back into the vacant lot. A ferocious exchange of rounds between a number of officers and the suspect occurred.

The suspect broke from the scene and began to run away. But this time Peake observed he was limping badly.

Running and firing at the pursuing officers, the wounded suspect—still brightly illuminated by the JetRanger's searchlight—headed across the street. He ran into a vacant series of buildings that was a labyrinth of connecting rooms and tunnels designed to receive railroad freight cars.

Peake lost sight of the suspect in the maze. With no other option, the pilot maneuvered his helicopter at the mouth of one of the tunnels and shone the searchlight down into the hole. It was a desperate move, and Peake knew that he was placing himself and Zavas in a precarious position should the suspect choose to open fire on them.

The Nightsun's beam turned the pitch-black tunnel into a surreal tangle of light and shadow. Peake spotted the suspect hiding behind a concrete pillar. While Peake kept the man holed up, other units surrounded the location. With that done and LAPD special weapons teams on the way, Peake broke away and headed to where the other two suspects had last been seen, less than a quarter of a mile away.

For several hours that night Peake would travel back and forth between the two locations in support of the ground units. It was during this period that a determination was made to have the Air Division place SWAT team members on the roof of the abandoned building. Peake returned to the Air Division base to remove all excess items from the JetRanger and for fuel. He intended to use the unit's Huey for the job, but as luck would have it, that particular helicopter was out of service.

Three JetRangers were set up for the mission. Using an open lot near the scene, two SWAT members would stand on the skids on the outside of the helicopter for each trip to the roof. The three JetRangers involved made three trips each to the top of the abandoned structure.

That done, Peake returned to the junkyard where two of the robbers had last been seen. He was asked by ground units to broadcast a warning over the PA system that the two men should surrender or K-9 and SWAT units would be going in. A few minutes after making the broadcast, one of the ground units reported that two men had come out of a nearby building with their hands up. It took a while to figure out that those two were just some local burglars who figured all the commotion was their doing and surrendered! And then a few moments later another two burglars were captured in the same area, equally uninvolved with the original robbery team.

The two robbers should have been as smart as the four

crooks who gave up before them. The ground units sent the dogs in. It didn't take them long to find the two suspects, whose guns were empty—lucky for both them and the officers searching for them—and who wound up being bloodied up in the process of the K-9's "arresting" them.

With the capture of those two there still remained the suspect who disappeared down a tunnel in the abandoned buildings, plus one other male. While special weapons units and K-9s looked for the former suspect, Peake was asked by ground units to fly back over to the getaway vehicle and shine his light on it.

As he had done throughout the entire night, the pilot put his aircraft in a vulnerable hover barely a hundred feet above the car—the only thing between any gunman hiding inside and the Air Division officers being air and the grace of God—and turned on his light. Inside he could clearly see the body of a single person lying on his side.

Two officers on the ground ran up to the car and yanked the door open. They saw the man inside had taken a blast from a shotgun in the head and wouldn't be robbing Rusty's Hacienda or anyplace else ever again.

Later it was determined that the fatal round was fired when the pursuit was first initiated. The young officer sitting in the passenger side of the black-and-white had fired the shot. It was his first night on patrol after graduating from the LAPD Police Academy.

When the dead robber's body was autopsied, the coroner found an addition bullet in his body. That projectile's striations—identifying marks—matched those that came from the gun of a police officer who had been involved in a gunfight with that robber two years earlier. Among the many coincidences of the night was that Peake remembered being present in his department helicopter over that incident as well.

After five hours of searching, the SWAT unit members had to reconcile themselves to the fact that the fifth man of the robbery team had escaped the complex of abandoned tunnels and buildings. As the search was about to end, a call came in regarding a person suffering a gunshot wound who had gone into a local county hospital five miles away.

The sergeant sent a unit to check the report out. By the

time the officers arrived, the man had fled. The doctor told them that the victim—who was later positively identified by hospital personnel from previous arrest photos as the man they were looking for—had suffered an extremely serious and unusual wound. A bullet entered the man at the base of the neck, traveled straight down his torso, and exited out his left testicle. He also told the officers that if the man didn't get treatment soon he was going to die.

From the description the doctor gave of the bullet's track, the shot would appear to have come from somewhere above the suspect. However, it couldn't possibly have come from Peake and Zavas's JetRanger, as firing from a department helicopter would have been a serious violation of the LAPD and Air Division rules.

At the debriefing that morning, Peake carefully went over his helicopter looking for bullet damage. By some miracle none of the estimated three hundred rounds fired by the robbers had found the JetRanger. The total number of rounds exchanged by the officers and suspects can only be guessed at.

Peake learned that the female member of the team had been arrested while still in the restaurant. When her companions left her, she attempted to mingle with the rest of the patrons. She found a single man and pretended she was with him. Her ploy didn't work.

Peake also was told that among the patrons in Rusty's during the robbery was an off-duty LAPD officer. Seeing himself badly undergunned, he tried to hide his firearm and police identification when the robbery started. It was to no avail, as one of the robbers discovered his shield, which the officer kept on a chain around his neck. Two members of the robbery team got into an argument over who was going to have the pleasure of killing the officer. Just a moment before he was to be executed, the noise of Peake's helicopter hovering outside caused the band of robbers to panic and the five men ran from the restaurant and into their getaway car.

At the trial of the four men and one woman, the presiding judge wanted to know what happened to the fifth man. He was told that as far as the police were aware, he had died.

Not satisfied with that response, the judge interviewed one of the man's family members, who told him the man had fled over the border to Mexico and had died and was buried in Tijuana. The judge responded by telling the officers to send somebody over there, dig up the body, and bring him back to court!

Appendix

How They Fly

HEAVIER-THAN-AIR OBJECTS HAVE FLOWN SUCCESSFULLY above the surface of this planet for the last several hundred million years. First there were the great flying reptiles, which soared in the prehistoric skies. They were ultimately replaced by birds, who in turn must now share the sky with man. Controlled flight in a heavier-than-air craft was first successfully performed before the turn of the century. Using gliders, Otto Lilienthal made numerous successful flights in aircraft of his own design. He came to understand well the basic principles of flight and the mastery of the directional control of his devices before he was killed during one of his experiments.

The first successful, controlled, powered heavier-than-air flight is generally credited to the Wright brothers. Often mythically viewed as a pair of simple bicycle makers who in their spare time invented the airplane, the fact is, they were self-taught aeronautical engineers with a sophisticated understanding of the principles of flight.

The Wright's airplane at Kittyhawk was able to fly for the same reason a Boeing 747 flies today. Both machines utilize wings that generated lift when air is moved over them. Some of the air is pushed down by the underside of the wing, forcing the wing up, while some air going over its top causes a decrease in pressure. The net result is called lift.

289

APPENDIX

The wings of airplanes are fixed in place. For centuries people had tried to work out the problems inherent in using wings that rotated in order to succeed in achieving heavier-than-air flight. The obstacles were formidable and it wasn't until the 1930s and early forties that rotary-wing aircraft—helicopters—had been developed to the point where they could be considered practical flying machines. First it was the German aircraft designer Heinrick Focke who produced workable flying machines. Soon Americans Larry Bell and Igor Sikorsky followed suit.

The majority of aircraft flown in airborne law-enforcement missions are helicopters. There's good reason for the preference shown by such agencies for these versatile, albeit expensive, machines. Nothing else, nothing, can do what a helicopter can accomplish. There is simply no other practical device that can fly to an unprepared site, remain motionless overhead or land as required, and/or perform meaningful tasks as needed as well as helicopters can.

The helicopters mentioned in this book all fly utilizing the same principles of flight. A single rotating wing—hence the term rotary-wing aircraft—sits over the pilot and passengers. It is the lift generated by air moving across this wing (blades) that enables helicopters to hover, takeoff, fly, and land. Heading is maintained by the rotating wing—called the disk area when the blades are in motion—being tilted by the pilot in the desired direction of flight.

For every action there is an equal and opposite reaction. The smaller tail rotor, seen at the rear of these aircraft, is needed to compensate for the twisting force of the main blades as they whirl around. There are some helicopters of newer design that are attempting to eliminate the tail rotor altogether and use forced air to perform the same directional control function. When the pilot adds power to the main rotor blade, the helicopter's nose will move off to one side. When power is reduced, it will head in the opposite direction. By pushing on the tail rotor's control pedals—or forced-air system controls, as the case may be—the pilot keeps the nose of the machine pointed as desired.

Helicopters can do what no other heavier-than-air vehicle can accomplish. These devices can not only fly, but perhaps more importantly, they can hover (remain motionless) in respect to their position over the ground. And unlike conventional aircraft, which requires a minimum of a thousand feet of clear area to take off and land in, these machines can do the same thing in remarkably smaller spaces.

By their very nature these machines are more complex to manufacture and maintain than conventional fixed-wing aircraft. Most of the modern helicopters in use by police agencies utilize turbine or jet engines. These engines have internal rotating parts that sometimes reach speeds of 50,000 revolutions a minute.

The turbine's incredible turning motion must then be transferred to the helicopter's main rotor system, whose blade-tip speed is perhaps 400 rotations per minute. Modern helicopters perform such mechanical miracles millions of hours a year with a great safety record. But the price of this complexity may be found in the fact that these machines are extremely costly to both operate and maintain. While these engines are known for their reliability, due to the fine tolerances and exotic metals required in their manufacture they are also quite expensive to repair and overhaul, as is the transmission required to move their power to the main rotor system.

Once I calculated how much the New York City Police Department had spent on training me to fly their JetRangers. It cost the city somewhere around $90,000 before I was permitted to perform any unsupervised work in one of its helicopters. The numbers below tell the story:

Fifty Hours JetRanger Dual (Unit minimum needed before solo flight permitted)	$25,000
Fifty Hours JetRanger Dual and Solo (Unit minimum required before pilot permitted to take the mandated Commercial Pilot test)	$20,000

One Hundred Hours JetRanger Dual and $45,000
Solo (Required to meet the unit's 200-hour
minimum before I was permitted to work without
another pilot aboard the helicopter)

The need for airborne law enforcement can only continue to grow. With no other flying machine visible on the horizon able to perform the job of helicopters, they will continue to be the dominant vehicle used by Sky Cops for the foreseeable future.

The helicopters used by airborne law enforcement are many and varied. Following is a list of those mentioned in *Sky Cops,* along with the names of those departments in the book in which they are either currently or have been formerly operated. In addition there is a brief description of their capabilities and roles.

The Machines

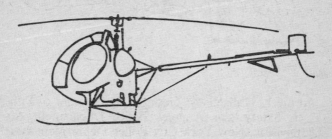

Hughes 300
McDonnell Douglas 300
Schweizer 300

Currently Utilized by: City of Baltimore Police Department

The three names preceding the Model 300 are the three companies that over the years have produced this light utility helicopter. The ship is distinctive in appearance, having a wide Plexiglas cabin with a comparatively thin-looking tail boom jutting out behind.

Powered by a four-cylinder internal combustion engine, the craft has a top speed of approximately one hundred miles per hour, but pilots will admit that its real world-cruising speed is closer to eighty. Able to carry three people, but most often flown with a pilot plus one passenger, it makes a reliable and relatively inexpensive observation aircraft, well-suited for law-enforcement purposes.

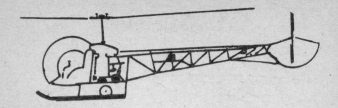

Bell 47 Series

Formerly Utilized by: Georgia Department of Public Safety, Los Angeles Police Department Air Division, New York City Police Department Aviation Unit

This was the first model helicopter purchased by the New York City Police Department Aviation Unit in 1947, thus becoming the first helicopter ever to be put in police service. The basic design lasted into the early 1970s, and thousands of these reliable three-passenger internal combustion-engine-powered aircraft are still flying and working today.

Made in many variations, the vast majority of these models utilized a distinctive round bubble to enclose the cabin. Until recently, whenever the word "helicopter" was uttered, the image of a Bell 47 would come to people's minds.

The large surface area of its bubble gives the helicopter a practical cruising speed of about eighty-five miles an hour. The after-market Soloy conversion, which replaces the Bell 47's standard internal combustion engine with the same turbine engine found in JetRangers and McDonnell Douglas 500s, has been a popular modification, adding years to the useful life of the design. Speed is not enhanced by the modification, but lifting capacity and reliability are significantly improved.

Its primary mission has been in the observation and patrol roles but when properly equipped, and before more modern craft were available, these helicopters had done service in untold thousands of medical evacuations (Medevacs).

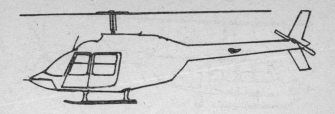

Bell 206B JetRanger

Currently Utilized by: Arizona Department of Public Safety, Georgia Department of Public Safety, Los Angeles Police Department Air Division, New York City Police Department Aviation Unit

An immensely popular design dating back to the early 1960s, these were the first turbine-powered (jet engine) helicopters to be placed into wide civilian service. These machines are known to be particularly safe aircraft, statistically the safest single-engine *aircraft*—fixed or rotary-wing —flying today.

Now considered somewhat light and cramped for medical evacuation purposes, the JetRanger remains in service as an observation, patrol, rescue, and transport helicopter.

Capable of carrying five adults (pilot plus four) at a practical cruise speed of 120 miles an hour, and with a maximum range of nearly 400 miles, these aircraft will remain in use by law-enforcement agencies well into the next century.

Bell 206L LongRanger

Currently Utilized by: Arizona Department of Public Safety, Los Angeles Police Department Air Division

The LongRanger is a larger version of the JetRanger, and was brought out in 1975. From a distance, the two machines appear almost identical. The LongRanger has a larger inte-

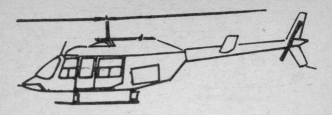

rior cabin—the aircraft can carry the pilot plus six—than the JetRanger, and is equipped with a more powerful engine, which enables the model to carry a greater load.

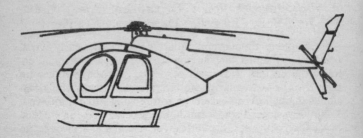

Hughes 500
McDonnell Douglas 500

Over the years, this helicopter has had two manufacturers, hence the two names shown above. In use by many police departments around the nation, this aircraft utilizes the same turbine engine as is in the Bell 206B. Somewhat smaller in overall size then the JetRanger, what this model lacks in interior space is made up by the helicopter's fast cruise speeds. The 500 series finds use in observation, patrol, and rescue roles.

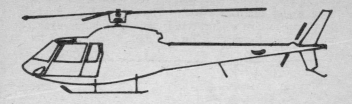

Aerospatiale AS350B

Currently Utilized by: Maryland State Police, Los Angeles Police Department Air Division

This is a recent newcomer to the airborne law-enforcement field. Of French design, this helicopter's interior is larger than the JetRanger's, an aircraft which it competes with. The ship also boasts a more powerful engine with modern interior appointments. The advantage the design offers over the Jet-Ranger is the machine's ability to better carry the necessary, and heavy, ancillary equipment—emergency floats, multimillion-candlepower searchlights, Forward Looking Infra Red, etc.—found on modern police helicopters.

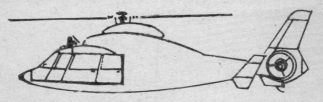

Aerospatiale AS365 N2 Dauphin

Currently Utilized by: Maryland State Police

Also of French manufacture, this helicopter is a large, fast, and powerful twin-engine turbine-powered aircraft. This model has found good acceptance among those public safety agencies needing serious Medevac capability. The comfortable interior of the ship permits them to be set up as a minihospital emergency room. Thus, critically injured patients can receive sophisticated medical attention even before reaching the destination hospital.

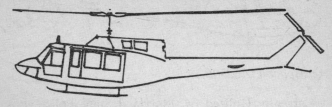

Bell 412

Utilized by: New York City Police Department Aviation Unit

This twin-engine turbine-powered helicopter, similar in design to the Huey, has a gross weight of 12,000 pounds. The machine is designed for lifting a great deal of weight and serves admirably for personnel transport, medical evacuations, and deployment of SWAT officers. Two are currently in use by the New York City Aviation Unit. A single 412 costs more than four million dollars.

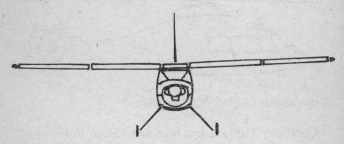

Helio-Courier

Formerly Utilized by: Georgia State Patrol

A unique piece of flying machinery, this fixed-wing aircraft was designed with safety as its primary goal. Using a sophisticated wing design, the Helio-Courier can be flown at speeds of around forty miles an hour. While out of production for nearly twenty years, they are still in demand where an aircraft is needed that can safely get in and out of small unimproved airstrips.

Cessna T-41

Formerly Utilized by: Georgia State Patrol

Formerly used in military service, a number of these planes eventually found their way into the inventories of public safety agencies when declared as surplus. This design is a modified —with a larger internal combustion engine —version of a civilian fixed-wing aircraft. Able to seat four persons, its primary mission is in observation and patrol.

Cessna 210

Formerly Utilized by: Los Angeles Police Department Air Division

A powerful and fast six-passenger aircraft—using a 300 horsepower internal combustion engine—this model has been used for purposes of transport and surveillance by a number of agencies.

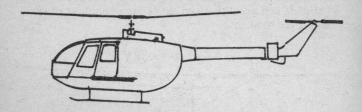

MBB Bolkow 105

Currently Utilized by: New York City Police Department Aviation Unit

This machine is considered a light twin among two-engine helicopters. The aircraft uses two of the same Allison turbine engines found in the Bell 206 series; this redundant power makes for safer flying, particularly around urban areas. And because its engines are identical to those of the popular JetRanger helicopters, aviation units equipped with both aircraft need to keep few additional spare parts for their engines on hand.

Terminology

Nontechnical Explanation of Some Common Terms Used in the Book

This book was written with the general public in mind. Still, when discussing a technical subject such as helicopter flight, it is inevitable that some terms must be used that are not readily recognized by the nonfliers among us. Below are some of these words and phrases explained in what I hope is a lucid and easily understood manner. Flight instructors and professional pilots will forgive me if they detect that I have taken some liberties with the explanations or that they are less than complete.

Aircraft and Engine Instruments/Gauges: The various gauges used by the pilot to determine the aircraft's position, the working and operating condition of the engine, and the condition and functioning of the aircraft's ancillary equipment as well as the flight attitude of the aircraft in relation to the ground.

Airspeed: The speed an aircraft makes through the air. Ground speed is the speed it is traveling in relation to the ground. For example, an aircraft showing a 100 mile an hour airspeed on its airspeed indicator, and that is flying with a wind of 10 miles an hour blowing on its nose, would be covering ground at the speed of 90 miles an hour.

301

TERMINOLOGY

Modern aircraft speeds are normally measured in knots, or around 1.15 miles per hour. Ninety knots is around 103 mph.

Autorotation: The ability of a rotary-winged aircraft to come to a safe landing without use of its engine. Air moving across the helicopter's blades as it descends to earth continues to permit them to generate lift. The inertia stored in the moving blades enables the pilot to maintain control over the machine and to safely land the aircraft.

Collective: The lever on the pilot's left side used to control the angle the rotating blades strike the air, as well as to control the amount of power being generated by the engine. Simply put, it is the primary control that is used to make the helicopter climb and descend.

Commercial Pilot License: A license requiring the demonstration of substantially greater aeronautical knowledge and flying skill then the Private Pilot license. Most police agencies require their pilots to possess this level of license.

Cyclic: The control stick—sometimes referred to as "joy stick"—directly in front of the pilot. It is used to establish the direction of flight the helicopter takes, and does so by moving the aircraft's main rotor blades.

Fixed-Wing Aircraft: An aircraft whose wings are fixed to the flying machine's body. An airplane.

Ground Speed: The speed of the aircraft in relation to the ground. If an aircraft were flying at an airspeed of 100 miles an hour, and the plane had a tail wind of 10 miles an hour, it would cover the ground at a speed of 110 miles an hour.

Helicopter: A rotating wing aircraft capable of taking off and landing with zero forward speed and that can hover above a fixed point on the ground.

Hot Start: The introduction of fuel into a turbine engine before the engine has come up to sufficient speed to run within its design temperature limits. A hot start requires an expensive and time-consuming engine teardown and inspection.

Instrument Flight Rules (IFR): Flight by reference to an aircraft's attitude instruments and while in mandatory contact with ground controllers.

Main Rotor Blade: The main blade (the rotating wing) of a helicopter.

Navigation Instruments: Instruments used to determine where the aircraft is located and to aid it in getting to its desired destination.

Over-Torque: Pulling up excessively or too abruptly on the collective and thus stressing parts of the helicopter beyond their design limits. Torque is frequently measured at the helicopter's transmission, but can also be measured at the main mast.

Propeller: A small winglike device used to push or pull an aircraft through the air and thus enable its wing to generate lift.

Rotary-Wing Aircraft: An aircraft whose wing rotates; for example, gyro-copter, helicopter.

Skids: The piece under the helicopter that the machine rests on when on the ground. Some helicopters utilize wheels in lieu of skids.

Tail Rotor: The small rotor to the rear of the helicopter's tail boom, used to counteract the twisting forces of the main rotor when there is either a decrease or increase in the power applied to the main rotor blade.

Terminal Control Area (TCA): A restricted airspace found around larger airports. Now called Class B airspace.

Torque: A twisting or rotating motion.

Turbine Engine: An engine utilizing rotating compressor stages, which operate at high RPM. These engines consume jet fuel (kerosene) and are very light for the power produced. The turbine engine on the JetRanger is the Allison Model 250–20 series and weighs approximately 158 pounds, but is capable of generating 420 shaft horsepower. These engines close tolerances, and the exotic materials they must be made of to withstand the tremendous temperatures and rotational speeds they generate make these motors quite expensive to buy and maintain. They are noted for their reliability.

Visual Flight Rules (VFR): Rules that permit the pilot to fly without contact with ground controllers and without need to reference on-board attitude instruments.

Yaw Pedals: Tail rotor controls used to keep the nose of the helicopter pointed in the direction of flight, to counteract torque or aid in maneuvering the machine when near the ground.